William Taylor Thom

Shakespeare and Chaucer Examinations

William Taylor Thom

Shakespeare and Chaucer Examinations

ISBN/EAN: 9783337055080

Printed in Europe, USA, Canada, Australia, Japan

Cover: Foto ©ninafisch / pixelio.de

More available books at **www.hansebooks.com**

SHAKESPEARE AND CHAUCER

EXAMINATIONS.

EDITED, WITH SOME

REMARKS ON THE

CLASS-ROOM STUDY OF SHAKESPEARE,

BY

WILLIAM TAYLOR THOM, M.A.,
PROFESSOR OF ENGLISH LITERATURE IN HOLLINS INSTITUTE, VIRGINIA.

BOSTON:
PUBLISHED BY GINN & COMPANY.
1888.

DEDICATION.

---o---

To those to whom it is due,

TO MY PUPILS,

I dedicate their own work and whatever is of worth in mine with an affection whose bonds are drawn the closer by the loss of the two pure spirits that have passed from us into the haven of their rest.

TABLE OF CONTENTS.

	PAGE
PREFACE TO SECOND EDITION	7
INTRODUCTION	9
HAMLET EXAMINATION	15
LETTER OF F. J. FURNIVALL, ESQ.	62
MACBETH EXAMINATION	63
CLASS EXAMINATION IN HAMLET, 1887	105
KING LEAR EXAMINATION	107
OTHELLO EXAMINATION	157
THE MERCHANT OF VENICE EXAMINATION	189
CLASS-ROOM STUDY OF SHAKESPEARE	237
CHAUCER EXAMINATION	275
WOMANHOOD IN CHAUCER, SHAKESPEARE, AND TENNYSON	307

PREFACE TO SECOND EDITION.

A SECOND edition of this book is offered to the public in response to what seems to be a genuine demand for it as shown in the sale of the first edition. The chief usefulness of the book will be found in its suggestiveness as to the Study of Shakespeare — is not that indeed the most valuable element in all school work on Shakespeare? — in addition to which a good deal of technical information very helpful to understanding Shakespeare's English will be available to those not having time or inclination to work over a Shakespeare grammar. The book has been enlarged by the Examinations on *King Lear*, *Othello*, and the *Merchant of Venice*, to which the Examination on Chaucer has been added with the hope of stimulating the study of our delightful old story-teller whose poetic fame is too much talked about for his works to be so little read. Every-day readers could easily know what a splendid poet Chaucer is, if they would only choose to take a little trouble at first with his unfamiliar words; and Dr. Morris's edition of the *Prologue* (see within) or one of Professor Skeat's beautiful editions (*Clarendon Press Series*) will amply repay any one for buying and reading it. I hope the Examination here given may urge on some of my fellow-teachers who have not yet done so, to put some of Chaucer's works, the *Prologue* especially, into their course of English Literature. They will not regret doing so, particularly if the time necessary be taken from the study of one of the numerous hand-books of our literature, which we can neither use satisfactorily nor do without altogether in most schools; for, at school, time taken from *reading about* a good author and spent in *actually reading* his best works, is time well taken and well spent.

It is a great pleasure to believe that this little book has been helpful in promoting the study of Shakespeare in our schools, and I am grateful to the friends, known and unknown, from whom such assurance has come to me. It is mournful to think that prejudice still keeps out of some of our schools, as a text-book, the greatest artist of our race, who is also one of the greatest moralists of the world.

W. T. T.

HOLLINS INSTITUTE, VA.
   May, 1887.

INTRODUCTION.

THAT a teacher should print the work of his pupils is, perhaps, extraordinary; that he should accompany their work with an appendix in the nature of a discussion of his own method of teaching is, doubtless, so extraordinary as to need explanation. The explanation is as follows: In the autumn or winter of 1880, I learned that the "New Shakspere Society" of England conferred annual prizes upon schools for good work done on Shakespeare in them, and that Miss Stark had gained this prize in the Logan Female College, Russellville, Kentucky. I wrote to Dr. Stark, President of the Logan College, and obtained from him the Examination Papers, and also the permission, courteously given by him and by Mr. Furness of Philadelphia, to use the questions. These examination questions, with, I think, one omission and five additions of my own, were used in this Institute for the "Prize Examination on *Hamlet*" printed herewith. *Hamlet* was the play read that session in my senior Literature class. The Examination Papers were printed, sent to England, the New Shakspere Society's prize was gained, and a very gratifying letter received from Mr. F. J. Furnivall, the Director of the New Shakspere

Society, accompanied by an extra complimentary prize for each of the young ladies. This award was noticed in the London *Academy*, which notice was copied into several papers in America. In consequence, I soon began to receive applications for the Examination; then came letters asking information as to my method of teaching; for advice as to how to study Shakespeare and how to make him interesting in little clubs; requesting me to instruct by correspondence; to go through a play by letter as I go through one orally with my class; and so on. In the summer of 1882, the *Macbeth* Examination was also printed to be sent to England, secured a continuance of the prize, was subsequently noticed in this country, and called forth additional letters. These letters have come chiefly from teachers and have shown a wide-spread interest in the school study of Shakespeare. To answer them fully and satisfactorily has been — with the best will in the world — beyond my ability, as can be readily imagined. Yet I have regretted keenly this inability, and have been troubled to think that a few words of direct, practical suggestion, even from so humble a student of Shakespeare as myself, might fall upon good ground and bring forth much fruit, and that these words were not uttered.

To this consideration have been added the influence of advice, public and private, to print the Examinations in a form accessible to the public, and the promptings of my own vehement desire to do all within my power to encourage the study of Shakespeare in schools throughout the country, especially in schools for girls. For I believe that Shakespeare can and will do a work for our youth, just at this period of our national life, not to be done in any other way.

Hence it is that this little book is in existence: a work done chiefly by women, published chiefly for women.

I hope that my remarks on "Class-Room Study of Shakespeare" may serve as a reply to the letters which I have received; that the Examinations, taken with these remarks, may form a suggestive working commentary on the two plays discussed; and that my fellow-teachers and fellow-students may find themselves helped by a comparison of methods.

These Examinations are the result of such careful study of Shakespeare as precluded, it is hoped, any "cram" in the ordinary sense of the word; though, doubtless, none of the young ladies examined would be found as ready now as when they were working on the Examination. The questions are identical in kind with the ordinary class-work, and give the results of that same work carried on in a post-graduate way; and, for any independent progress in Shakespeare study, that is the proper method.

In giving these Examinations to the public, I beg that it be borne in mind that they are printed as they were written, — errors and all, a few clerical errors excepted, — and that they present their authors in an examination light, consequently to some disadvantage. Yet I think I may be permitted to say that I would be fully content could I hope to get one such piece of work each year from among my pupils, to work with whom and for whom affords such sincere satisfaction and enjoyment.

My own remarks do not pretend to be a correct theory of how Shakespeare should be taught; do not even pretend to be stated in an exhaustive and systematic way. They are filled with repetitions, are rough in style, and are fragmentary in form. The atmosphere of the class-room is strong upon them. But it seems best to me to leave them in this half-colloquial form, as they may be on that account more readily available to those who find profit in them, especially to young people studying alone. I shall be very glad to learn from the experience of others, and my desire is to modify my views if I shall be thereby enabled to do my work more effectually. Each teacher must work independently; but almost any teacher may help almost any other teacher to do his work better. Criticism of my method will be welcome.

Indeed, no claim of originality is intended to be made in speaking of my method of teaching as peculiar to myself. Rather am I making a report on the methods of Abbott and Aldis Wright and Hudson, than setting up any method of my own. The small volume of essays by Mr. H. N. Hudson, "English in Schools," of which more hereafter, should be in the hands of every Shakespeare teacher in America.

My own experience had brought me to many of his conclusions before I saw the book; but it is all the more welcome on that account.

My earnest hope for this little book is, that it may prove suggestive and useful. Its pronounced *personality* was unavoidable.

I desire to express my high appreciation of the generous conduct of the New Shakspere Society, and my conviction that they are doing much to foster the study of Shakespeare in the schools; and to acknowledge my obligations to Mrs. E. F. Bemis, of Malden, Mass., of the "Society to Encourage Studies at Home," for her kindness in promoting the production of this little volume. Especially do I wish to record my hearty thanks to Mr. Joseph Crosby, of Zanesville, Ohio, for the generous sympathy, the sound counsel, the prompt aid which he has given me, — indeed, who in America earnestly desiring to study Shakespeare has not something to thank Mr. Crosby for? And finally, my thanks for efficient help of every kind in this undertaking are due to her whom, of all his friends, the nearest and dearest, a man loves best to thank.

W. T. T.

HOLLINS INSTITUTE, ROANOKE CO., VA.
February, 1883.

SHAKESPEARE

PRIZE EXAMINATION.

HOLLINS INSTITUTE, VA.

1881.

NOTE.

THE young ladies studying in the Literature Department of Hollins Institute were notified during the session that a prize examination in *Hamlet* would be held in the spring, and the papers forwarded to the "New Shakspere Society" of England, for the purpose of obtaining, if possible, the prize offered by that Society for the encouragement of the study of Shakespeare in schools. Two young ladies offered to compete, both of whom received their training in this Institute. They worked on the examination after the regular recitation hours, and were given ample time to think over their work. They had no idea of what the questions would be, and prepared the whole play. The questions were arranged by Mr. H. H. Furness of Philadelphia, and were first used by Dr. Stark at Logan Female College, Kentucky. By the courtesy of both gentlemen I was permitted to use them again, and, in doing so, I added questions [56], [57], [60], [61], [67]. The papers were submitted to Mr. Joseph Crosby, of Zanesville, Ohio, for examination. He considered both as worthy of being forwarded to England, and both are herewith given. The young ladies, Miss Mertins, of Alabama, and Miss Wilson, of South Carolina, wrote entirely unassisted, and their work, except a few clerical corrections, is given as they produced it.

WM. TAYLOR THOM,
Prof. English Language and Literature.

HOLLINS INSTITUTE, VIRGINIA.

PRIZE EXAMINATION IN HAMLET.

HOLLINS INSTITUTE, VIRGINIA, MAY, 1881.

Questions by Horace Howard Furness, Esq., of Philadelphia. Examination Papers of Miss Emma A. Mertins, of Alabama, and Miss Hannah Wilson, of South Carolina.

HISTORICAL AND BIBLIOGRAPHICAL.

1. On what story is Shakspere's tragedy of *Hamlet* founded?
2. Did Shakspere get it from the Danish historian?
3. What is the date of the earliest edition of Shakspere's *Hamlet*?
4. What is the date of the second edition?
5. Is there much difference in bulk between these two editions?
6. When was the first edition said to have been acted?
7. And probably on what occasion?
8. How was the copy of the first edition probably obtained for the printer?
9. Does Francis Meres mention it?
10. What is the theory of the editors of the Clarendon Press Edition in regard to the quarto of 1603?
11. Is there any difference between the first and second editions on the score of Hamlet's madness?
12. Is there any difference in the names of the characters?
13. Is there any contemporaneous play of *Hamlet* in any other language than English?
14. What is the date of the first edition of Shakspere's collected works?
15. How many years after Shakspere's death was it published?
16. And by whom was it published?

1. The story upon which Shakspere founded his *Tragedy of Hamlet* is as follows : —

Roderick, king of Denmark, having divided his kingdom into sections, placed over them governors, among whom were two brothers, Horvendile and Fengon. At that time the greatest honor was obtained by piracy, and in this Horvendile excelled all others. Collere, king of Norway, aware of this fact, and perhaps envious of his fame, challenged Horvendile to a combat in which the winner was to gain all that was in the other's ship. In the contest Collere was killed. Horvendile returned home with his booty, a great part of which he gave to King Roderick, from whom he received his daughter in marriage. Their son is the hero of the story. Fengon became envious of his brother's good fortune, and resolved to kill him. The murder of Horvendile by Fengon, the marriage of the latter with his brother's widow, Hamlet's feigned madness, the various means employed by Fengon to discover Hamlet's secret, Polonius' death, Hamlet's remonstrances with his mother, and his banishment to England, are all found in the *Histoire of Belleforest*, which goes on to say how, after his uncle's death, Hamlet became king of Denmark, how he went to England again, married two wives, by one of whom he was betrayed, after having returned to Denmark, into the hands of his maternal uncle, Wiglerus, and was finally slain in battle. The denouement of this story differs essentially from Shakspere's *Hamlet*, otherwise the action of the play is very much the same in both. The names in the "Historie," with the exception of Hamlet himself and of his mother, Geruth, have no resemblance to Shakspere's. The scene is laid in Denmark, before the introduction of Christianity there, and when the Danish power held sway over England. The story is rude, uncouth and unredeemed by any artistic touches of the narrator, and is typical of the corrupt morals of the time.

2. The story of Hamlet is told by Saxo Grammaticus, in his *Historia Danica*, written between 1180 and 1208, but not published until 1514. This story is found incorporated in Francis Belleforest's *Histoires Tragiques*, printed at Paris about 1570. A translation of the story from the *Histoire* brought it upon the English stage. It was first printed in London by Richard Bradocke, in 1608, and had probably been adapted to the stage before Shakspere took it up. Upon one of these old plays he no doubt built his own tragedy, though he does not follow in all the details any particular version of it. Shakspere was probably familiar with Holinshed's treatment of the subject.

3. The earliest edition of Shakspere's *Hamlet* was printed in 1603, and was acted by his Highness' servants in London, at Cambridge and Oxford.

4. The date of the second is 1604.

5. It was enlarged to "almost as much again as it was according to the true and perfect copy." That of 1603 contained about thirty leaves, whereas the edition of 1604 contained fifty, exclusive of the title.

6. The first edition was acted in London, and at the two Universities of Cambridge and Oxford.

7. Probably at the coronation of James I.

8. The copy of the first edition was probably obtained by some short-hand reporter while the play was being acted, or from the actors themselves — passages were jotted down — some from memory, and, when memory failed, the passage was supplied by some stupid blockhead, and in this condition the play was hurried to the press.

9. Francis Meres does not mention the play of *Hamlet* in his *Palladis Tamia* of 1598, because it had not been written then. He mentions *Two Gentlemen of Verona, Errors, Love's Labor's Lost, Love's Labor's Won, Midsummer Night's Dream*, and *Merchant of Venice*, for comedy; and for tragedy *Richard II., Richard III., Henry IV., King John, Romeo and Juliet*, and *Titus Andronicus*. He would certainly have included *Hamlet* in the list in preference to some there mentioned, being decidedly superior to them, had it existed, for he was an ardent admirer of Shakspere.

10. The theory of the editors of the Clarendon Press Edition is based upon subjective considerations. For a long time a play on the subject of Hamlet had existed, and these editors think that about 1602 Shakspere took such a play, and began to revise it and rewrite, as he had done others — that in this work he advanced little further than to the third act, which fact can easily be ascertained by examining the two quartos — that further examination will show that the inferiority of some parts of the quarto of 1603 to that of 1604 cannot be accounted for on the supposition that they were written at different periods of the author's life, especially as the first could scarcely have been written before 1602.

The inferior portions of the quarto of 1603 are hence attributed to some lesser artist, and regarded as the remains of the old tragedy.

11. The first edition differs from the second with regard to Hamlet's madness, in that, in the first, it is decidedly more marked, more pronounced than in the second.

12. Polonius, in the edition of 1603, is Corambis, Reynaldo is Montano, and Voltimand is Voltimar.

13. There is a play contemporaneous with Shakspere's *Hamlet* in the German language, not derived from Shak-

spere's play, but founded on same old story as was his. Polonius in this play is Corambis.

14. The date of the first edition of Shakspere's collected works was about 1623.

15. From Shakspere's death, 1616 — seven years.

EMMA A. MERTINS.

1. Shakespeare's *Tragedy of Hamlet* is founded on a story from the Danish Chronicles of Saxo Grammaticus, who wrote probably from 1180–1208. They were first printed at Paris in 1514, and incorporated into Belleforest's *Histoires Tragiques*, thence translated into English. The earliest English translation extant, of the volume in which the story of Hamlet is found, is that of 1608. The characters in this story bear no resemblance in name to those of Shakespeare, except in the case of Hamlet, who is Hamblet, and that of his mother, who is called Geruth; Polonius is Corambis, and Reynaldo, Montano. The story is one of horrible intrigue and murder, unrelieved by a single touch of art or fancy. It is substantially this: The Kingdom of Denmark was divided into provinces, over two of which the war-like brothers, Horvendile and Fengo, were Governors. In that age piracy was esteemed not only legitimate but honorable, and Horvendile's famous feats moved Collere, King of Norway, to challenge him to combat, the victor being awarded as spoils, the vessel and its contents, of the vanquished. Horvendile being victorious, returned in triumph to Denmark, and rendered up his treasures to the King, who thereupon rewarded him with the hand of his daughter, Geruth, in marriage, and, upon his death, left him on the Danish throne. From this marriage sprang Hamlet, the hero of the story. Fengo, being filled with envy

at his brother's good fortune, corrupted his Queen, and then murdered him secretly. Hamlet, naturally fearing for his life, feigns madness. Corambis (the Polonius of Shakespeare) warns the king, and together they plot against him, contriving an interview between Hamlet and the Queen, to which Corambis was a secret listener. Hamlet, suspecting treachery, keeps up his assumed madness, and beating on the arras with his arms, discovers his hidden foe, on which, crying "a rat, a rat," he thrusts him through with his sword, and drawing him out half dead, finishes the bloody deed in the presence of the Queen. Geruth declares her innocence of the murder of Horvendile, and tells Hamlet that she had often interfered to save his (Hamlet's) life. Fengo now despatches Hamlet to England, in charge of agents who are instructed to have him executed. Hamlet succeeds in delivering himself, and returns to Denmark, where, after marrying two wives, he is finally slain in battle. Hamlet's melancholy is prominent in the old story, and there is an episodical narrative to the effect that the northern country was under the dominion of Satan, and it is obscurely hinted that Hamlet, like other young men of the time, held some communion with spirits.

2. Shakespeare probably took his play from the English translation of this old story, and from an older play, of unknown origin, founded on it.

3. The first that we hear of Shakespeare's *Hamlet* is from an entry in the Stationers' Registry, in London, July 26, 1602, of a book, "The Tragicall Historie of Hamlett, Prince of Denmarke," by William Shakespeare. This is probably the book which appeared in print the following year, 1603.

4. 1604.

5. That of 1603 contained thirty-two pages, the second edition twice as much.

6. In the city of London, the Universities of Cambridge and Oxford, and elsewhere.

7. Probably on the accession of James I., as is suggested by the editors of the Clarendon Press Series.

8. It was probably taken down by a short-hand writer from the stage.

9. Francis Meres, a great admirer of Shakespeare's genius, in his "Palladis Tamia," or *Wit's Treasury*, written in 1598, fails to mention among the list of Shakespeare's plays then current, that of *Hamlet*, which is a significant sign that it was not then in existence.

10. That it represents Shakespeare's *Hamlet* in a transitional state, from its beginning in an old play, which Shakespeare took and fitted for the stage by some alterations and additions of his own, and afterwards expanded into the quarto of 1604, which is the play that we have.

11. Hamlet's madness is more pronounced in the quarto of 1603.

13. In the German.

14. The first collected edition was made in 1623.

15. Seven years.

16. Heminge and Condell.

HANNAH WILSON.

GRAMMATICAL.

17. Explain the use of "*sensible*," in I. i. 57.[1] Give other instances of adjectives similarly used in this play. In *Macbeth;* in *Merchant of Venice*.

18. What is the meaning of "*still*" in I. i. 122? Can you recall any other instances in this play? Any in *Macbeth?* In *Merchant of Venice?*

---

[1] The references here and elsewhere in these examinations are to the *Clarendon Press* editions of the plays.

19. What was Shakspere's use of "*thou*" and "*you*"? Illustrate by references to *Hamlet*.

20. What ellipsis is there in "That father lost, lost his, and the survivor bound"?

21. Can you recall any instances of suffixes appended to nouns for the purpose of signifying an agent? In *Macbeth?* In *Merchant of Venice?*

22. Can you give any instances of the use of the prefix *a* before nouns? before participles?

23. Give instances of Shakspere's use of double comparatives?

24. Can you recall any instances where Shakspere neglects the inflection of the pronoun *who?* In *Macbeth?* In *Merchant of Venice?*

25. Give some instances of the conversion of one part of speech into another.

26. Give some account of the rise of the use of *its*.

27. What is Marsh's rule about the use by Elizabethan writers of *sith* and *since?* Does the rule hold uniformly good in Shakspere?

28. Explain the meaning of the line: "When we have shuffled off this *mortal* coil." What peculiarity in the use of the adjective? Illustrate by examples.

29. "The glow worm shows the matin to be near, and 'gins to pale his *uneffectual* fire." What is the meaning of *uneffectual?* Give examples of adjectives used proleptically.

17. The use of *sensible* in this line is an example of what Mr. Abbott calls the passive use of adjectives. The word means *that which can be perceived*, real, actual, tangible. It is not used now in that sense.

Other instances like this occur, as *plausive manners*, meaning manners that can be applauded, and hence pleasing. The expression *dreadful secrecy*, also in this play, is a similar use of adjectives in this sense. In *Macbeth* is the expression, "To throw away the dearest thing he owed as 'twere a *careless* trifle," also "the *sightless* couriers of the air."

18. *Still*, here means *constantly*. From the original signi-

fication of *quiet, unmoved;* then continuing in this state of rest, and hence *constantly.*

Other instances occur in, "Thou *still* hast been the father of good news."

"I should *still* be plucking the grass to find where the wind sits." — *Merchant of Venice.* "The world is *still* deceived with ornament." — *Merchant of Venice.*

"*Still* gazing in a doubt." — *Merchant of Venice.*

"Remove from her the means of all annoyance, and *still* keep eyes upon her." — *Macbeth.*

"Your good advice, which *still* hath been both grave and prosperous."

19. *Thou*, in Shakspere, is used in familiar address; *you*, in formal address. *Thou*, also, was used in speaking to inferiors. Thus, in the gravedigger's scene, Hamlet always addresses the clown as *thou*, and the clown replies with a respectful "*You*, my Lord." Hamlet, having killed Polonius, says: "*Thou* rash, intruding fool, I took *thee* for *thy* better!" Here *thou*, because he took him for his better, and now discovers his real character.

When the King asks Laertes, "What wouldst *thou* have, Laertes?" he probably uses *thou*, because Laertes begs a favour, and is, in this sense, his inferior.

Perhaps *thou*, in the exclamation of the Queen, "O! Hamlet, *thou* has cleft my heart in twain!" contains a touch of affection which *you* would not express.

20. "That father lost, lost his," &c.

The ellipsis seems to be, "that father, *who was* lost, lost his." The relative is frequently omitted in Shakspere, where the meaning is evident, and the ellipsis can be easily supplied. In the expression, "Now follows *that* you know"; that is, "*that that* you know," the relative and demonstrative pronoun being the same, the ellipsis is quite natural. The neuter verb is also frequently omitted in such cases as this. A similiar omission of relative and neuter verb occurs in the passage : "And they, in France, of a most select," &c., omitted, because of the pronoun before, and the prepositional clause coming after, "And they *who are*," &c.

21. Suffixes used by Shakspere for converting a noun into an agent, are *er, or*, as *truster, ling*, as *groundling— Hamlet; sleepers — Macbeth.*

22. The prefix *a* was primarily *on, in*, a preposition contracted by rapidity of pronunciation, and hence occurs with those words most commonly in use. Thus *a-work, a-waking, at gaming, a-cursing*, in *Hamlet; a-brewing, a-bleeding, Merchant of Venice; a-foot, Macbeth; "on* brood," *Hamlet;* stand *an* end, *an* for euphony.

23. *More nearer* is an instance of the use of double comparative where the force of the *er* as sign of comparative having been lost, the word was compared by *more* and *most. More richer* also occurs in *Hamlet, more elder* in *Merchant of Venice;* "*my* sudden and *more strange* return," *Hamlet;* also *worser.*

24. *Who* is not inflected in the expressions "Between who?" "Saw? Who?" *Hamlet.*

25. The following are instances of the conversion of one part of speech into another, "as *hush* as death," "I doubt it *nothing*," "in *few*," "*moment* leisure," "*music* vows," "*region* kites," *wont*, past participle of Anglo-Saxon *wunian, woned, wont* used as noun, *instant* instantly, "most select and generous *chief* in that," *hatch, disclose, remove, Hamlet;* "*trifle*" is used in *Macbeth* as a verb (active), "to *top* Macbeth," same use of *top* occurs in *King Lear;* "*vinegar* aspect," "*exceeding strange*," "childhood *proof*," "will you *pleasure* me," *Merchant of Venice.*

26. *Its* was not used very often by Shakspere, as in the expression, "It lifted up it head, &c.," in *Hamlet,* and in *King Lear,* "It had it head bit off by it young." *His* was genitive masculine and neuter of the pronoun *he, heo, hit.* When a thing was personified there was danger of mistaking the *his* used in personification for the neuter *hit.* Milton frequently uses the feminine form in such cases, as "*his form* had not yet lost all *her* original brightness."

The inconvenience of this became great and the writers made use of *hit's, it's, its,* instead of the neuter form *his.*

27. Marsh's rule about the use of *sith* and *since* is that *sith* has an *illative* force and *since* merely expresses *time after.* Shakspere makes no such nice distinction, but uses them interchangeably.

28. "Shuffle off this *mortal coil.*" A metaphor from anything that winds in coils, entanglements. A similar use of the adjective *mortal* is found in *Macbeth: mortal words,* mortal thoughts.

29. "The glow-worm shows the matin to be near, and 'gins to *pale his uneffectual fire.*"

Fire may here be said to be uneffectual, because in the superior light of the sun the feeble light of the glowworm is as naught. In the use of prefixes having a negative force, *in, un,* and the like, Shakespeare makes no distinction, though he seems to prefix *un* before dentals. *Un* is perhaps stronger. *Uneffectual* is used proleptically. Other examples of this use of the adjective occur in the expressions "rose of the *fair* state"—*fair* because the rose adorns it. "Takes off the rose from the *fair* forehead of an innocent love," in *Hamlet,* and in *Macbeth,* "ere humane statute purged the *gentle* weal"—*gentle* being the effect of purging.

EMMA A. MERTINS.

17. We find adjectives, especially those ending in *ful*, *less*, *ble*, and *ive*, used sometimes in an active and sometimes in a passive sense.

> Hamlet I. i. 57.—
> "I might not this believe
> Without the *sensible* and true avouch
> Of mine own eyes."

Sensible, which we use in a neuter sense, is here passive, meaning "real, tangible, that may be felt or perceived by the senses."

> Merchant of Venice II. viii. 48.—
> "And with the affection wondrous *sensible*
> He wrung Bassanio's hand."

Sensible is here active, and means "feeling."

> Macbeth I. vii. 23.—
> "Upon the *sightless* couriers of the air
> Shall blow this horrid deed in every eye."

Sightless is here passive, meaning "unseen."

> Hamlet I. ii. 207.—
> "This to me
> In *dreadful* secrecy impart they did."

Dreadful, meaning "frightened," is here used in a passive sense.

> Hamlet I. iv. 30.—
> "The form of *plausive* manners."

Plausive, meaning "that may be applauded," is here passive.

18. Hamlet I. i. 122.—
> "As harbingers preceding *still* the fates."

Still here, according to its original meaning of "unmoved," "in one place," has the force of *always, constantly*.

Hamlet II. ii. 42. —
"Thou *still* hast been the father of good news."

Macbeth III. i. 21. —
"We should have else desired your good advice,
Which *still* hath been both grave and prosperous."

Merchant of Venice I. i. 17. —
"I should be *still*
Plucking the grass, to know where sits the wind."

19. The Elizabethan use of "thou" is the same as that of the German "du." It was the pronoun (1) of affection towards friends, (2) of good-humoured familiarity towards servants, (3) of contempt for strangers. This use of "thou" commenced to be broken down in Shakespeare's time, and subsequently "thou" became the rhetorical pronoun, while "you" was commonly used in conversation. In *Hamlet* [sc. ii.], beginning at line 40, in the interview between Laertes and the King, he, in speaking to Laertes, begins with the formal "you," and then, rising in his professions of esteem for Laertes, uses the affectionate "thou," — again returning to formal questioning, resumes the use of "you,"— and, once more, in granting a gracious permission of the desired favor, returns to "thou." In the same scene, the King, in his argument with Hamlet, uses the formal "you," the Queen the affectionate "thou."

20. "That father (who was) lost, lost his, and the survivor bound."

The Elizabethan desire for brevity caused them often to omit words, which to our minds are important to the construction, and which omission sometimes leads to great obscurity. In this case the missing words may be readily supplied from the context.

21. Hamlet I. ii. 172.—
"Nor shall you do mine ear that violence,
To make it *truster* of your own report
Against yourself."
Merchant of Venice III. iii. 1.—
"*Gaoler* look to him; tell me not of mercy."
Macbeth I. vii. 65.—
"Memory, the *warder* of the brain."

22. In the formative period of the language adverbs were frequently formed from nouns, adjectives, and participles, by prefixing "a," which represented an earlier "in" or "on."
Hamlet II. ii. 685.—"And fall *a-cursing*"—(part.), "a" has the force of "on" or "in the act of."

Hamlet II. ii. 473.—
"Aroused vengeance sets him new *a-work*."
Lear III. iv. 136.—
"Poor Tom's *a-cold*."
Macbeth III. iv. 33-4.—
"The feast is sold
That is not often vouch'd, while 'tis *a-making*."

23. The use of the double comparative by Shakespeare does not convey a negative force, as with us, but was simply intensitive. The comparative was first formed by the addition of "er" or "re," but in the transitional state of the language, this termination lost its force, and "more" was frequently added to intensify.

Hamlet II. i. 10-11.—
"By this encompassment and drift of question
—come you *more nearer*."

24. Hamlet II. ii. 195. —
"Between *who?*"

Macbeth IV. iii. 170. —
"The dead man's knell
Is there scarce ask'd for *who.*"

25. We find great license in the Elizabethan usage in this respect; almost any part of speech can be used as another, — nouns as adjectives and verbs, pronouns used as nouns, transitive verbs used intransitively, etc.

Hamlet II. ii. 470. —
"The bold winds speechless and the orb below
As *hush* as death." — [interjection for adjective.]

Macbeth I. v. 6. —
"Who *all-hailed* me." — [interjection used as verb.]

Macbeth II. iii. 18. —
"The *primrose* way." — [noun as adjective.]

Macbeth II. iii. 118. —
"To show an unfelt sorrow, is an office
Which the false man does *easy.*"
— [adjective for adverb.]

Hamlet I. iii. 132-3. —
"I would not, in plain terms, from this time forth,
Have you so slander any *moment* leisure."

Here we have a noun used for the adjective, where we should probably use the genitive or some other adjective.

Hamlet I. v. 90. —
"And 'gins to *pale* his uneffectual fire."
— [adjective as verb.]

26. In Shakespeare's time "his" was generally used as the genitive of "it," and we find this use prevailing until the time of Milton.

27. Marsh's rule was that "sith" was the illative adverb, and "sithence" or "since" the temporal adverb. Shakespeare uses them changeably.

> Hamlet III. iii. 53-4.—
> "That cannot be; *since* (illative) I am still possess'd
> Of those effects for which I did the murder."
>
> Hamlet III. ii. 58-59.—
> "*Since* (temporal) my dear soul was mistress of her choice
> And could of men distinguish, her election
> Hath sealed thee for herself."

28. "When we have shuffled off this *mortal* coil."

It seems to be a euphemism — to express, in an elegant way, the act of dying. "Coil" is used as of a rope, to express folds or entanglements.

29. "The glow-worm shows the matin to be near,
And 'gins to pale his *uneffectual* fire."

"*Uneffectual*" is used for "ineffectual." The meaning of the expression is, the glow-worm's fire, which could only be seen in darkness, was beginning to grow pale in the growing light of day, and that it would by broad daylight be of no effect.

> Hamlet III. i. 152.—
> "The expectancy and rose of the *fair* state."

The state was *fair* because it was so adorned.

> Macbeth III. iv. 76.—
> "Ere humane statute purged the *gentle* weal."

Here the weal is represented as *gentle* because it has been purged.

HANNAH WILSON.

PHILOLOGICAL.

30. What is the meaning of, "I'll make a ghost of him that *lets* me"?
31. What is the meaning of *unhousel'd, disappointed, unaneled*?
32. What is the meaning of *windlasses and assays of bias*?
33. Is Shakspere's use of the word *closet* the same as ours?
34. What is the meaning of, "The clown shall make those laugh, whose lungs are *tickle o' the sere*"?
35. Explain: "I am but mad north-north-west. When the wind is southerly, I know a hawk from a handsaw."
36. What is the meaning of *extravagant*? I. i. 154.
37. What is the meaning of, "No fairy *takes*"? I. i. 163.
38. Is Shakspere's accent of *Hyperion* (I. ii. 140) correct?
39. Explain the meaning of "*dearest foe.*" I. ii. 182.
40. What is the derivation of "*nickname*"? III. i. 144.
41. Was a "*jig*" anything more than a dance in Shakspere's day?
42. Explain "black and *grained spots.*" III. iv. 90.
43. What is the meaning of "*curb and woo*"? III. iv. 152.
44. Explain the allusion in "the owl was a baker's daughter."
45. What was Shakspere's opinion of politicians, as inferred from his use of the word?
46. What is the meaning of, "Woo't drink up eisel"?
47. Explain: "I would have such a fellow whipped for o'erdoing Termagant. It out-herods Herod."
48. Explain: "Would not this, sir, and a forest of feathers — if the rest of my fortunes turn Turk with me — with two provincial roses on my razed shoes, get me a fellowship in a cry of players, sir?"
49. Explain: "The king doth wake to-night and takes his rouse, keeps wassail, and the swaggering up-spring reels."
50. What does Bernardo mean by calling Horatio and Marcellus "the *rivals* of my watch"?
51. Explain: "Methought I lay worse than the mutines in the bilboes."
52. What is Shakspere's use of "*ecstasy*"?
53. What is the meaning of *eager*, in "like *eager* droppings into milk," and in "a nipping and an *eager* air"?
54. Explain: "They *can* well on horseback."

55. What does Hamlet mean by saying to Rosencrantz and Guildenstern, "Let me *comply* with you in this garb"?
[56.] Explain: "To split the ears of the *groundlings*."
[57.] Explain: "For, O, For, O, the hobby-horse is forgot."

30. "I'll make a ghost of him that lets me," means, I'll make a ghost of him that hinders, prevents me from going. This word *let*, though having the same form, is derived from an Anglo-Saxon verb, different from the word *let*, which means to permit. (Anglo-Saxon *lætan* means *permit* and *lettan* means *prevent*.)

31. The meaning of "*unhouseled*," is not having received the eucharist. It is from the Anglo-Saxon noun *husel*, verb *unhuslian*. *Disappointed* means *unprepared*. *Unaneled* signifies not having received extreme unction.

32. "*Windlasses* and *assays of bias*" mean *circuitous* and *indirect ways* or means. *Assays* of *bias* is a metaphor from the game of bowls where the bowl, by a circular movement, is made to reach the "queen," instead of by a direct line.

33. Shakspere uses the word "*closet*" to mean one's private apartments as it does in the Scriptures. I think it is now used to mean a small recess adjoining a larger room.

34. "The clown shall makes those laugh whose lungs are *tickle o' the sere*."

The *seare*, or *sere*, was part of or attached to the trigger of old matchlock guns, so arranged that the slightest movement would make the gun discharge. Lungs, then, "tickle o' the sere," are those easily excited to laughter.

35. "I am but mad north-north-west; when the wind is southerly I know a hawk from a handsaw."

Handsaw is probably a corruption for *heronsaw, hernsaw*. In some dialects of England *harnsa* is used, and it is but a step from this to *handsaw*. The meaning generally given to this passage is, that birds generally fly with the wind, and, when the wind is northerly, the sun dazzles the hunter's eye, and he is scarcely able to distinguish one bird from another. If the wind is southerly, the bird flies in that direction, and his back is to the sun, and he can easily know a hawk from a handsaw. When the wind is north-north-west, which occurs about ten o'clock in the morning, the hunter's eye, the bird, and the sun, would be in a direct line, and with the sun thus in his eye he would not at all be able to distinguish a *hawk* from a *handsaw*.

36. "*Extravagant*," compounded from Latin *extra*, and *vagare-vagans*, originally meant wandering beyond due bounds, limits, in the broadest sense, but now is restricted to meaning wandering beyond bounds as regards expenditures.

37. "No fairy *takes*."

Takes is an astrological term, like *strikes*. In *King Lear* occurs the *taking* air — the term refers to the malignant influence supposed to be exerted by the phenomena of the natural world, and the invisible spirits popularly believed to exist.

38. "*Hyperion* to a satyr."

Shakspere, in the word *Hyperion*, throws the accent which should be placed on the penult back one syllable on the antepenult.

39. "*Dearest foe.*"

Dear, in Shakspere's time, was not restricted as now, but was used to express intense feeling, whether of hatred or love. Thus, in *As You Like It*, Shakspere writes : " My father hated his father *dearly*."

40. "*Nickname.*"

The derivation perhaps is from an *eke-name*, an agnomen, the "*n*" having possibly slipped from the article, and become joined to the *eke*-name, as similarly an *adder* was originally a *nadder*, an *apron* was a *naperon*.

41. A "*jig*," in the days of Shakspere, besides being a dance, was also a song, perhaps quick and rapid in movement in imitation of the dance.

42. "Such *black* and *grained* spots as will not leave their tinct."

Grained, primarily meant dyed in *grain*. *Grain* was the name of a dye obtained from the coccus insect, a scarlet dye, which retained its color. Gradually this meaning was lost, and the term came to be applied to all colors that would "not leave their tinct."

43. "*Curb* and *woo*," are explained as meaning to *bow* and *beg;* *curb* being from French *courber*.

44. "*The owl was a baker's daughter.*"

As the legend goes, Christ begged hospitality of a baker's wife, who would have given it, but was prevented from doing this act of charity towards the seeming beggar by her daughter, who was, in consequence, changed into an owl.

45. Shakspere evidently did not have a very exalted opinion of politicians, for he frequently speaks of them in the most disparaging terms — "one who would circumvent God," says Hamlet, as he muses on the skull of a dead man, whom he imagines was once a politician.

46. "*Woo't drink up eisel?*"

This probably means "wouldst thou drink vinegar?" as *aisel* in Anglo-Saxon means vinegar. Some commentators think *eisel* refers to a lake somewhere in the Scandinavian peninsula, but as no such lake can be found, or rather, appears to have been found, it is safe to rely upon the other explanation. The meaning seems to be "Would you do a monstrous thing, an impossibility? I'll do it, too, and more than that."

47. "*Termagant,*" supposed to have been a god of the Saracens, a very violent character, was employed very often in the plays of the middle ages, but no such character has been found in any English plays. The Italian is *Trivigante*. Derivation probably *ter*, three, and *magnus*, great.

Herod was also a favorite character of the time, very noisy and turbulent, hence to "out-herod Herod" would be to be excessively violent.

48. "Would not this ... get me a fellowship in a cry of players?"

"*Forest of Feathers.*" The allusion is to the fact that a great many feathers were worn by actors in Shakspere's time.

"*Turn Turk,*" that is, if my fortunes undergo a complete revolution for the worse. Englishmen evidently had not a very high opinion of the Turks, for the expression occurs in Othello and other plays of Shakspere.

Provincial roses in this case were nothing more than rosettes worn on the shoe. The roses of Province were noted for their beauty. *Razed*, that is slashed, inlaid with different colored silks, stitched and embroidered perhaps. *Cry of players* means a company of players. *Cry* was commonly applied to a pack of hounds, though seldom to people.

49. "The king doth *wake* to-night and takes his *rouse,*" etc.

Wake means *feast, carouse,* used now to mean a *watch over the dead.*

Rouse means *bumper,* from Danish *ruus,* meaning a surfeit in drinking.

"Keeps *wassail*" perhaps contains the same idea of revelry, *wassail* being from the Anglo-Saxon *waes hael,* be of good health.

Upspring was part of an old German dance. *Hüpfauf* is the German, I believe,—a wild sort of dance.

50. "The *rivals* of my watch."

The word *rivals* used here in its primary signification of *partners*, those who lived by the same *rivus* or *stream*, and who both had use of it for purposes of irrigation.

From contentions which perhaps arose between the partners, the word came to mean those who vie with each other in anything.

51. "Methought I lay worse than the *mutines in the bilboes*."

Those confined by fetters and all chained together, so that the slightest movement of one would arouse all the others from sleep. *Bilboes* is derived from the name of the place *Bilboa*, in Spain, where the iron fetters were made.

52. Shakspere used *ecstasy* to mean *insanity, madness*. It occurs very often in *Hamlet* with this meaning, in *Macbeth* and elsewhere. Used now, I believe, as an expression of intense feeling, joy, or grief.

53. "*Eager*," from French *aigre*. Anything sour dropped into milk will make it curd, coagulate. "In *eager* and nipping air" the derivation of *eager* is the same French *aigre*, and means *keen, sharp, bitter*.

54. "They *can* well on horseback."

That is they are well skilled in horsemanship, *can* being used in its original meaning, to know how to do a thing, to be able, like the German *können*, Anglo-Saxon *cunnan*.

55. "Let me *comply* with you in this garb," that is, let me use ceremony with you—courtesy—lest my *extent, condescension*, etc. *Comply* is used once again in this play in the same sense.

[56]. "Split the ears of the *groundlings*."

The *groundlings* were those who were in the pit of the theatre, who paid a penny or more for entrance. A very boisterous, noisy rabble.

[57]. "For, O, the *hobby-horse* is forgot!"
The hobby-horse was a figure in the May games and Morris dances.
The Irish *hob* means *pony*.

EMMA A. MERTINS.

---

30. "I'll make a ghost of him that *lets* me." *Let* is derived from O. E. *lette*—to hinder.

31. "Unhousel'd, disappointed, unanel'd."
Unhousel'd without the eucharist. "Housel" is from Anglo-Saxon *housel*, eucharist, from which are formed the verb *huslian* and participle *gehusliad;*—*disappointed*, unprepared, as we speak of appointments in the sense of preparations,—*unanel'd*, without having received extreme unction; Anglo-Saxon *aell*-oil, from which the verb *anele*, to give unction. The whole phrase indicates that the King, in his sudden death, had been deprived of those last rites which in the Romish Church are considered necessary to prepare the soul for the future world.

32. "*Windlasses* and *assays of bias*"—winding and circuitous ways. The phrase "*assays of bias*" refers to a game of bowls in which the player strikes at his ball, not directly, but in a curved line, by which this ball is reflected upon the one aimed at. Perhaps the phrase is best explained by Polonius's own interpretation in the next line: "By indirections find directions out." It is noticeable here that Shakespeare uses the word "assay," which we use of trying metals, in the sense of our modern. "essay" or "attempt."

33. *Closet* has in modern times the literal meaning of the Latin "clausus"— *close, concealed*. Shakespeare uses it of a lady's private apartment.

34. "*Tickle o' the sere.*" The *sere*, variously spelt *sere, sear*, or *scear*, was the catch in a gunlock which kept the hammer in half or full cock, and was released by the trigger. In the old matchlock muskets, the sear and trigger were in one piece, hence, "lungs tickle o' the sere," meant lungs easily moved to laughter, like a gun that went off at the slightest touch.

35. In the provincial dialects of England *heron* was variously corrupted into *heronshew, harnsa*, etc.,—from the latter we readily trace "handsaw." The expression obviously refers to the sport of hawking. A bird, especially one of heavy flight like the heron, when roused by the falconer or his dog, would fly down or with the wind, in order to escape. If the wind were northerly, the heron would fly towards the south, and the sportsman, having his face towards the sun, would be dazzled by its rays and be unable to distinguish the heron from the pursuing hawk—on the other hand, if the wind were southerly the heron would fly towards the north, and the sportsman, now having his back towards the sun, would easily distinguish between the two birds. Further, we may notice that a wind from the precise point, "nor-nor-west," would be in the eye of the sun at half-past ten in the forenoon, a likely time for hawking.

36. "*Extravagant*," derived from two Latin words, "extra" *out, beyond*, and "vagans," *wandering*, is used by Shakespeare in this literal sense of wandering beyond limits, while we have restricted it to the sense of wandering beyond the bounds of economy.

37. "*Takes*" is here used in the sense of *infecting*, as in Lear II. iv. 158 —

> "Strike her young bones,
> You *taking* airs, with lameness."

38. "*Hyperion.*"—The accent in the original (Greek) is on the third syllable, which Shakespeare, as in the modern English manner, changes to the second.

39. "*Dear*" was used by Shakespeare of whatever touches us nearly, either in love or hate, joy or sorrow.

40. "*Nickname.*" Formerly an *eke*-name, or an added name. We can readily see how "an eke-name" was collided into "a nickname."

41. "*A jig*" seems to have consisted of a little farcical acting, introduced either at the end of a play or between heavier pieces.

42. "Black and *grained* spots." *Grain* from the ovarium of the coccus insect, which from its shape was called in Latin *granum*. This produced a bright scarlet, an unfading dye. The name was afterwards applied to any dye that will not wash out; hence, "black and *grained* spots" would mean dark stains that were indelibly impressed.

43. "*Curb* and *woo.*" *Curb*, from French *courber*, to bend; hence, to bend, or to bow and beg.

44. There is said to have been an old tradition in Gloucestershire to the effect, that the Saviour while on earth was churlishly refused by a baker's daughter, of whom he asked bread, and that she was, for this offence, changed by him into an owl.

45. Evidently a low opinion. We learn from history that the politicians of his time were low political tricksters, who would stoop to any means to accomplish their ends. Shake-

speare speaks of the politicians, as desiring, if it were possible, to overturn even the decrees of Providence.

46. Numerous attempts have been made to explain this phrase, "*Woo't drink up eisel.*" Some have thought that it refers to a lake, Eysel, in Scandinavian mythology, which one of their gods was supposed to have drunk up. But this, on competent authority, is shown to be false, as there was no Lake Eysel in that country, and the only feat of that kind was performed by Thor, the God of Thunder, who was challenged to drink up a river, but the other end of the horn from which he was drinking being turned into the ocean by his opponent, he only succeeded in drinking it to its edge. The idea is probably that Hamlet challenges Laertes, as in the following words "eat a crocodile," to perform some impossible feat. The phraseology indicates supreme contempt; "woo't," a corruption of "wilt thou," being used either contemptuously or as a mark of great affection.

47. "*Termagant*" was a famous character in the old Miracle or Mystery plays, a supposed god of the Saracens, son of the earthquake and of the thunder. He is represented as a great swearer, swaggerer and boaster, raving and ranting up and down the stage. Herod, the Slayer of the Innocents, was also a favorite character in these plays, very similar to that of the Termagant. These characters represent what was called the tyrant's part on the stage, which was a very noisy, boisterous one, as Bottom (in M. N. D.) says — "My chief humor is for a tyrant: I could play Ercles rarely, or a part to tear a cat in, to make all split."

48. Hamlet, referring to the success of his plot, asks Laertes if his fortunes *turn Turk* (that is, change as completely as if one should turn from an infidel to a Christian), with the help of the various appurtenances belonging to an

actor's wardrobe would obtain for him a position in a cry (or company) of players. The feathers spoken of were used for adornment. The *Provincial roses* are the rosettes, in imitation of the roses of Provins, or Provence, a brilliant, red rose, worn by the actors on their shoes, and the custom, as well as that of *razed shoes*, was said to have caused great extravagance. These *razed shoes* are described as being fanciful leather tops, cut or slashed in various designs, and lined with a color to display the design.

49. "The king doth *wake* to-night, and takes his *rouse*, keeps *wassail*, and the swaggering *up-spring* reels." *Wake* means here, keeping a late feast; *rouse* is from the Danish "ruus," a bumper; wassail, from Danish "*waes hael*" — be of good cheer, hence wild revelry; "*up-spring*" is said to be the English rendering of the German "*Hüpfauf*," the last and merriest dance at a merry-making.

50. It is curious that the quarto of 1603 uses "partners," which is the meaning of *rivals* here. The word is derived from Latin "rivus," which means a stream, and was applied to persons living beside the same stream and having equal rights to its use for irrigation; hence arose frequent contentions, and hence the metaphorical use of the term so much more used, both in Latin and in modern languages.

51. "*Mutines*"—a contracted form of mutineers; "*bilboes*"—a frame with iron stocks for holding the feet of prisoners on board the vessel, so called from Bilboa, a city in Spain, where iron was first manufactured. We understand how accurately the phrase represents Hamlet's restless condition, by remembering that the slightest motion of one of these imprisoned sleepers would arouse all the others.

52. Shakespeare uses "*ecstasy*" as synonymous with madness.

53. "Like *eager* droppings into milk "— a "nipping and an *eager* air "— *eager*, from French "aigre," means sour, biting, sharp.

54. "They *can* well on horseback " — *can*, from Anglo-Saxon " cunnan " — to know, to be able, means *well-skilled*.

55. " *Comply* with you in this garb," seems to be a sample of the Euphuistic style of language originated by John Lyly, an immediate predecessor of Shakespeare, who sometimes adopts it to ridicule it. The meaning of the phrase seems equal, " use ceremony with you after this fashion."

[56.] The *"groundlings"* were those who occupied the pit or ground-floor at the theatre, and were generally a rude, uncultivated set, whom Ben Jonson describes as "hissing everything above their grounded judgments."

[57.] " For O, for O, the *hobby-horse* is forgot." This, the *hobby-horse*, was probably a figure in the Morris dances. During the Puritan sway all public amusements were forbidden, which of course roused great resentment among their powerless opponents, and it is conjectured that this is a line from an old ballad satirizing the Puritan tyranny.

HANNAH WILSON.

ÆSTHETIC.

58. What is Gœthe's view of Hamlet?
59. What is Coleridge's?
[60.] What is Taine's and Hudson's?
[61.] What is your own?
62. How do you account for Hamlet's levity after his interview with the Ghost?
63. Does Hamlet or Horatio say: "The rest is silence"?
64. Are the flowers which Ophelia distributes to the King, Queen and others, real or imaginary?

65. Was the Queen an accessory to her husband's murder?
66. Was Hamlet mad?
[67.] What is your opinion of Hamlet's treatment of Ophelia in III. i.?

58. Gœthe thinks that, in the character of Hamlet, Shakspere evidently intended to depict a noble soul under the pressure of a duty which it is incapable of performing. " 'Tis a delicate vase," he says, "in which may blossom only beautiful flowers — an oak is planted there, grows, and the vase is shattered." "Thus cracks a noble heart." "Hamlet has no plan," says Gœthe, "but the piece is full of plan." Hamlet advances, recoils, resolves and re-resolves, but never acts, and when finally his uncle lies dead, the deed is done, not from any premeditated plan-scheme, but is merely accidental.

59. Coleridge thinks that in portraying Hamlet's character, Shakspere displayed his profound knowledge of metaphysics. That he desired to show the effect of an undue preponderance of thought over action, the unequal balance of the real and imaginary; that Hamlet by indulging in deep speculations in "thoughts that wander through eternity," loses the power of action. According as the exercise of power is hindered in its development in one direction it will be the more strongly and fully developed in another. The principle of correlation of forces which exists in the physical world, Mr. Coleridge thinks, holds good in the metaphysical. To this excessive thinking then he attributes Hamlet's incapacity for action.

[60.] Mr. Taine thinks that Hamlet's character is intended to show the effect of a moral poisoning, as also Macbeth's. That within classic halls he had known none of the strife and misery of the world. A dear father, who to him was the very ideal of manhood, and the sweet Ophelia, upon whom he had placed his affections, his mother and a few others — these were all he had known before he was summoned to his father's grave. Two months elapsed and his mother married her husband's brother. The discovery of the murder of his father by his uncle, his mother's marriage, were enough to make him lose faith in men and become disgusted with the world. He is morally deranged. Already in his soliloquy: "O, that this too, too solid flesh would melt," etc., there are earnests of hallucination. After the Ghost appears he is in a state of frenzy, he staggers, his knees are knocking together, his teeth chattering — indications of the monomania to come. Taine thinks that in this state Hamlet had no need to look for "wild and whirling words" — he could utter none other. Hamlet is the child of events — borne along he has no control over circumstances. With him the Ghost need not have objectivity — it already existed as a subjective reality.

Mr. Hudson, by a sort of eclectic process, has devised a theory of Hamlet from the different opinions of Shaksperian scholars, Gœthe, Schlegel, Coleridge, etc., and has succeeded, we think, in culling a good deal of truth, though we differ with him on the score of Hamlet's madness. Hudson finds the opinions of the above mentioned critics inadequate to express Hamlet's character. They have each looked at Hamlet from one particular point of view. Mr. Hudson thinks that Hamlet was not lacking in capacity for acting, as is shown by the quickness with which he sent Rosencrantz and Guildenstern to their just doom — by his determined resolve to break all connection with Ophelia, hard though it might be, and the carrying out of that resolution, though seeing how disastrous would be the consequences. His opinion, and I agree with him, is that Hamlet's hesitation to kill his uncle arose not from excessive thinking, not from lack of strong will, determination, but rather from the struggle which takes place in every noble heart when contemplating such a deed. I think Hamlet the nobler for this struggle, and if he had killed Claudius without any scruple, one might entertain a doubt as to whether he himself was as noble and good as he should be. To do his father's will was Hamlet's greatest desire. From his memory he had promised to wipe all "trivial fond records," and write there only the revenge of his father's death, and yet the still "small voice" of conscience kept crying to be heard, questioning the right, the justice of taking the life of one who to him was more than kin. He knows not but that the Ghost may be some evil spirit in a pleasing shape come to "abuse him in order to damn him."

When Hamlet finds Claudius praying, though thirsting for revenge, he does not kill because he thinks it will only be sending him to heaven, while in his memory is branded as with a scorching iron the picture of his "dear father murthered," condemned to "sulphurous and tormenting flames." That last "Remember me" rings in his ear, he cannot forget it. It would not be revenge then to murder Claudius as he kneels in prayer, 'twould be "hire and salary," and so Hamlet delays revenge.

[61.] In giving the views of the above writers, I have in general expressed my own.

62. Hamlet's levity, after the interview with the Ghost, is due to the terrible shock which the revelation of his father's murder produced — a thing which he may have suspected, but had not definitely known. I dare say any of us would be stunned were we to receive such a message from the other world. Deep grief, coupled with such a revelation, seems to

shake his whole frame, his delicate, sensitive soul. His words are like the smile, or hysterical laugh of a dying man, and his mind, which *will* ever be active, when not in a healthy state, will produce unwholesome thoughts. No disrespect is intended towards his father, whose ghost he calls "*old mole*," "*truepenny*," and the like — 'tis a jest of one in torture, in agony, pale, a ghastly smile on his countenance.

This, to me, seems the cause of Hamlet's levity on this occasion.

63. Does Hamlet, or Horatio, say " the rest is silence "?

It seems to me these words should belong to Horatio, though they are generally given to Hamlet. They accord so well with everything that Horatio ever said, with the whole tenor of his life. No bursts of grief ever came from him, always sane, calm in exterior, he bore alike the smiles and buffets of fortune, and when the soul of Hamlet wings its flight — perhaps as he is muttering, " O, I die Horatio," etc., and before he is able to finish, Horatio adds " the rest is silence "; words so calm, yet with a depth of meaning in them. " Flights of angels sing thee to thy rest," Horatio continues.

64. I do not see how it is possible to decide whether the flowers Ophelia distributed were real or imaginary. There is no internal evidence to decide.

65. I do not think that the Queen was accessory to her husband's murder, or knew anything at all about it until the deed had been done. The Ghost, though it reproaches her for her faithlessness to him, her frailty, does not intimate that she was at all implicated in his murder. Again, it is not probable that Claudius, a man of considerable intellect, would disclose to Gertrude his intention of killing her husband, to whom she seemed to be devoted. 'Twould not be a very

safe method of procedure. When the king rises, unfeignedly surprised, disturbed and excited by the player king and queen, surely Gertrude, a woman, would have felt the stings of conscience, the pangs of remorse, and would have given some indication of her guilt had she really been in the plot to murder her husband, for "conceit in weakest bodies strongest works." Again, when in their interview Hamlet tells his mother that his killing Polonius is "almost as bad as kill a king and marry with his brother," she exclaims in true innocence and amazement, "As kill a king!" When her heart was so wrung by Hamlet, we doubt not but that she would have declared herself guilty of the crime if she really were.

66. Was Hamlet mad?

Despite what commentators have to say on the subject, I cannot think Hamlet mad. That he was deeply moved with grief, afflicted with melancholy, hypochondria, I agree, but that Hamlet's mind, his intellect, was at all affected, I cannot entertain for a moment. I think he was morally affected, not mentally, and his madness, as he himself says, was feigned, and I fail to see how his feigning madness so well could prevent it from being distinguished from a real case of the disease, as some commentator supposes, for I am sure the poet presents Hamlet to us more than once as the most sane of men. He does at all times put on an "antic disposition." With Horatio, his only true friend, he casts aside this mask of insanity, and his eagerness to be alone, when he would not be compelled to assume the guise of madness, when he can commune with his own thoughts, and be himself, certainly indicates saneness of mind. "Oh! these tedious old fools!" he exclaims, when Polonius leaves, and he is alone.

Again when the players — when Rosencrantz and Guildenstern retire, Hamlet exclaims: "Now I am alone!" and falls into a reverie, that is not born of madness — then devises a means for "catching the conscience of the king."

Hamlet's conversation with his mother, though his words be "wild and whirling" — metaphor following metaphor — is most sane. The frenzy of grief is over him — nothing more. This exhortation to his mother is not the voice of a madman. 'Tis an earnest heart, sending up a prayer that the one whom he had through all his youth cherished may be reclaimed from sin and error.

Again the king — the one guilty of the murder of Hamlet's father — is the only one who at all suspects that Hamlet's madness is feigned; and I think it should be so, for he, whose hand was stained with a brother's blood, would no doubt watch closely Hamlet's every movement, and words that Hamlet uttered, though unintelligible to others, were to him fraught with the deepest meaning.

Hamlet's rushing into Ophelia's presence, seizing her by the arm, staring long into her face, some think is madness. I find no insanity in it. Perhaps in solitude, the desperateness of his condition and his grief overpowered him, he rushed in to learn if Ophelia could keep his secret, and help him bear the burden of his grief, if she still were true to him, and were not leagued on the side of his enemies — a tool in their hand; or, even more.

As eye meets eye in agony he reads in the depths of her soul her incapability of sharing his sorrows. Not a word is said, 'tis the first great silence of this king of words, — the second is death, and this silence expresses more than a volume of words. Those who favor the view of Hamlet's being mad generally hold that position because they think his treatment of Ophelia would be brutal and fiendish were he not mad, but as it will be seen Hamlet had manifold and good reasons for acting as he did towards Ophelia. Could any one say that Hamlet, in his conversation with Horatio, Act III. Scene ii., has strayed from sanity, that his words are not full of sobriety and good judgment? These are not qualities of madness.

Surely, Shakspere would not have put into the mouth of a madman such superb, profound thoughts, such exquisite, far-reaching speculative soliloquies. His depth of character and of mind seem to me incompatible with madness. Albeit a certain commentator says that madness and the richest intellect may exist in harmony, — that is not madness. Of course by the suppression of one faculty predominance is given to another, which is thereby sharpened and its action quickened. If such a one is mad, then are all mad, for in none is there such a balance of faculties. Different occupations and pursuits require different powers of mind.

"Had I but time — as that fell sergeant, death, is strict in his arrest," says Hamlet, "O, I could tell you." Again he says to Horatio, "absent thee from felicity awhile to tell my story." What story could it be, if, as the world thought, Hamlet was mad, and things were as they seemed?

Because Hamlet said things incomprehensible to us, I cannot think him mad. One must not presume to know the heights nor sound the depths of his soul, and we may rejoice that we get but a vague, dim outline of the story he so earnestly prayed Horatio to tell to the unknowing world when he himself was dead.

[67.] I think Hamlet's conduct towards Ophelia perfectly justifiable knowing the circumstances of his life, how, through the frailty of his mother — whom no doubt he had loved devotedly, and the only woman whom he had known intimately except Ophelia — he had seen the whole of womankind. This of itself would be sufficient to disgust him with the whole sex, and to make him infer that the rest were no better than his mother. Again, the tie between parent and child in those days was closer, stronger than now. Hamlet felt himself obliged to perform the duty imposed upon him by his father. He knew that Ophelia would likewise be compelled to comply with her father's desires, and that father was his enemy, in the service of the king. Ophelia's father would no doubt interrogate her concerning Hamlet, and force her to yield up his secret, or tell whatever she knew of his true state of mind, and hence it is that he acts the madman before her, stinging her with bitter sarcasms.

Perhaps also Hamlet kept his real state of mind from Ophelia because he did not wish to poison her own pure heart, to make her taste of that bitter cup which he himself was to drain to the dregs.

No doubt Hamlet was devoted to Ophelia, but, as we said, he held his duty to his father above all other ties; one must not think, however, that he lightly, heartlessly broke the connection between himself and Ophelia. He bore his grief with manliness, she, a more delicate and sensitive nature, ended life in hopeless insanity.

We have heard some sanctimonious people say that even if Hamlet was oppressed by grief amounting almost to agony, although it was good policy to keep from Ophelia, and consequently from the king, his plans, yet nothing can justify him in his brutal treatment of Ophelia. Human nature cries to be heard at such an accusation, and it will manifest itself in spite of everything. If for ten years one should stand gazing up at the clouds to refine and purify his soul, and so far forget the world as to almost extinguish human passions, even then one would not be an angel. Man will be human — he cannot submit so quietly always to destiny with a "Thus saith the Lord." Human feelings and human motives will come into play.

I have neither given nor received information on this examination.

EMMA A. MERTINS.

---

58. Goethe's view of Hamlet, in brief, is that he is a most lovely, pure, and moral nature without the strength of nerve that makes a hero — sinking beneath the weight of a task which is to him an impossibility. To him all duties are holy, the present is too hard; he winds and twists, now advancing to the accomplishment of his purpose, and as often recoiling, until, at last, in his indecision, his purpose all but fades from his thoughts. He likens Hamlet, or Hamlet's mind, to a beautiful vase which should have borne a rose in its bosom but has instead an oak tree planted in it. As the roots expand the frail receptacle trembles, and at last lies a shattered ruin.

59. Coleridge's idea is that Hamlet is a being gifted by nature with noble mental and moral endowments; a man whom we admire, yea reverence, and whom we would fain know and understand, but whose hidden springs of thought and action resist our utmost efforts of penetration. He compares him to a mighty stream whose surface-objects we can see, but can only guess as to the unfathomable depths below.

[60.] Taine's idea is that all of Shakespeare's great creations are the victims of some species of monomania, as in the cases of Lear, Macbeth, Othello, Hamlet. He thinks that Hamlet's is a case of moral poisoning. His nature is of a high moral tone, so delicately sensitive to impressions from without, that where no tangible evidence of things existed his powerful imagination supplied its want. Upon such a nature, the mystery surrounding his father's death and the evident defection of his mother, were enough to conjure up such images in his brain that the revelations of his father's ghost were scarcely more than seals to his haunting fancies. These ideas prey so sorely upon his moral nature that his mind fairly totters under the strain. He becomes a prey to morbid thoughts which tinge the whole universe with their dark colors, so that everything becomes distorted to his mental vision. Reason remains, but the mind is so loosely hinged that it sways horribly under every added shock. His father's ghost appears and he is aroused to dedicate his life to vengeance, but resolution and action are alike lost in the fatal melancholy which palsies every faculty.

Mr. Hudson gives a very exhaustive and common-sense view of Hamlet's character, which is ripe with the study of years and with a practical directness that charms us with its reality. He thinks that we become acquainted with Hamlet as we do with persons around us — that is, that we know him progressively, and that our views of him change as we reach different stages and experiences of our own lives; and thus his varied and complete personality appeals to the feelings and sympathies of all. He says that it often happens that the more we study Hamlet, the less we shall feel that we understand him. Just so we often find it in our own lives; we are often completely astonished by some new revelation in the life of a friend whom we have known for years, perhaps all our lives, which causes us to realize how little we can ever know of the inner lives of those around us. Mr. Hudson says, very truly, that Shakespeare has painted Hamlet in sentiments and manners far in advance of his age, and even of his immediate surroundings, as we see in the play: for instance, how bitterly he deplores the drinking customs of his countrymen — and, besides, his superior moral elevation which made him averse to shedding blood (of which we see he was only capable in moments of strongest excitement). He accounts for Hamlet's apparent weakness of purpose partly by the peculiar difficulties of his situation. Should he kill the king, he would be committing in the eyes of the world the very crime which he desired to avenge. For who would believe the testimony of a Ghost, whose ghastly revelations no mortal ear but his own had heard? But Mr. Hudson believes that Hamlet is mad, and devotes much of his argument to proving that fact, backing his views by scientific and philosophical opinions from learned authorities versed in mental phenomena. He thinks that Hamlet is the victim of a peculiar and subtle type of insanity, which, being perfectly compatible with seasons of entire sanity, only attacks him at certain times and under certain circumstances. A madness which the person is perfectly aware of, and which he would guard if possible from the knowledge of others. So Hamlet, when his reason has been dethroned by the awful revelations of the Ghost, meets his friends with uncontrollable and idiotic ravings, which, as he becomes calmer, he seeks to excuse, by hinting that, at some future time, he may see fit to assume madness, for a purpose which he cannot explain.

Again — Mr. Hudson notices that Hamlet is violently affected by meeting certain persons who naturally call up exciting thoughts; as, for instance, the King, Polonius and Ophelia; the first as the author of all his woe — Polonius as being perhaps accessory to the plot against his father, and certainly as influencing Ophelia against him, and hurt and angry at rebuffs which he had received from the latter, and perhaps suspecting her as a willing tool in the hands of his two enemies in the plot against him. In this way he (Mr. H.) explains Hamlet's silly badgering of the puzzled old courtier, his malicious mockery of the king, and his cruel violence towards Ophelia, in all of which cases he is, as it were, beside himself, literally crazy for the time being, and only becomes himself again when the irritating cause is removed.

[61.] I agree fully with Mr. Hudson in his estimate of Hamlet's character (independently of his madness), which I have tried (tho' with imperfect success, his views being so exhaustive) to sketch. I think with him that Hamlet's intense humanity is that which above all things endears him to us, that in Hamlet's woes we learn to sympathize as with a brother man, and it seems to me that if we try to estimate his character exactly as we do those of other men around us we shall find its inconsistences due to those human weaknesses that are common to all. Hamlet is a man in whom we find the noble qualities of mind and heart, which we are led, from the implied rather than expressed testimony of the play, to attribute to the murdered king, allied to the womanly delicacy and weakness of will which we discover in the fair, frail Gertrude. Thus we find him, though recognizing the sacredness of the duty imposed upon him, voluntarily resigning all the happy memories of the past, the possibilities of the future, to dedicate himself alone to vengeance; yet, in the next instant, we hear the wail of human agony:

"The time is out of joint: O cursed spite,
That ever I was born to set it right!"

At one time we find him listening with cool disdain and contempt, showing not a trace of the angry passion that the long, unfeeling harangue of his "uncle-father," must have stirred within him — anon we would scarcely recognize him as the same man, when alone he pours out, in abject sorrow, the woes of his unhappy soul. It is mostly in these soliloquies that we see best the wonderful depths of Hamlet's character; they are as mirrors of the soul, in which we see at the same time his greatest strength as well as his greatest weakness, — his noble sense of duty, his brave resolves to overcome the weakness that paralyzed his actions, and at the same time his vain longings for rest and quiet, for deliverance from this very duty. The fact is, that Hamlet saw so clearly what the result of an action would be, that he would, for fear of a future evil, neglect the present good. But we like, besides this, to think that Hamlet was morally incapable of deliberately performing a deed of murder, that it was only by a sudden emergency that he was capable of sending into that "undiscovered country, from whose bourne no traveller returns," the soul of his fellow-man.

62. That it was the natural result of the tremendous shock to his nervous system, which Hamlet experienced from the revelations of the ghost, added to the necessity he felt of concealing his real feelings from his friends. We often observe similar reactions where the mind has been subjected to an unnatural tension, and seeks to relieve itself. Sometimes we see it in the form of hysterical laughter, sometimes in unmeaning talk, or anything that is foreign to the subject on which the mind is brooding. As we notice in Hamlet, while he is nervously awaiting the appearance of the ghost, he talks of the weather, of the hour, of the King's revel, moralizes on the drinking habits of his countrymen, — anything but the ghost.

63. I think that these words should properly belong to

Horatio, though either interpretation may be maintained. Hamlet has said above in lines 320–21:

> "Had I but time — as this fell sergeant, death,
> Is strict in his arrest — O, I could tell you."

If these words be attributed to him, I think they would probably mean a repetition of the same idea, a sad regret that he is unable to clear up the mystery that clings around his life and death. On the other hand, if we attribute these words to Horatio, which I think more natural (in that Hamlet must have felt satisfied that his story would be safe in the keeping of this faithful friend), I think it is susceptible of a two-fold meaning — either somewhat of the same meaning that it has from Hamlet's lips, that death prevents his further utterance, or it is as a sigh of relief from this loyal friend, who has witnessed with a harrowed soul this awful and unexpected finale, that silence has at last fallen upon the scene.

64. I think it is more entirely in consonance with the representation of Ophelia's madness to suppose that the flowers are real. She is represented as singing snatches of old songs, and her mind seemingly only sensible to impressions from within, insensible to those from without. She seems to have lapsed into the past and to recall those old songs and stories which she had heard in childish days; so it seems to me, that, as a child, she would have gathered the flowers which she is represented as distributing. Besides we have very significant proof of their reality in the description of her death by the Queen, who speaks of her as having "fantastic garlands" of flowers, with which she sought to crown the "envious slivered willow."

65. I think not, for Gertrude does not possess the force of character which one to do a deed like this must have.

We find Gertrude "the beauteous majesty of Denmark," a woman of exceeding grace and courtesy of manner; a fascinating woman who has inspired such idolatrous love in the hearts of two men, that the one remembers her even beyond the grave, the other, for love of her, has sold his soul. A woman who, at best, could so dishonor the memory of a noble man whom she had loved, as *such a heart* could love and could so far forget her own self-respect as to marry another "within a month." And this from the weakness of a character which could not say "*no*" and stand to it. It might be said that such a woman could be brought to commit almost any crime, but I think that Gertrude shows a moral cowardice which rendered her incapable of such a crime as murder. In her interview with Hamlet, the woman who was to have taxed him with his "pranks," soon sinks in abject remorse and begs mercy of him who has shown her her true self in colors so dark that she cannot bear the sight. But in that interview I think she clears herself of the guilt of her husband's murder. What denial could be more emphatic than her amazed repetition of Hamlet's words: "As kill a King!" She has also, I think, proved her innocence at the play, where the King, who has before this worn a "front of brass" to the world, rises in the uncontrollable anguish of a suddenly aroused conscience and rushes from the scene; we have no sign of guilt from this weak woman who shortly after quailed before Hamlet's charges.

66. I do not agree with Mr. Hudson that Hamlet is mad, and I can best express my views on this subject by attempting to answer his instances of what he considers Hamlet's madness. I think in the first place that Hamlet's hint to Horatio, Bernardo and Marcellus, that at some future time he might assume madness, was literally and simply what he

meant to do. Even while the ghost was speaking, Hamlet, with that keenness of foresight with which he was so peculiarly gifted, saw as in a vision the difficulties of the position into which destiny forced him. He suddenly thinks of, and as quickly decides upon madness as the cloak under which disguise his plans may be matured. Again, his sudden madness at sight of Polonius and the king is perfectly consistent with his intention of deceiving them, and surely we cannot be surprised at the evident malice and deliberate contempt which he shows towards the former, the keen ridicule with which he dares to chafe the latter. Mr. Hudson thinks too that the keen womanly perception of the Queen and Ophelia would not have been deceived by the pretended lunacy of Hamlet. On the contrary it seems to me that these two, of all others, would have been most easily deceived. Gertrude we find represented as a woman of a yielding, plastic nature, susceptible to all impressions, and this, added to the natural anxiety of a mother, would cause her to be easily misled by signs which to a disinterested eye would seem but trifles. Ophelia is only a young girl, one whom her father calls a "green girl," one who besides her intense love for Hamlet reverences him as a hero. She would be the last to suspect him of deceit. Turning from Hamlet's madness to the positive evidences of his sanity, what could be more reasonable, more complete, more adapted to the purpose than Hamlet's admirable advice to the players? What could be more ingenious, more carefully planned than his plot to catch "the conscience of the king"? What could be more genial, more whole-souled, more sane and natural than his noble tribute to Horatio? But why multiply instances? In short, I think that Shakespeare did not intend to lower so noble a conception as the character of Hamlet, but that he is only, as Hamlet says for himself, "mad in craft."

[67.] Some one has truly said that Shakespeare's dramas are of a two-fold nature — the visible drama or that which appears on the surface, and the invisible, which we can only perceive when we study for ourselves the characters and attempt to appreciate their motives. I think that reading, as it were between the lines, in the famous scene between Ophelia and Hamlet, we may see that he acted the part of a real hero in his seeming cruelty. We cannot think that his conduct was that of a degraded trifler, ruthlessly trampling upon the holiest feelings of the gentle girl before him, nor that his cruel words were those of a madman, however glad we feel to think that Ophelia solaced her bleeding heart with the thought that it was Hamlet's madness, and not Hamlet, that had spoken thus. It was impossible that the old relation should continue, and feeling this, as an honorable man, the stern duty of sundering the tie between them devolved upon Hamlet. He would fain perform the task as shortly and effectually as possible, and we feel in our hearts that the cruel words: "I loved you not," were as full of pain to the speaker as to the hearer. Who can doubt the reality of his words at the open grave of Ophelia: " I loved Ophelia ; forty thousand brothers could not, with all their quantity of love, make up my sum."

I have neither given nor received information on this examination.

HANNAH WILSON.

CASTELL FARM, BEDDGELERT, N. WALES,
September 8, 1881.

MY DEAR SIR:—

After a long morning's ramble . . . over the hills in this beautiful region, I read . . . the two printed Examination Papers and answers by Miss Wilson and Miss Mertins, that you have just sent me.

My first feeling was one of regret, that for so trifling a prize as the "New Shakspere Society" can afford to give to each of the thirty Colleges and Schools that have them — only a yearly guinea's worth of its Publications — you should have gone to the expense of printing this pamphlet of thirty-six pages.

My second feeling was one of satisfaction, that your Examination Papers were not . . . mere cram-questions, but contained at least seven questions which implied your belief that your pupils had minds as well as memories, and could form an opinion of their own on the chief characters of the play.

My third feeling was one of pleasure at the general goodness of the answers, and at the fact that the Answerers tho' evidently overpowerd and opprest by Hudson's view of Hamlet, had yet judgment and independence enough to reject Hudson's notion of Hamlet's madness, and see that it ruins the character. Neither of the Answerers has apprehended the purport of the play as I see it, that God *will* have his purposes carried out, and *will* make this jibing, kicking Hamlet pass the goal of his uncle's death though he dies himself in the effort, — see my Introduction to the "Leopold Shakspere,"— but I think the answers so good on the whole that I ask Mr. Griggs to post you two copies of the Fac-simile *Hamlet* quartos first and second, and shall feel obliged if you will hand one couple to Miss Wilson and the other to Miss Mertins, with my best wishes. The Society's books will reach you in due course.

With best wishes for the success of your classes and College, and heartfelt hopes that your noble and long-suffering President Garfield may soon be restord to health, I am truly yours,

F. J. FURNIVALL.

TO PROF. WM. TAYLOR THOM.

SHAKESPEARE

PRIZE EXAMINATION.

HOLLINS INSTITUTE, VA.

1882.

NOTE.

THE Shakespeare Prize was awarded to Miss N. B. Bowman, of Lynchburg, Virginia, upon an examination in *Macbeth*. Miss Bowman was allowed to refer to the unannotated text of *Macbeth*, and also of *Hamlet* and *King Lear*, as given in the "*Globe*" Shakespeare. She wrote without knowing what the questions were to be, and without assistance, and her papers are herewith given as she wrote them, four or five unimportant corrections excepted.

This Examination was given to show the best results attained in the study of Shakespeare in the Institute, and will be forwarded to the "New Shakspere Society" of England, whose prize for the encouragement of the study of Shakespeare was awarded this school last year on a similar examination in *Hamlet*.

Respectfully,

WM. TAYLOR THOM,
Prof. English Language and Literature.

HOLLINS INSTITUTE,
Roanoke Co., Va., June, 1882.

PRIZE EXAMINATION IN MACBETH.

HOLLINS INSTITUTE, VIRGINIA, JUNE, 1882.

TEXTUAL.

1. When was *Macbeth* first published, and in what form?

2. At what period in Shakespeare's artist life would the general style and characteristics of verse place the play?

3. How are the upward and downward limits of the date of the play fixed?

4. What incident may have suggested the subject of *Macbeth* to Shakespeare?

5. Dowden, following Malone, places the date of the play about what year, and on what internal evidence?

6. What is the opinion of the Clarendon Press editors on this subject?

7. Whence did Shakespeare get the materials of the play?

8. And what incidents, not belonging to the original story of Macbeth, has he incorporated in the play?

9. Is there anything historical in the play?

10. What is the theory of the Clarendon Press editors as to interpolation, and by whom?

---

11. Explain use of "*of*" in "*of* kerns and gallowglasses is supplied." I. ii. 13.

12. Explain use of "*on*" in "eaten *on* the insane root." I. iii. 84.

13. Explain constructions — "*in viewing* o'er the rest," &c. I. iii. 94; — "like *the leaving* it." I. iv. 8; — "*old turning* the key." II. iii. 2.

14. Explain force of "*who*" — "*who* was the thane lives yet." I. iii. 109.

15. Explain construction—"*as* 'twere a careless trifle." I. iv. 11; —"*as* they had seen me." II. ii. 27; —"*An't* please heaven he shall not." III. vi. 19.

16. Explain construction —"a *careless* trifle." I. iv. 11; —"*sightless* substances." I. v. 47.

17. Explain use of "*to*"—"the late dignities heaped up *to* them." I. vi. 19; "And *to* that dauntless temper of his mind." III. i. 51.

18. What is peculiar in the adjective use in "Unto our *gentle* senses"? I. vi. 3; —"eaten on the *insane* root"? I. iii. 84.

19. Explain the use of "*but only*"—"*but only* vaulting ambition." I. vii. 26.

20. Explain "*would*"—"which *would* be worn now," &c. I. vii. 34; —"That *would* be howl'd out in the," &c. IV. iii. 194.

21. Construction of line, "Hear not my steps, *which way they walk*." II. i. 57.

22. Explain form *gives*, "Words to the heat of deeds too cool breath *gives*." II. i. 61.

23. Illustrate power of conversion of parts of speech by "Hath *trifled* former *knowings*." II. iv. 4.

24. Explain "Go not my horse *the* better." III. i. 25.

25. Explain "*while* then, God be with you." III. i. 43.

26. "There is none *but* he." III. i. 53.

27. "Unsafe the while, *that* we must lave," &c. III. ii. 32.

28. Explain "Imposters *to* true fear." III. iv. 64.

29. Explain "*To know* my deed, 'twere best not know myself." II. ii. 73; —"*To fright* you thus methinks I am too savage." IV. ii. 70; —"blame his pester'd senses *to recoil* and start." V. ii. 22.

---

30. What is the meaning of "*Aroint* thee, witch!"? I. iii. 6.

31. What beliefs are suggested in—

"But in a sieve I thither sail,
And like a rat without a tail"? I. iii. 8–9.

32. What is the meaning of *fantastical* in "are ye *fantastical?*" I. iii. 53; —"whose murder yet is but *fantastical*"? I. iii. 139.

33. What was a *harbinger?* I. iv. 45; and a *purveyor?* I. vi. 22.

34. Explain —
"Herein I teach you
How you shall bid God 'ild us for your pains,
And thank us for your trouble." I. vi. 12–14.

35. Explain "if the assassination could *trammel up* the consequence, and catch with his *surcease, success.*" I. vi. 2–4.

36. Explain "That memory, the *warder of the brain* shall be a *fume*, and the receipt of reason a *limbec* only." I. vii. 65–67.

37. What is the meaning of "*travelling lamp*"? II. iv. 7.

38. Meaning of "Nature's copy's not eterne"? III. ii. 38.

39. What is meant by "Our hostess keeps her *state*"? III. iv. 5.

40. Explain "*witches' mummy.*" IV. i. 23.

41. What is meant by "the *blood-bolter'd* Banquo"? IV. i. 123.

42. What courtier-like reference does Shakespeare make in bringing in "*the evil*"? IV. iii. 146.

43. Explain the meaning of "rise from her bed, throw her *night-gown* upon her." V. i. 4.

44. Explain —
"For their *dear causes*
Would to the bleeding and the grim alarm
Excite the *mortified man.*" V. ii. 3–5.

45. Meaning of "*pester'd* senses"? V. ii. 23.

46. Explain —
"They have tied me to a stake; I cannot fly,
But, *bear-like*, I must fight the *course.*" V. vii. 1–2.

---

1. *Macbeth* was first published in the folio of 1623, where it comes between *Julius Cæsar* and *Hamlet*, occupying pages 131–151 inclusive.

It was divided into acts and scenes, and the text, though not so corrupt as in some other plays — *Coriolanus* for example — was yet very defective as regards division of lines. The Clarendon Press editors conjecture that it was printed from a transcript, not copied from the author's MS., but written to dictation, since many of the errors are palpably those of the ear, not of the eye.

That it had not been published at an earlier date appears from the fact that it is entered by Blount and Jaggard in the Stationers' Record in 1623, as "one of the plays not before given to other men."

This folio itself is interesting, being "the first edition of Shakespeare's collected works, as set forth by his friends and fellows, John Heminge and Henry Condell." They speak contemptuously of certain "stolne and surreptitious copies," referring to some of the quartos, and claim that their work is printed from the original MS. It is certain, however, that in some instances the plays of the folios were printed from earlier quartos. Yet, in spite of the failure to realize the editors' claim, this folio is of great value — not only because in certain points superior to the quartos, but because it contains eighteen plays not found in quarto form.

This folio was dedicated to the earls of Pembroke and Montgomery, and contained all the plays found in modern editions, save *Pericles*.

In 1632 was published the second folio — a reprint of the first conjecturally emended, the emendations being more often wrong than right.

The third folio (1664) contained seven additional plays not found in the first, all of which, with the exception of a part of *Pericles*, are proved to be not Shakespeare's work.

The fourth folio appeared in 1685.

2. With Dowden, dividing Shakespeare's dramatic career into four periods, embracing all together the twenty years and upwards between 1588 or 1590 and 1612, the general style and characteristics of versification would place *Macbeth* in the third period, extending from 1601 to 1608, in which

were produced the grave and bitter comedies and the great tragedies — believed by many to be but the reflection of the author's own heart.

Having passed through the period of apprenticeship and experiment, in which he was at once a diligent workman, and a bright and cheerful one, leaving this impress upon the works of this period, he next began to exercise his imagination upon affairs of real life, and to perceive that there is "sterner stuff of poetry" in actual life than in all the prettinesses and affectations which had sometimes led him astray in his earlier career. This is the second period in which he is "*in the world*" — and of the world too. The works belonging to this period are the "joyous comedies" and the "historical plays." Before the close of this period he had known sorrow — death had removed some dear to him — his friend of the sonnets had wronged him. His imagination now finds employment in sounding the depths of the human heart, piercing the mysteries of evil itself. At this period it is that *Macbeth* is to be placed. It is one of the group of "Later Tragedies," along with *Lear* and *Othello*.

3. The upward limit of the date of the play is fixed by the words of Macbeth, in Act iv. Sc. i. —

"And some I see
That two-fold balls and treble sceptres carry."

—which refer to the union of the two kingdoms of Great Britain and Scotland, under James I., who acceded to the English throne in March, 1603, while the union took place in October of the following year (1604). The play then could not have been written before this event.

On April 20, 1610, Dr. Simon Forman saw *Macbeth* acted at "the Globe," and, in his Diary, he gives an elaborate description of the play. It was certainly, therefore, written before 1610.

4. When King James visited Oxford in 1605, there was represented before him a Latin play or interlude on the subject of *Macbeth*. Farmer thinks this may have suggested the subject to Shakespeare; but the Clarendon Press editors think this not probable, believing that Holinshed furnished the material to the Latin dramatist as well as to Shakespeare, and in each case a subject was selected from Scottish history to please the Scottish monarch, and Shakespeare's play would be none the less acceptable for representing the rightful heir restored to his throne by a victorious English army.

5. Dowden maintains that the characteristics of versification forbid us to place *Macbeth* after *Pericles* and *Anthony and Cleopatra*, or very near *The Tempest*. " Light endings " begin to appear in this play for the first time in any considerable number (twenty-one being the exact number). There are but two " weak endings." The predominance of light and weak endings and of double or feminine endings in a play is an indication that it is of Shakespeare's later works, when he was growing in freedom and naturalness of style. On the other hand, rhyme, as a rule, indicates an early date. There are, however, exceptions, since conditions of the drama itself may sometimes require rhyme.

Upon the whole, Dowden thinks the internal evidence favors the opinion of Malone (also adopted by Steevens and Chalmers), that the play was written about 1606. They all agree, as do Gervinus and Collier (upon second thought), that the reference to the union of the two kingdoms, mentioned above, would have lost much of its force had the play not been written soon after. Again, in the *Porter-Scene*, " the farmer who hanged himself upon expectation of plenty," is thought to be an allusion to the scarcity of corn in the autumn of 1606, and the "equivocator" to the trial, in 1606, of Henry Garnett, superior of the order of Jesuits, for implication in the gunpowder plot, and to his perjury on that occasion. Some base the argument further on the "tailor stealing out of the French hose," explaining it as a reference to the scantiness of pattern then fashionable in that article of apparel, as contrasted with former voluminousness. The habit of tailors in this respect seems to have been a common subject of ridicule. Finally, the practice of "touching" for "the evil" had been revived by James, which may throw some general light upon the date.

6. The Clarendon Press editors maintain that the union of the two kingdoms was a matter of such importance that it would not soon pass from the minds of men. Therefore it is not necessary to suppose *Macbeth* written immediately after that event; that the Jesuitical doctrine of equivocation was an established fact and common subject of complaint with ministers of the age, hence no need to suppose that it refers specially to Garnett. "The farmer who hanged himself upon expectation of plenty" might refer to the abundant harvest of any other year as well as to the scarcity in 1606. When Dr. Simon Forman saw *Macbeth* in 1610, he would scarcely have been at the pains to make an elaborate summary of the plot, had it not been then a new play. Moreover, so great, at that time, was both the demand for and supply of new plays, that even the most popular had not such a run, nor were so frequently revived as at the present day. There is nothing to justify the inference, much less to prove that *Macbeth* was produced at an earlier date than this (1610). In Beaumont and Fletcher's "Knight of the Burning Pestle," there is an obvious allusion to the ghost of

Banquo, which also favors the view that *Macbeth* was then a new play and fresh in the minds of the people.

7. Shakespeare got the materials of the play entirely from Holinshed's Chronicle, who in turn got them — through Bellenden's Scotch translation — from the "*Scotorum Historiae*" of Hector Boece (1465–1536), first principal of King's College, Aberdeen. Boece followed Fordun, adding to him largely.

8. The details of Duncan's murder were taken from Holinshed's account of the murder of King Duffe by Donwald,— an incident of earlier date.

Between the histories of King Duffe and Donwald, and of Duncan and Macbeth, Holinshed has a few pages devoted to Kenneth, a brother and successor of Duffe, who in order to secure the throne to his own son, poisoned Malcolm, the son of Duffe. Holinshed relates how, at night, Kenneth heard a voice saying: "Think not, Kenneth, the murder of Malcolm Duffe, by thee contrived, is hidden from the eye of the living God." This probably is the original of the "terrible voice" of the murder scene in *Macbeth*.

The incident of the death of Siward's son is taken from Holinshed's history of England.

9. The Clarendon Press editors say the only points in which the drama coincides with real facts are the murder of Duncan and Macbeth's connection therewith (either as principal or accessory), and the character of Lady Macbeth.

The rebellion of Macdonwald, and the invasion of Sweno, during the reign of Duncan, are fables, and Banquo and Fleance, ancestors of the Stuarts, are inventions of the chronicler. These editors declare it is difficult to make one's way through the maze of tradition and fable which has come down to us. The single point upon which historians agree is that the reign of Macbeth was one of prosperity and vigorous government.

10. In 1779 Steevens—it is generally conceded to have been Steevens, I believe—discovered a manuscript play, "The Witch," by Thomas Middleton, which was found to bear a striking resemblance, in some respects, to Shakespeare's play of *Macbeth*, so that the question of plagiarism was raised and discussed in a spirited manner.

With reference to this, the Clarendon Press editors affirm that, were they convinced that Shakespeare wrote the whole of *Macbeth*, they would unhesitatingly pronounce Middleton the plagiarist. But, they go on to say, though the "least mannered of all poets," Shakespeare has always a manner peculiar to himself, and there are some parts of *Macbeth* in which we can find no trace of this manner. Some of these are Act I. Sc. ii.; Sc. iii. ll. 1–37; Act II. Sc. i. l. 61; Sc. iii. ll. 1–47 (specially); Act III. Sc. v.; Act IV. Sc. i. ll. 39–47; also ll. 126–132; Sc. iii. ll. 140–159; Act V. Sc. ii.; Sc. v. ll. 47–50; Sc. viii. ll. 32–33; and the last forty lines of the play.

Having given what they think conclusive arguments in support of this opinion, they account for these passages upon one of two hypotheses — first, that Shakespeare wrote the play in conjunction with some one else as "collaborateur"—that having formed the general scheme, he reserved for himself those parts in which Macbeth and Lady Macbeth were to appear, and consigned the rest to Middleton, largely re-writing and correcting the work of his assistant, though good-naturedly allowing some of Middleton's suggestions in his own work.

But these editors think that Shakespeare would never have permitted the second scene of Act I. to remain, so prefer the theory that, after the death of Shakespeare, or after his withdrawal from connection with the stage, some one — probably Middleton — remodeled *Macbeth* — extending the parts assigned to the Weird Sisters, adding a new character, Hecate; putting in the *Porter Scene* "to please the groundlings"; possibly also substituting the scene of the "bleeding sergeant" for the supposed original conversation between Macbeth and Banquo.

---

11. The difference between the Shakespearean and the modern usage as regards prepositions, and indeed many other words, may be often explained upon the principle of division of labor, which has been in action since that time. The manifold duties then performed by a single word, have been divided out amongst other words. Thus, "*of*" originally meant "*from*" — a force still retained in the strong form "*off.*" In the meaning "*from,*" Shakespeare not only uses "*of*" to express the *agent from whom* the action is regarded as proceeding — where we should use "*by*," — but also uses it to express the *instrument*, where we should use "*with.*" Especially is this the case with verbs and adjectives of "constructing," "filling," and the like, expressing not only the thing *with which*, but that *out of which* the thing is made. We still use "*of*" with verbs and adjectives of construction, and with adjectives of fullness.

For "*of*" in sense of "*from*" see Hamlet III. iii. 31–33 —

> "'Tis meet that some more audience than a mother,
> Should o'erhear the speech, 'of' vantage."

In Hamlet IV. ii. 12 — " Besides, to be demanded 'of' a sponge !" where 'of' denotes the agent. Ham. I. i. 25 — "This dreaded sight twice seen 'of' us." And especially

Lear III. ii. 59 — "More harder than the stones whereof 'tis raised."

12. "*On*" signified "juxtaposition," — was frequently used for "*of*" in sense of "*about*."

Compare the indifferent use of "*on*" and "*of*" in Hamlet IV. v. 176-177 —

> "God ha' mercy '*on*' his soul!
> And '*of*' all Christian souls I pray God."

So too, Hamlet III. ii. 88-89 —

> "How fares our cousin Hamlet?
> Excellent, i'faith; '*of*' the chamelion's dish."

King Lear I. iv. 98-99 —

> "Why, this fellow has banished two *on's* daughters."

Hamlet I. i. 55 —

> "What think you *on't*."

On in sense of *about*.

13. "*In viewing* o'er the rest," etc. As to the nature of these words in "*ing*," it seems difficult in some cases to determine whether they are *nouns* or *verbals*. The history of these forms seems to be as follows. In Anglo-Saxon the verb had an abstract noun ending in "*ung*," and a present participle in "*ende*," which two forms later became confused. There was also a gerund or dative infinitive, ending in "*enne*," preceded by "*to*," and this too was confounded with the present participle, and thus with the noun. Finally, there resulted from all this confusion a single form in "*ing*," having the force now of a *noun* — being both preceded by an adjective and followed by a preposition, as, "shaking of," Hamlet II. i. 92 — "At last a little *shaking* of my arm," etc., — but again of a *verbal* governing a direct object — "like

the *leaving* it"; "old *turning* the key," where the article and adjective preceding are accounted for by the confusion with the noun as explained above.

The whole thing is a result of the general tendency towards the discarding of inflections and the simplification of grammatical structure, so largely accelerated by Norman influence after the conquest in 1066.

See Hamlet III. ii. 60 —

"For thou hast been
As one, in suffering all, that suffers nothing."

"Or by pronouncing of some doubtful phrase."
— Ham. I. v. 175.

"As checking at his voyage." — Ham. IV. vii. 61.

"Did my father strike my gentleman for chiding of his fool."
— King Lear I. iii. 1.

"Mumbling of wicked charms." — Lear II. i. 39.

"One that slept in the contriving of lust."
— Lear III. iv. 86.

14. *Who* here illustrates the definite use of the relative, referring to a special person, compare the indefinite use in *Othello*:

"*Who* steals my purse steals trash."

Who was originally the interrogative pronoun (A.-S. "*hwa*" masc. and fem., "*hwaet*" neuter) ; *that* was the relative (A.-S. se, seo, thaet). The transition from the interrogative to the relative meaning of "*who*" may be illustrated by *Henry V.* Act IV. Prologue :

"O, now, who (interrog.) will behold
The royal captain of this ruined band . . . ?
Let *him* cry 'Praise and glory on his head!'"

This would easily become, "Let him who (rel.) will behold," etc.

The lingering memory of the old interrogative force, when it was used to standing alone, is shown in the omission of the antecedent. Omission of antecedent also explained by some as the result of the emphatic position of the relative.

15. The usual explanation of the constructions makes "*as*" equivalent to "as if," "*an*" (which they say is the imperative of "*unnan*," "to grant"—incorrect, since "*an*" and "*and*" are the same word used interchangeably, meaning merely "with the addition of") equivalent to "if." The fact is, the "if"—the contingency—is contained in the subjunctive mood, which was formerly inflected and expressed alone all the subjunctive relations. After a while the same forgetfulness or disregard of the force of inflections which produced "more better," "most unkindest," etc., led to the insertion of "*if*" after "*as*," "*an*," etc.

Compare :

"Smile you my speeches *as* I *were* a fool."
—Lear II. ii. 78.

"He must speak truth! *An* they will take it, so."
—Lear II. ii. 95.

"*An* thou *hadst* been set in the stocks for that question."
—Lear II. iv. 61.

16. These words illustrate what Mr. Abbott calls the *active* or *passive* use of adjectives ending in *less*, *ive*, *ble*, etc.— such words being sometimes equivalent to an active participle, again to a passive. *Careless* trifle, i.e. "uncared-for" trifle ; *sightless* substances — "invisible," that *cannot be seen*.

Compare :

"Without the *sensible* (that can be perceived by the senses) and true avouch of mine own eyes."
—Hamlet I. i. 57.

"In *dreadful* (frightened) secrecy impart they did."
— Hamlet I. ii. 207.

"Let it be *tenable* (that may be retained) in your silence still."
— Hamlet I. ii. 248.

"Or by some habit that too much o'er-leavens
The form of *plausive* (pass.) manners."
— Hamlet I. iv. 30.

"Who I am sure is kind and *comfortable* (act.)."
— Lear I. iv. 297.

"Scarf up the tender eye of *pitiful* (act.) day;
And with thy bloody and *invisible* (pass.) hand."
— Macbeth III. ii. 47-48.

17. "*To*," radical meaning "motion towards," hence "rest near," hence "addition," as here — "heaped up *in addition to* them; "and *in addition to* that dauntless temper."

This meaning of "*to*" is now retained only with verbs of motion, and the strong form "*too*" (*cf.* "of" and "off," above) alone has by itself the meaning of "*in addition to.*" For "*to*" in this sense we use "*besides.*" But Shakespeare could use "*to*" without any verb at all with this meaning of "*in addition to.*"

There were other forces of "*to*" arising from this radical notion of "motion towards," "rest near"; hence "by the side of," "in comparison with," "up to," "in proportion to," "according to"; then "like," from which comes the meaning of "equivalent," "apposition," etc., as found in the expression "taken *to* wife:" Ham. I. ii. 14. Meaning "*motion*," it comes, also, to mean "motion with a view to," "for a purpose" —

"Worthy to be a rebel, for *to* that (end)
The multiplying villanies of nature
Do swarm upon him."   — Macbeth I. ii. 10.

"As flies *to* (compared to) wanton boys, are we to the gods,
They kill us for their sport."   — Lear IV. i. 38-39.

18. These examples illustrate what is termed the "proleptic use" of the adjective. What would be fully expressed by a whole clause following the noun, is condensed into a single word and placed before the noun. "The *insane* root "— *i.e.*, the *root which produces insanity* (as the effect of eating it) ;— "our *gentle* senses" are our senses made gentle (soothed) thereby— *i.e.*, by the pleasant air.
Compare —

"And 'gins to pale his *uneffectual* fire." — Ham. I. v. 90.

19. The same forgetfulness of the original meaning of words, referred to above as producing "more better," &c., led to the redundant use of " but only " = " only only."

But — Early English and Modern Northern English "*bout*," A.-S., "*bi-utan*," where "*bi*" is modern *by;* "*utan*" = *out* or *without*. Hence, *but* is formed on the analogy of *without*, and meant "*out take*," "*except*," — having force both of active participle governing the accusative case, and of a passive participle taking a nominative absolute. (See below, 26th question : "There is none *but he*.")

All the meanings of *but* can be explained from the original meaning of "out take" or "except." Sometimes it was used to except a whole clause, for instance : —

"And *but* she spoke it dying, I would not have believed her."

This illustrates the transitional use of *but* from " except" to the adversative (the most common modern use) "on the contrary," " by way of prevention." Thus : " If she had not spoken (except she spoke) it dying, I would not believe," and again " I would not believe, but (adversative) she spoke," &c.

All uses of "*but*" arise — 1. From variation between the meaning of "except" and the adversative "on the other hand"; 2. From the fact that the negative before *but* is sometimes omitted — "but ten came," may mean "ten however came," or "*none* but ten " — *i.e.*, *only* ten came. Thus "but only" of the question is shown to be no other than "only only."

"Bring me *but* to the very brim of it."
— King Lear IV. i. 75.

20. *Would* carries the idea of *will*, in the sense of *wish*, *purpose*. The attempt to realize a wish is very apt to take the form of a requirement. We wish a thing; then consider the thing as a duty, obligation; then require its performance. 1. I would, 2. I should, 3. I must.

In the examples "which *would* be worn now," "That *would* be howl'd out," there is conveyed the notion of *requirement*, derived as described above; showing that Shakespeare had not, though we have, forgotten the force of the A.-S. *wilnian* = *to wish, to require*.

"It *would* be spoke to."   — Hamlet I. i. 45.
"That *would* be scanned."   — Hamlet III. iii. 75.

21. "Hear not my steps, which way they walk." An example of the redundancy of Shakespeare's language adopted for the sake of emphasis. He introduces a single (unnecessary) object, thus making the real clause-object a mere explanation of this intruding object. Compare his use of the double negative for the purpose of strength.

"But wilt thou hear me how I did proceed?"
— Ham. V. ii. 27.
"I know you what you are." — Lear I. i. 262.

22. Mr. Abbott says the use of "gives" in this case is probably for the sake of the rhyme. But this verbal inflection in *s*, with plural subjects, is a perfectly common occurrence in Shakespeare's writings, and may be very readily explained. It is merely an additional instance of the lingering memory of the then rapidly disappearing, and now almost entirely gone, inflections of the Anglo-Saxon, and of the dialectic peculiarities of the Early English, where we find for the plural of verbs three forms, one in each dialect: Northern *es*, Midland *en*, Southern *eth*. Hence Shakespeare's apparently singular verbs are generally to be explained as the natural and legitimate descendants of the old Northern plural in *es*.

"All that *lives* must die." — Ham. I. ii. 72.
"For women's fear and love *holds* quantity."
— Ham. III. ii. 142.
"The great man down, you mark his favorites *flies*." [1]
— Ham. III. ii. 179.
"What, *has* his daughters brought him to this pass!"
— Lear III. iv. 61.
"Which very manners urges." — Lear V. iii. 235.

23. There was the utmost license in this respect. Almost any part of speech could be used as any other part of speech, at pleasure. Formerly the infinitival termination (M. E. *en* (*e*), A.-S. *an*) could convert almost anything — noun, adjective, &c., — into a verb. When this inflection was lost, the power of conversion still remained, — nouns, adjectives, &c., being used as verbs — generally in an active sense — without any verbal termination at all.

Besides, passive verbs were used as active verbs; nouns,

---

[1] For this reading, *cf.* Furness, *Var. Ham.*, and Abbott's *Shak. Gram.* § 333. T.

verbs, adjectives, participles, and even conjunctions, interchanged in the most liberal manner. "*If* (verb) me no *ifs* (noun)."

Here: "Hath *trifled* former *knowings*"—*trifled*, an intransitive verb used transitively, or, perhaps, a noun used as verb; "*knowings*," participle used as noun and given the plural inflection.

"Sweno, the *Norways*' king, craves composition."
—Macbeth I. ii. 59.

"*Nothing* afeard of what thyself didst make."
—Macbeth I. iii. 96.

"So nightly *toils* the subject of the land."
—Hamlet I. i. 72.

"*Shark'd* up a list of lawless *resolutes*."
—Hamlet I. i. 98.

"Are of a most select and generous *chief* in that."
—Hamlet I. iii. 74.

"In *few*."　　　　　　—Hamlet I. iii. 126.

"As *hush* as death."　　—Hamlet II. ii. 471.

"The honey of his *music* vows."　—Hamlet III. i. 156.

"Dowered with our curse and *strangered* with our oath."
—Lear I. i. 196.

"Thou losest here, a better *where* to find."
—Lear I. i. 253.

"*Straight* took horse."　　—Lear II. iv. 34.

"He *childed* as I *fathered*."　—Lear III. vi. 109.

24. "Go not my horse the better." In *go* we have the old force of the subjunctive inflection,—not requiring "*if*."

"*The*" is the instrumental case of the old demonstrative or relative (A.-S. *thi*, *the*, from nom. *se*, *seo*, *thaet*). With comparatives, it is used to express the measure of excess or defect. In this use *the* varies between the meanings, "on this account," "therefore," "in this way."

Here we may explain (considering the distance), "if my horse go not *on that account* better"; or, considering it a race between the night and the horse, "Go not my horse the better of the two."

25. "*While*" used to be a noun meaning *time* [A.-S. *hwil* = "time," dat. plur. *hwilum*, whence E. E. adverb *whilom*, meaning *formerly*, a form still retained].

We may still hear, "he stayed a long while," where "*while*" means "*time.*" Generally, however, *while* with us means "during the time when"; with Shakespeare it meant "up to the time that." Here, "while then" has a future signification.

26. "There is none *but he*" = "there is none, *he being excepted.*" (See answer to question 19, above.)

27. "Unsafe the while, *that* (in which)." *That*, as representative of the Anglo-Saxon relative, *se, seo, thaet*, having itself lost the different case forms, nevertheless retains their force. An instance of "inflection lost, power retained." There is probably some ellipsis to be supplied in this sentence. "Unsafe (is) the while (time) (for us), that (in which)," &c.

These ellipses are common in Shakespeare, who seems to have preferred brevity above everything; then strength (clearness); lastly, if possible, grammatical correctness.

28. "Impostors *to* true fear," *i.e.*, compared to true fear. (For derivation of this use from radical meaning of "motion towards," see answer to question 17, above.)

29. These examples illustrate what is termed the *indefinite and general use of the infinitive.*

The old infinitive termination (A.-S. *an;* M. E. *en*) having been lost, it was replaced by "*to*," the sign of the old dative infinitive or gerund (which denotes *purpose* — *cf.* Latin use of *ad* with gerund), and this new infinitive form was used in a very general sort of way, retaining all the forces of both parent forms (infinitive proper, and gerund). Thus, in following cases: "*To know* my deed," the infinitive has a comparative force. "'Twere best not know myself than know my deed—." "If the knowing myself implies the knowing my deed, it would be better," &c. "*To fright* you thus"—"for frighting you," &c.

> "blame
> His pestered senses *to recoil* and start,"

for recoiling and starting.

> "Which being kept close, might move
> More grief *to hide* than hate *to utter* love."
> —Hamlet II. i. 119.
>
> "Could you on this fair mountain leave *to feed*."
> —Hamlet III. iv. 66.

---

30. "*Aroint* thee, witch,"—a form of dismissal or exorcism when addressed to witches. Also used by milkmaids to their cows—"Aroint thee, lovey." Sometimes spelt *rynt*, *runt*. Various conjectures have been made as to the derivation of the word. Perhaps it is of Icelandic root. Some have supposed it connected with the adverb "*aroume*"= *abroad* (found in Chaucer). Others derive it from Latin "*averrunco*," as in "*Dii averruncent*"—"The gods forfend!"

31. It was a common belief that witches could and did go sailing in sieves, and there is found a notice how one Dr. Fian, a notable sorcerer (finally burned at Edinburgh), in company with a number of witches, went to sea in a storm—all in "cives." Witches were supposed, too, to be able to

take the form of any animal — the tail, however, being always wanting; which reminds us of the old descriptions left of the werwolf.

32. *Fantastical* means "imaginary" — "existing only in the imagination," "as a conception of the mind." It is an example of the Shakespearian use of certain words — as a rule, those recently introduced from foreign sources — in a literal and general sense, which we now use in a metaphorical and particular sense. There being already in the language a word which signified "imaginary," this new word became restricted. Compare "*metaphysical*" = (in Shakespeare) "supernatural."

33. A *harbinger* was one who went before to provide a place of abode for the king and his suite. Comes from our word "*harbour*," "harbourer," "harbinger." Perhaps *ng* crept in, as the *n* did in *passenger*, *messenger* (from *passage*, *message*), through carelessness of pronunciation.

A *purveyor* was one sent before to provide *food* for the king.

34. "God '*ild us*" — i.e., *reward us, pay us*; "'*ild*" is a corruption from *yield*, which is derived from A.-S. *gyldan* (or *gildan*), meaning "to pay," "to reward."

The whole expression means: "In having shown you that the trouble I give is due to the love I have for you, I teach you how you must ask God to reward me for that love, even though it be the source of trouble to you."

"*Bid*" (A.-S. *biddan*), used with its original meaning, "*pray*." We have a reminiscence of this in our noun *bead*, which was first the prayer, then the string of beads on which the prayer was said, finally the beads (round things) themselves. In "Saint Agnes Eve," we meet with the word — the old "*beadsman*."

35. "If the assassination could put an end to (or prevent) its natural consequences, and, by stopping these consequences, secure success," according to which interpretation the antecedent of *his* is *consequence*, — whence *his* is neuter genitive, where we should use *its*. [But A.-S. neuter pronoun was *hit* (nominative), *his* (genitive), and Shakespeare had not forgotten that entirely as we have. *Its* is said to have been formed on the analogy of the usual genitive case formation in *s*, when the *h* of the old nominative form having been lost and forgotten, it was felt that *his* was not the proper genitive for the neuter pronoun.] Several other interpretations of this passage have been suggested, but the one given above seems most satisfactory.

"Trammel up" means "ensnare, as in a net," "entrap," and so put a stop to. "*Surcease*" is not connected with *cease* (Fr. *cesser*), as might seem probable, but comes from Fr. *sursis*, and this from "*surseoir*" — a legal term, meaning "to put a stop to a suit." "*Success*" has also been interpreted, in its literal meaning, "succession," "issue." The modern meaning is a derived one. First, "succession," "issue" (Lat. *succedere*), now confined to "fortunate issue."

36. The old anatomists divided the brain into three ventricles; in the hindermost of which — the cerebellum, connecting with the spinal column, and so with the nerves throughout the body — they supposed the memory to be stationed to watch over the reason (in the fore part of the brain) and guard it from attack. Now, when by drink the memory was converted into a mere vapor, it would fill the whole brain, which would thus become like the cap of a still, into which the vaporized liquor passes before it goes into the condenser.

"*Warder*" is a word with which we do not often meet

now-a-days — equivalent in meaning to our word *guard*, — being in fact the same word. It was brought by the Saxons to England, where it remained as "warder"; and was also taken to France, where it seems the natives were unable to pronounce the pure "*w*" sound, and in the attempt let the "*g*" slip in. This "*g*" form was then brought to England by the Norman invaders in 1066, and finally superseded the equivalent English form in "*w*." A similar history is to be found in a good many other words; *cf.* "warrant" and "guarantee"; "wise" and "guise"; Eng. "war" and Fr. "guerre"; Eng. "warren" and Fr. "garenne."

"*Fume*" — originally *smoke* (Lat. *fumus*) — is probably used by Shakespeare in a metaphorical sense, as we speak of a man's reason being *clouded.*

"*Limbec*" — corruption of *alembic* (made of the Arabic article *al* and a Greek word) — a word borrowed from the Arabian alchemists, and meaning "the cap of a still, or retort."

The change seems to have been caused by mistaking the initial "*a*" for our indefinite article. Removing this, "*lembic*," by popular corruption, becomes *limbec.*

Other words taken from the Arabic are "almanac," "alchemy" itself, "algebra."

For the trouble with regard to the article, we have a good many similar examples in our language. Having two forms — *an* used before vowels, *a* before consonants, consequently before words beginning with "*n*" — changes were produced. "An adder" used to be "a nadder"; "an apron," "a napron"; "an orange," "a norange" (Persian); while "a newt" was "an eft (ewt)."

37. "*Travelling* lamp" — in the folio, "*travailing* lamp." Shakespeare rarely observed the modern distinction between

these words, using them interchangeably, and generally involving a combination of both ideas. Here "travelling lamp" probably means "the sun painfully struggling on its way." Compare the use of "human" and "humane," accent nearly always on the first syllable.

38. "The deed by which man (they) holds life of nature gives no right to perpetual tenure."

Nature is compared to a lord of the manor, under whom men hold their livings by copy-hold tenure. This is a tenure for which the tenant has nothing to show but the copy of the rolls made out by the steward of his lord's court. It is a legal metaphor which is kept up lower down, "cancel and tear to pieces that great bond." Shakespeare frequently employed these law terms.

39. The "state" was the elevated seat or throne with a canopy over it, placed for the hostess at the head of the table. It first meant the "canopy," then the whole arrangement.

40. "*Mummy*" was a favorite medicine for some time before and some time after Shakespeare's day. *Francis I.* is said to have kept it constantly about him as a panacea against all diseases. So great did the demand for this article become that it is said the Jews, who dealt in it largely, found it both profitable and practicable to manufacture mummy out of dead bodies — sometimes "gibbet leavings" — and give them some old king's name.

41. "*Blood-boltered*" Banquo, — *i.e.*, having his hair matted, — clotted with blood, as a natural consequence of the "twenty trenched gashes on his head."

The term is said to be still retained colloquially in some districts, — applied, I believe, to horses when their manes become knotted and tangled.

42. These lines in regard to "*the evil*," which have no connection with the regular course of the drama, are supposed to have been introduced as a compliment to King James, who believed himself endowed with the miraculous powers of Edward the Confessor, — the power of the healing touch, — an idea which seems to go along with that of the divine right of kings.

"The evil," or "the king's evil," was a term applied to the "scrofula," as being the special disease upon which the kings exercised this wonderful power.

Edward's claims were believed in by his contemporaries, or very soon after his death, and were claimed for his successors early in the twelfth century. Queen Elizabeth, James I., Charles I., Charles II., all touched successfully, it is said.

One of Dr. Johnson's earliest recollections was the being taken to be touched by Queen Anne, and the "touch-piece," hung by her about his neck is still preserved in the British Museum.

43. "*Night-gown*" in Shakespeare's time was equivalent to our "dressing gown." The word is used again in this play (II. ii. 70).

44. "Their *dear* causes," — the causes which touch each of them so closely. *Dear* indicated some close, intimate connection, — something of special interest.

"The *mortified* man," is explained by some as the "low-spirited" man, — the man subdued by feeling of shame or mortification; by others as "the religious," the recluse, the ascetic, who cares nothing for the world, and consequently could not be easily excited. But a stronger and better meaning still is given if we take "the mortified man" as the "dead man," — the literally *mortified* man. If this is the true meaning, it may embody the old notion that a dead body, when in the presence of the murderer, would bleed.

It has been suggested that "the mortified man" might mean "the Crucified" — "the Christ-man," which would give a very strong meaning. But this is hardly probable.

45. "*Pestered*" (Latin "*pes*"), literally "tied around the feet," — as "to hobble" a horse, — hampered in a physical sense, then metaphorically — "*troubled.*"

46. Reference to the old custom of "bear-baiting," so much practised by our ancestors. The bear was tied to a stake, and then baited with dogs — a certain number at a time, and each set or turn was technically termed *a course*.

———◆———

ÆSTHETIC.

47. What do you understand the "Weird Sisters" in *Macbeth* to be?

48. Does Macbeth, or Lady Macbeth, say (II. ii. 16): "Did not you speak?" And what do you think of Hunter's distribution of speeches adopted by Furness? —

"*Macbeth :* I have done the deed. Didst thou not hear a noise?
Lady Macbeth : I heard the owls scream and the crickets cry.
Macbeth Did not you speak?
Lady Macbeth : When? Now?
Macbeth : As I descended.
Lady Macbeth : Ay."

49. Give your impression of this whole Scene II., and of the effect of the *knocking*. L 57.

50. What is Coleridge's opinion of the *Porter-Scene* (II. iii. 1–37); and your own opinion? Can you recall anything similar elsewhere in Shakespeare?

51. How do you reconcile Macbeth's prompt murder of the grooms with his horror at the mere thought of killing Duncan, and his refusal to carry the bloody daggers back to the chamber?

52. Is Lady Macbeth's swoon, on hearing of the murder of the grooms, real or feigned — and the grounds of your opinion?

53. How do you explain the difference in Lady Macbeth's manner towards Macbeth after the Banquo ghost scene (III. iv.), as compared with her bearing after the murder of Duncan (II. ii.)?

54. Do you regard Lady Macbeth as a suicide? And what do you consider the causes of her death?

55. What effect does her death have upon Macbeth, and upon our feeling towards him?

56. The character of Macbeth in brief?

57. The lesson of the play?

---

47. The "Weird Sisters" in *Macbeth* seem to us neither on the one hand mere mortal witches of popular superstition, nor yet, as Holinshed states, and as their name would imply, do we see in them "goddesses of destiny" — "fates" determining human actions and issues without regard to that fundamental essence of personality, *will*. They know the future and can foretell events; yet they are not able of themselves to make those events come to pass. They also know the thoughts, tendencies, and purposes of human hearts, and herein lies the secret of their power over mortals. If there be not already the element of evil, the Weird Sisters never corrupt any man. It is that already in the heart which they draw out and develop.

I have been specially impressed by Mr. Hudson's idea of the symbolical character attached to the Weird Sisters — that they are but the poetical embodiment of that mysterious principle of action and reaction which constantly goes on between the evil mind and external nature.

As to special or real character of the Weird Sisters, Mr. Hudson finds nothing gross, sensual, or vulgar about them; deems them " the purity of sin incarnate — the vestal virgins, so to speak, of hell; in whom everything is reversed; whose ascent is downwards; whose proper eucharist is a sacrament of evil; whose law is violation of all law." Now, I like this idea very much; but, for some reason, find it impossible to divest myself of the feeling that there must be a certain and marked grossness about beings who could compile such surpassingly disgusting charm-potions as those upon which we find the Weird Sisters engaged in the latter part of the play.

Their relation to the play as a whole is no less important than to Macbeth as an individual. These creatures, whose proper element is the tempest, whose chariot is the whirlwind, whose religion is to do the evil, form a fit setting for a drama in which the very ground rocks beneath one's feet, in which the whole action is a stormy struggle between the powers of good and the powers of evil.

48. A question of this nature must, I suppose, be purely a matter of opinion. Still such questions will be raised and we are expected to possess an opinion. In this case Hunter's suggestion seems to me a good emendation. Macbeth had spoken, but it is probable that Lady Macbeth had recognized his voice and knew the fact perfectly. Moreover, in Macbeth's mouth these words acquire a deeper meaning, for they must be immediately prompted by and filled with the suggestion of that "terrible voice" of which Lady Macbeth knows nothing, and which had even forced from him the involuntary exclamation which she had heard. They are strikingly suited to Macbeth's character and state of mind, as exhibited in every word and in his whole manner throughout this scene. His bearing is that of eager, breathless listening, — waiting for that awful *something* which has not happened, but is going to happen, — for the repetition of those fearful ac-

cents, which have existed alone in his guilty imagination. The question is a despairing effort to find some natural and real explanation for the horrible creations of his excited imagination. For Lady Macbeth there could be in them nothing of all this. It would be either a matter-of-fact attempt to dispel her husband's fears, or at most might imply some dread on her part lest the sound, which she knew she had heard, might have come from some one else than Macbeth, indicating that they had been watched.

The further distribution is fitting too. Lady Macbeth, having just called his name, might naturally have concluded that he referred to that, and at once replied "Ay!" But there must have been a degree of anxious doubt in the question which led her to inquire: "When?" "Now?" His answer: "As I descended"—locates the time of the "terrible voice," and Lady Macbeth's final "Ay!" is accordant with facts.

49. This whole scene, in its relation to the rest of the play, is like a frightful nightmare in the midst of a troubled dream. The clear, sharp sound of the knocking, breaking through the weird silence — hitherto unbroken save by the irrepressible voice of the sinner's own conscience — is, for the instant, interpreted by the strained senses as the realization of that undefined "something" for which we, in sympathy with Macbeth, have been so breathlessly waiting. Such an acme of the terrible, in this way attained, cannot be endured; in another moment the knocking is repeated — we remember ourselves, and, with a lingering shudder, turn to laugh at the drunken Porter; while Macbeth washes the blood from his "hangman's hands," and goes forth in the strength of a desperate resolve to play an assumed part, foreign to his nature.

This knocking, viewed in its effects, seems to us completely analogous (continuing the comparison established at the outset) to an effort employed to restore the victim of a dire nightmare. At the first instant, in the half-unconscious state, blending with and intensifying the horrors, but proving in the end the effectual remedy and sure relief for the terrible malady.

50. Coleridge thinks that this low, vulgar soliloquy of the Porter, and the few lines following, were not written by Shakespeare, but interpolated by some inferior hand to please the ears of "the groundlings."

I cannot agree with Mr. Coleridge that an effect so essentially artistic as that produced by the introduction of this bit of comedy — coarse as it is — just at this point, would have been neglected by Shakespeare and finally supplied by a mere accident, as it were. Without the *Porter-Scene*, this portion of the drama — Scenes ii. and iii., with their intensely tragic nature, coming together as they do — would be utterly unendurable. But just at the moment when the feelings are wrought up to the highest pitch — a heinous murder having been committed almost before the eyes — here comes in this scene to afford the needful relaxation.

The eminent fitness between the drunken Porter's conception and the hellish deed, but then perpetrated within, has been urged, and I think justly, as an additional argument for its authenticity.

As far as the style is concerned, its broadness is conceded by the very best critics to be by no means un-Shakespearian; while "the primrose way to the everlasting bonfire" is far from being the only thing bearing the unmistakable impress of the mighty master.

Instances of the same sort of thing are multiplied in the writings of Shakespeare.

It seems to me that the witch scene (III. v.), coming as it does just after the terrible banquet scene, and the conversation between Lady Macduff and her little son (IV. ii.) just before their murder, have something of the same effect. Compare also, in *Hamlet*, the scene in the church-yard with the clowns (V. i.), followed by the frightful tragedy enacted at the open grave of Ophelia.

Also in *King Lear* compare the Poor Tom (Edgar) scene, which comes just before the putting out of Gloucester's eyes. And also perhaps the short clown scene in *Othello*, coming in as a sort of relief before the final catastrophe.

51. Macbeth is restrained from the murder of Duncan by the power of a sensitive conscience, working through imaginary terrors. Notwithstanding the assuring prophecy of the Weird Sisters, he is still haunted by the dreadful fear of the unknown, possible consequence. Immediately after the murder, conscience is still more active, and he cannot bring himself to face the horrors which imagination conjures up, — he cannot brave that "voice" again, — he dare not look on the murdered Duncan! It is the natural terror of a man "but young in deed," — "the initiate fear that wants hard use." His prompt murder of the grooms in the very next scene, though seemingly, is not really at variance with this shrinking which we have just noted. By utmost effort his wife has, in the interval, succeeded in rousing him to a realization of the immediate danger of detection in which they stand. Impressed with this idea, he comes forth to meet the nobles, and to play such a part upon the discovery of the murdered King, as shall entirely disarm suspicion. His whole conduct is governed by this desire, and is just what we should expect from a man whose face is "as a book where men may read things strange." His very language is

strained and unnatural, appropriate only in the mouth of a conscious murderer dissembling guilt. He talks to avoid his own thoughts, and to mislead others.

Exhibition of great grief for the death of the king and hatred for the perpetrators of the horrible deed seems to him the proper course, and in no way can this pious indignation be so effectually shown as in slaying the supposed culprits. It is possible, too, that he feared the grooms, who had been in the chamber, certainly roused, and may have seen more than he supposed.

52. We can readily understand how, upon a first reading of the play, having nothing upon which to base an opinion save Lady Macbeth's preceding words and conduct, one might think this swoon feigned, and but another exhibition of that presence of mind and determination of will by means of which she had succeeded in screwing her own and her husband's courage to the "sticking-place,"—which had not abandoned her during the murder scene (at first reading one might easily overlook the single unmistakable touch of womanly weakness shown in the words, "Had he not resembled my father as he slept, I had done it,"),—which had enabled her to take back the daggers and gild the faces of the grooms with blood, when the "infirm of purpose" refused to do it,—which even that terrible task could not destroy, since, upon her return, hearing the knocking, she remembered at once that to be found fully dressed would show them to be watchers. But, having gone through the play and heard Lady Macbeth's troubled sigh —

> "Naught's had, all's spent;
> Where our desire is got without content" —

(III. ii. 4-7); having observed her in the short scene with Macbeth after the banquet, and especially in the sleep-walking scene, we are satisfied that the swoon on this occasion is real. Some one very appositely suggests that, had Lady Macbeth adopted this artifice as a means of further averting suspicion, she would, without doubt, have fallen when Duncan's murder was announced to her. The effect would have been greater, and, moreover, knowing nothing of the murder of the grooms, she could not have anticipated this further opportunity. And just here, it seems to us, lies the explanation of this unexpected exhibition of weakness. She knew all about Duncan's murder and was on her guard, but this other was a thing thoroughly unexpected, for which, consequently, she was not prepared, and her nature gave way under the shock. May it not be, too, that her woman's heart felt even then that the husband, who so lately had leaned upon her entirely, in doing this deed without consulting her, was drifting away from her?

53. May not an explanation of the difference of her manner on the two occasions be found in the following considerations? Just after the murder of Duncan there was no time for the employment of gentler means — no time to seek the sleep which she entreats in the second instance. The nobles were even then at the gate; her husband must be recovered, and that both effectually and without delay, lest, in his phrensy, he divulge the whole terrible secret, and thus bring ruin upon them both (as was threatened again *during* the banquet scene — which may account for the contrast between her manner during that scene and after the scene is over). Lady Macbeth realizes this, and has both the clear-sightedness to know what to do, and, in her excitement, the strength to do it. Let us note too that she is under the influence of artificial stimulants.

In the second case, the guests are gone, all the harm done

that can be done, hence no such need for peremptory measures as on the previous occasion. It is permitted that her conduct be in accordance with her womanly feelings, and so we find it. Besides tenderest sympathy for him, there is a depth of pathos in her very words — a weariness in her voice and manner, which point possibly to another explanation to be found in the sad change — the gradually deepening melancholy fallen upon her own spirit since that former occasion.

54. On this subject commentators differ. Coleridge asserts, "she dies in suicidal agony." Gervinus thinks "she ends her life with suicide." Dowden's opinion is, "her thread of life snaps suddenly." Mrs. Jameson believes that, "In a mind constituted like that of Lady Macbeth, conscience must awake at some time or other, and bring with it remorse closed by despair and despair by death." Mrs. Siddons, agreeing in general with Mrs. Jameson, thinks that the woman's fragile constitution finally broke down under the weight of remorseful agony which she so resolutely shut up in her own bosom. Hudson says: "A mystery hangs over her fate. We do not know — the poet himself seems not to have known, whether the gnawings of the undying worm drove her to suicidal violence or themselves cut asunder the thread of her life." And it would seem not improbable that Mr. Hudson's candid acknowledgment of ignorance is, after all, the most just conclusion. But somehow — call it sentimentalism if you will — we cannot bring ourselves to believe that Lady Macbeth took her own life. It is true that Malcolm makes such an announcement; but he only states it as "'tis thought." It is true also that the Doctor orders that " the means of all annoyance " be removed from her, showing that he feared something of the sort; still, knowing Lady

Macbeth as the Doctor could not, we think the idea of suicide incompatible with her character as developed in the play.

The woman who, when the moment came, could not murder the sleeping king,—who fainted upon the announcement of the slaughter of the grooms, would have paused upon the threshold of eternity, daunted by the dreadful reality of the unknown which confronted her. I do not agree with Mrs. Jameson that Lady Macbeth's anguish is merely remorse —horror of the past, unmingled with terror of the future. That fearful sleep-walking revelation ("What's done cannot be undone," like everything else she says, is but an echo of the same words used on a former occasion, when, feeling herself beginning to sink, she strove by the expression of such fatalistic doctrines, not only to cheer her despondent husband, but to regain her own lost peace of mind by convincing herself of their truth) seems rather the prelude to a shrieking death-bed scene, where occurs a prolonged and desperate struggle between death and its guilty victim,—a frantic clinging to life with its horrible dreams, rather than face the still more horrible certainty which she knows awaits her.

Now, as to the causes of her death. It seems to us the combined effect of two fatal wounds upon a naturally delicate physical constitution. What has been said above is sufficient to show where we locate one of these,—violated conscience avenges itself. But we believe another, and possibly that which in the outset afforded a basis for the former, is to be found in the hidden wound rankling in her heart. Although we do not agree with Gervinus in thinking her *whole* ambition was "for and through her husband," we do believe that her courage was, in a great measure, based upon the strength of her own love for him, and her confidence in his love for and need of her. As long as this confidence remains, she is firm to endure anything,—at the first moment that it is shaken her apparently superhuman strength begins to yield (upon the announcement of the murder of the grooms, mentioned above). Conscience, up to this time stifled in the constant excitement attendant upon her efforts to spur her husband on, finds now an opportunity to assert itself, and death is but the legitimate result of these two causes.

55. One commentator sees in Macbeth's language at the announcement,

"The queen, my lord, is dead,"

the perfect indifference of a heartless criminal to the fate of the wife who had been so faithful to him.

Another thinks Lady Macbeth's death touches him in the only remaining vulnerable point, and calls forth some "deeply serious, solemn, elegiac strains." To us there is spoken a different story still. In these words is embodied a degree of combined bitterness and contempt which could only be wrung from a strong heart driven to the last extreme of desperation. The bitterness is that of a hopeless anguish which the victim feels has been drawn down by his own hand. To the natural grief for the loss of the wife whom he really loved, there is added, most probably, the stinging consciousness of his own selfish forgetfulness of her in the season when she needed him most sorely. The contempt is that of a man who has "supped full with horrors," and whom "the faint odour of blood has disgusted with all else." We behold in silence the unmistakable evidence of the inevitable but hidden workings by which justice *will* be satisfied. Our indignation is appeased. We now feel sincerest pity for the deep misery which we know rends the heart of a fellow being.

56. The development of the character of Macbeth in this play is the history of a struggle, fierce and prolonged, between the power of good and the power of evil found in each human heart. And a sharp fight it is, too, in this case, before the evil finally prevails. Schlegel's idea that Macbeth, with his noble nature, is irresistibly forced to crime by a supernatural power, wholly external to him, cannot, we think, be supported from the text. Upon his very first appearance, in the interview with the Weird Sisters, Macbeth displays a signal weakness — a susceptibility to impressions of the imagination, which by contrast with the matter-of-fact Banquo, is the more marked.

While Banquo, in amazement, questions the report of his own eyes, Macbeth drinks in their words, and when, almost immediately, one prediction is fulfilled, looks forward to the time when " the golden round and top of sovereignty " shall encircle his noble brow. Now begins the conflict — " This supernatural soliciting cannot be ill, cannot be good." Already is he so shaken by that " thought whose murder yet is but fantastical, that function is smothered in surmise, and nothing is but what is not." And when recalled to consciousness by a reproof from the observant Banquo, he shows still further weakness — in the desire to conceal his guilty thoughts, he sinks still lower and stoops to falsehood. All which things seem to us inconsistent with Schlegel's view.

We think with those commentators who believe Macbeth's sin the offspring of his own heart. Mr. Hudson's presentment of the progress of this leaven of evil seems to us excellent. He thinks that from the moment of meeting with the Weird Sisters, the idea of hastening the fulfilment of the third prophecy by the murder of Duncan was constantly before his mind; that the subsequent hesitation was due to the curious conscience of the man, powerfully active, though hiding itself under the mental disturbance which it occasioned; that there was needful yet another force before conscience could be made to yield — his domestic affections were enlisted, his manhood and valor impeached by the woman he loved — than which nothing is harder for a soldier to bear. When Lady Macbeth has thus made it a theme of domestic war and reduced the matter to this alternative — he must either do the deed or cease to live with her as wife, then and then only does he fully resolve to murder Duncan. He goes through this first crime with an assumed ferocity borrowed from his wife; but, as soon as this is done, he oversteps her designs and stains his hands still deeper in the blood of the helpless grooms. From this time forth, conscience, in imaginary terrors, becomes the instigator to new murders. Having given others cause to suspect him, he, in turn, suspects them, and seeks safety and peace in using the sword — every thrust of which adds a new wound to the agony he already suffers. Such is the horrible madness to which crime has driven him. Slaughter is heaped upon slaughter, — the most innocent are the chief victims. Trusting implicitly in the equivocal prophecy of the Weird Sisters, yet never losing sight of his own freedom, he rushes on with the blindness of desperation — forgetful alike of friends, of wife, of God — to the dreadful punishment which awaits him. And when it finally comes, we feel a stern satisfaction in the knowledge that justice, which we saw almost appeased in the restless agony at the death of his wife, is now fully satisfied.

In the powerful conscience and vivid imagination of Macbeth, we recognize a tinge of Hamletism, and therefore the comparison and contrast drawn between the two characters by Gervinus, is specially interesting to us. Herein is brought out strikingly one decided characteristic of Macbeth, upon which Hudson does not dwell. Macbeth is placed over against Hamlet as the man of action, opposed to the man of thought. Conscience is found equally strong in both, — but with this difference, that in Macbeth it has not only to reflect and doubt, but to do, to struggle — active to the last. Imagination too — a common heritage — while holding Hamlet back, urges Macbeth on, since to him " present fears are ever less than horrible imaginings." The essential difference between the man of thought and the man of action is seen in the results. In Hamlet's case, everything urges to the murder of Claudius — still, he hesitates ; while Macbeth slays the innocent Duncan in the face of consience and every external consideration.

57. Perhaps, as some suggest, this play may have served as a warning against the popular superstitions so rife in Shakespeare's time — beliefs in witchcraft and in supernatural agencies in general. It assuredly speaks, too, of the evils consequent upon inordinate ambition in particular. But do we not find therein a lesson more general, and at the same time more individual, saying to each of us in unmistakable accents, "'Keep thy heart with all diligence, for out of it are the issues of life '; and pray without ceasing, ' Lead us not into temptation, but deliver us from evil ' ! "

I have received no assistance in this examination.

N. B. BOWMAN.

INTERMEDIATE EXAMINATION.

SENIOR LITERATURE CLASS. JANUARY, 1881.

HAMLET.

I. Where did Shakespeare get the story of Hamlet, and when did he write the play? What is Gœthe's opinion of its aim?

II. Explain the following passages and words: —

Act I. Sc. i. 127. I'll *cross* it, though it *blast* me. — Sc. ii. 10, with a *defeated* joy. — Sc. ii. 42–50. Use of *thou* and *you;* *ib.* 70, thy *vailed* lids; *ib.* 92, to do *obsequious* sorrow; *ib.* 127, the King's *rouse.* — Sc. iv. 1, the air bites *shrewdly;* *ib.* 9, the King doth *wake* (what is modern *wake?*); *ib.* 65, at a pin's *fee.* — Sc. v. 77. *Unhousel'd, disappointed, unaneled.* Act II. Sc. i. 103. Whose violent *property fordoes* itself. — Sc. ii. 6. *Sith,* use of, and *since; ib.* 158, the *centre* — Shak.'s astronomy; *ib.* 337, whose lungs are *tickle o' the sere; ib.* 397–8, I am but . . . *handsaw; ib.* 443–5, your *ladyship — chopine.* (Meaning, and to whom applied.) Act III. Sc. ii. 12, the *groundlings; ib.* 15, *out-herods Herod; ib.* 131, your only *jig*-maker. (*Jig* was what?); *ib.* 142, the *hobby-horse,* was what? — Sc. iv. 38, *proof* and *bulwark* against *sense* (derivation of *bulwark*); *ib.* 98, a *vice* of kings.
Act IV. Sc. iii. 33, *go a progress.*
Act V. Sc. i. 299. *Woo't drink up eisel.* — Sc. ii. 6, the *mutines* in the *bilboes; ib.* 10–11, There's a *divinity* — how we will. (Explain this metaphor; its source.)

III. What three cardinal points must we observe in regard to the inflections of Elizabethan English? Give the grammatical explanation of the following expressions, according to Shakespeare's use?

Act I. Sc. iii. 126, how *prodigal* the soul. — Sc. v. 94, grow not *instant* old.
Act II. Sc. ii. 510, sets him *new* a-work.
Act I. Sc. i. 57, the *sensible* and true avouch; *ib.* 164, so *gracious* is the time. — Sc. iv. 30, The form of *plausive* manners.
Act III. Sc. i. 180, *variable* objects.
Act I. Sc. ii. 207, In *dreadful* secrecy. — Sc. i. 114, the *mightiest* Julius. — Sc. iii. 46, But, *good my* brother. — Sc. i. 8, For this relief *much* thanks. — Sc. v. 180, mercy at your *most* need. — Sc. iii. 133, slander *moment* leisure.
Act II. Sc. ii. 508, As *hush* as death.
Act III. Sc. i. 164, the honey of his *music* vows.
Act I. Sc. v. 19, to stand *an* end.
Act II. Sc. i. 58, There was *a-gaming*. — Sc. ii. 510, sets him new *a-work*; *ib.* 615, fall *a-cursing*.
Act III. Sc. i. 173, sits *on brood*.
Act I. Sc. iii. 135, come your *ways*.
Act III. Sc. i. 145, thou wilt *needs* marry.
Act I. Sc. ii. 218, *even* then the morning cock crew.
Act IV. Sc. iii. 22, are e'en at him; *ib.* your *only* emperor for diet.
Act II. Sc. ii. 42, Thou hast *still* been the father of good news.
Act I. Sc. iv. 57, *Why* is this? *Wherefore?* What should we do?
— Sc. ii. 11, *An* auspicious and *a* dropping eye.
Act V. Sc. ii. 92, impart *a* thing to you.
Act V. Sc. ii. 276, These foils have all *a* length.
Act I. Sc. iii. 95, And that *in way* of caution. — Sc. v. 65 enmity *with blood* of men.
Act III. Sc. ii. 394, Almost *in shape* of a camel.
Act I. Sc. iv. 21, though performed *at height*.
Act V. Sc. i. 100, Did these bones cost no man *the breeding?*

NOTE. — The following references to the Prize Examinations will be found useful in explanation of some of these grammatical questions to those who have not Abbott's *Grammar:* For Act I. iii. 126, see *Hamlet* 25; *Macbeth* 23; *King Lear* 11, 12; *Othello* 13. — Act I. i. 57: *Ham.* 17; *Macb.* 16; *Oth.* 4. — Act II. ii. 510: *Ham.* 22; *Oth.* 19. — Act I. ii. 218: *Mer. of Ven.* 11. — Act II. ii. 42: *Ham.* 18; *K. Lear* 14. — Act V. i. 100: *Macb.* 13; *Mer. of Ven.* 20.

SHAKESPEARE EXAMINATION:

KING LEAR.

MISS MAGGIE C. WILLIAMS,
OF TAZEWELL COUNTY, VIRGINIA.

HOLLINS INSTITUTE, VA.

1883.

NOTE.

THE three following Examinations, on *King Lear*, *Othello*, and *The Merchant of Venice*, were written, respectively, in the years 1883, 1884, 1886, under substantially the same conditions; that is to say, each young lady was given a few of the questions at a time; each was allowed to refer to the unannotated text of the *Globe Shakespeare;* each was allowed to read over and revise her work after the first writing; no one received any other assistance; and, a few trifling corrections affecting form, not substance, excepted, the work of each is printed as she wrote it.

WM. TAYLOR THOM.

HOLLINS INSTITUTE, VA.
May, 1887.

SHAKESPEARE PRIZE EXAMINATION IN KING LEAR.[1]

JUNE, 1883.

TEXTUAL.

1. When and in what form was *King Lear* first published?
2. How, according to Dowden, do we fix the order of the plays?
3. When was *Lear* written, and how can you establish the time?
4. Where did Shakespeare get the materials of the play?
5. How do the original stories differ in conclusion from Shakespeare's play?
6. Was *King Lear* an original or an adapted play?

Explain the following constructions and usages : —

7. I. i. 99. "Return *those* duties back *as* are right fit."
   I. iv. 63. "With *that* ceremonious affection *as* you were wont."
8. I. i. 153. "*Answer* my life my judgement."
9. I. i. 163. "Thou *swear'st* thy gods in vain."
10. I. i. 194. "*Hath* rivall'd for our daughter."
11. I. i. 207. "And *stranger'd* with our oath."
12. I. i. 223. "That *monsters* it."
13. I. i. 227. "*If for* I want that glib and oily art."
14. I. i. 234. "A *still-soliciting* eye."
15. I. i. 251. "*Since that* respects of fortune."
16. I. ii. 43. "The contents are *to blame.*"
17. I. ii. 106 and 125. "I pray *you* . . . it shall lose *thee* nothing."

---

[1] References to the *Globe Shakespeare*.

110   EXAMINATION IN KING LEAR.

18. I. iii.   1.   "For *chiding of his fool.*"
19. I. iv.   40.   "Not *so* young, sir, *to* love a woman."
20. I. iv. 112.   "*An* thou *canst* not smile."
21. I. iv. 204.   "I would not be *thee*, nuncle."
22. I. iv. 221.   "But *other* of your insolent retinue."
23. I. iv. 225.   "*To have found* a safe redress."
24. I. iv. 306.   "Her *brow of youth.*"
25. II. iv. 277.   "If it be you that *stirs* these daughters' hearts."

Explain the following expressions:—

26. I. i. 125.   "And thought to *set my rest.*"
27. I. ii. 4.   "Permit the *curiosity of nations.*"
28. I. ii. 149.   "*Fa, sol, la, mi.*"
29. I. iv. 18.   "And to *eat no fish.*"
30. I. iv. 282.   "More hideous when thou show'st thee in a child than the *sea-monster.*"
31. I. v. 2   ⎧   "these *letters.*"
            7   ⎩   "your *letter.*"   How are *letters* and *letter* used?
32. II. ii. 16–20.   "*Three-suited, worsted-stocking, lily-livered, one-trunk-inheriting* slave."
33. II. ii. 84.   "Turn their *halcyon beaks.*"
34. II. ii. 90.   "I'ld drive ye cackling home to *Camelot.*"
35. III. ii. 10.   "*Court holy-water* in a dry house."
36. III. vi. 78.   "Poor Tom, *thy horn is dry.*"
37. ⎧ IV. v. 29.   "Take this *note*," cf. IV. v. 33.
    ⎩ V. iii. 27. "Take thou this *note*," cf. V. iii. 245.
38. IV. vi. 187.   "This (is) a good *block.*"
39. IV. vii. 17.   "*Child-changed* father."
40. IV. vii. 80.   "To make him *even o'er* the time he has lost."

41. I. i. 126.   "Hence and avoid my sight." To whom was this addressed?
42. I. i. 151.—
           "Reverse thy doom" (Q)
           "Reserve thy state" (F)
                              The best reading, and why?

43. I. ii. 104, 105. "To his father that so tenderly and entirely loves him." Is this in keeping with the character of Gloucester? Why should it be regarded as an interpolation?

44. II. iv. 213, 214.—
"To be a comrade with the wolf and howl
Necessity's sharp pinch," or,
"To be a comrade with the wolf and owl,—
Necessity's sharp pinch."
Best reading?

45. IV. ii. 62. —
"Thou changed and *self-covered* thing, for shame,
Be-monster not thy feature."

46. Mr. Spedding's division of acts IV. and V. What is your opinion of it?

47. V. iii. 305. "And my poor fool is hang'd." Is Lear, in the incoherence of dying grief, confusing the Fool and Cordelia?

48. III. vi. 21–91. What do you understand to take place which causes Lear's outbreak in ll. 57–59?

49. III. 7. How do you understand that Gloucester's eyes are put out, and what do you think of the propriety of this scene?

———

ÆSTHETIC.

50. The Fool in *King Lear*. His function in the play. Was he a boy or a man?

51. What do you think of Cordelia's refusal to respond to Lear's desire for flattery? And had she probably made any further choice between France and Burgundy than appears on the surface?

52. Your idea of Goneril physically, intellectually, and morally.

53. Does Shakespeare overstep the bounds of the natural — of human nature — in Goneril and Regan?

54. What is your opinion of the condition of Lear's mind in the opening scene? What effect does his increasing passion seem to have upon his faculties? Character of the king.

55. Cordelia's character and influence in the play, upon the characters, and upon our estimate of them?

56. What is the view of human society in *King Lear?* What the conflicting principles of human nature? The causes, destructive and conservative, of the prodigious upheaval in the play?

57. Your idea of the aim and lesson of the play?

---

1. *King Lear* was first published in 1608, in quarto form. Two quartos appeared in that year, differing in punctuation, spelling, pagination, and text so much as to make the fact evident that one quarto was not merely a corrected copy of the other. The titles of the two quartos were identical with the exception that the imprint "London: printed for Nathaniel Butler and are to be sold at his shop in Paul's churchyard at the sign of the pied bull near St. Austin's Gate, 1608," is replaced by "Printed for Nathaniel Butler, 1608." The variations in these two quartos and in the copies of them gave rise to the opinion — entertained by Mr. Hudson, I believe — that there was a third quarto edition. The theory has been found false, and we hear of no more publications, until *King Lear* shares with *Othello, Macbeth,* and *Cymbeline* the honor of being divided into acts and scenes in the folio of 1623. It is thought that the quartos were among the "stolne" and "surreptitious" copies of Shakespeare's plays, condemned by Heminge and Condell, the editors of the first Folio. The Folio is superior to the quarto editions with regard to text, but the quartos contain about 225 lines not found in the Folio, including Act IV. Sc. iii.

2. According to Mr. Dowden, there are three ways of fixing the date of a play: (*A*) By evidence wholly external. (*a*) The entrance on the stationer's register always bearing

in mind that the play was sometimes entered before it was written, and sometimes not until it had been in circulation for some time. (*b*) Reference to the play by a contemporary writer, the date of whose work is known: for instance, mention is made of twelve of Shakespeare's plays in Meres's *Palladis Tamia*. (*c*) By quotations from the play in a work whose date is known, remembering that Shakespeare *may* have quoted from his contemporary instead of *vice versa*. (*d*) Some information may be gained by ascertaining the company which acted the play, or the theatre at which it was performed: for instance, we can fix a downward limit to the date of Henry VIII., when we know that it was being acted when the Globe Theatre was burned.

(*B*) By evidence partly external and partly internal. (*a*) Reference to an historical event whose date is known. (*b*) Quotations from a book whose date is known: for instance, the devils in Edgar's speech, just before the trial scene, receive their names from Harsnet's *Declaration of Popish Impostures*. Hence we infer that *King Lear* was written after 1603 — the date of the publication of Harsnet's book.

(*C*) By evidence wholly internal. (*a*) Change in style and diction. At first Shakespeare clothes his thought in full, flowing language, — the dress is almost too loose. But as his imagination becomes more powerful and energetic, as his knowledge of life increases, language becomes inadequate for the expression of the ideas that throng through his brain. In the passionate earnestness and vehement action of his soul, thought changes so quickly that it is difficult to comprehend, to the full extent, the meaning of his expressions. (*b*) His judgment and taste become more refined. (*c*) Characterization changes. (*d*) Entire reflective power deepens. (*e*) Sympathy with the passions of men and the power to express them increases. (*f*) Humour becomes more refined, and works in conjunction with his (*g*) deepening pathos. Finally (*h*) his entire moral reach is expanded. His understanding of his fellow-being matures by experience, his conception of woman is more delicate and refined, and the general spirit of his works changes from the joyous, careless happiness of the comedies to the grave, bitter, yet intensely brilliant genius of the later tragedies.

Mr. Dowden divides Shakespeare's dramatic authorship into four periods. Commencing with 1588 or 1590, he assigns the period up to 1595 to dramatic apprenticeship and calls the period "In the workshop," because now Shakespeare is employed on light and fanciful plays and is adapting old plays. From 1595 to 1601 the poet was employed on comedies and histories, exercising the plastic energy of his imagination on the world as seen through a poet's spectacles. Now he is "In the world," amassing a fortune, and drinking deep draughts of worldly pleasure. From 1601 to 1608 was the period of the sterner comedies and most powerful tragedies. He has known sorrow now, and it has taught him to probe the human heart, and to express its varied passions. Life's restless billows have swept over a soul that re-echoes "Out of the depths" the hoarse roar of the ocean's tumult. Next comes the period when the poet reaches a calm which is only attained by passing through and beyond the turmoil of life's conflicting elements. From 1608 to 1613, the Romances were produced by a mind freed by trial from the dross which, while it could not dim the lustre of genius, yet concealed the strength and purity of the moral faculty.

Besides the tests already given, Mr. Dowden gives "End-stopped and run on verses, rhyme, weak endings," and a few others.

3. *King Lear* was written, certainly, between 1603 and 26th Dec., 1606. The play was entered on the stationer's register 26th Nov., 1607, with the statement that it had been acted at Whitehall on St. Stephen's night in the Christmas holidays of the year before. The downward limit therefore is fixed at 26th Dec., 1606. The upward limit is accurately fixed by the publication in 1603 of Harsnet's *Declaration of Popish Impostures*, from which Shakespeare gets the names of the devils mentioned by Edgar, IV. i. Gloucester and Edmund each mention [I. ii.] late eclipses which probably refers to the eclipse of the sun October, 1605, preceded within a month by an eclipse of the moon. This eclipse had been foretold by John Harvey of King's Lynn, writing in 1588 against the superstitious dread of the consequences of such an event. Possibly Gloucester's mention of "machinations, treachery, etc.," was suggested by the Gunpowder Plot of November, 1605. The change from "English" of the Folio to "British" of the Quarto owing to the union, under James I., of England and Scotland under the name of Great Britain, can be of no use in fixing the date, since "English" might have been inadvertently written after the union, and even while the memory of it was still fresh in men's minds, and while the ephemeral literature of the day abounded in references to the subject. Mr. Wright does not recognize this change as an aid in fixing the date of the composition of the play. So we decide that *King Lear* was written between November, 1605, and December, 1606. In the "high-grown fields" the "fumiter" and "darnel" we have an indication of summer. But in III. ii. 68 Lear says, "Art cold? I

am cold myself," and the Fool, III. iv. 80, "This cold night will turn us all to fools and madmen." An attempt to approximate to the date of the play by such tests denies to Shakespeare an imagination sufficiently strong to conceive of an object or event without its actual presence. That *Lear* was written at or about the forty-second year of the poet's life, when sorrow had deepened the sources from which he drew his materials, that it is the play in which passion assumes its largest proportions and acts upon the widest theatre, is sufficient to place *Lear* among the later tragedies, along with *Macbeth* and *Othello*.

4. The story of King Lear was told in its main outlines by Geoffrey of Monmouth in his *Historia Britonum*. He probably derived his information from some Welsh legendary source. We find something like it in Layamon's *Brut*, in the *Gesta Romanorum*, in Spencer's *Faerie Queene*, in Camden's *Remaines*, and in a ballad in Percy's *Reliques;* also in an old play, entered on the stationer's register in 1593. Mr. Furness thinks that this play was re-entered in in 1605 under the name of "*The Tragicall History of King Lear*," and that it furnished the original from which Shakespeare drew the plot of his play. But knowing Shakespeare's fondness for Holinshed, Mr. Wright decides that it was to this source that the poet went for the incidents of the drama. After a careful examination of the extracts as given by Mr. Furness of both Holinshed's story and the old play, we can but express our conviction that Mr. Wright is right.

The story of Gloucester is taken from an episode in Sidney's *Arcadia*. Gloucester takes the place of the blind king of Paphlagonia, and Edgar that of Leonatus. Like the history with which it is incorporated, it only furnishes the incidents — the spirit and characterization are Shakespeare's own.

5. The story of King Lear, as given by Holinshed, is as follows : —

Leir was made king of Britain in 3105, while Joas ruled in Judah. He governed his kingdom in great wealth and power. His wife had died, leaving him three daughters, but no son. When he became old and unwieldy, he called his children to him, to divide his kingdom according to the measure of their love. Having asked Gonorilla how much she loved him, she called her gods to witness that she loved him more than all things. When he questioned Regan, she too swore great oaths that she loved him more than her life. Well pleased with these answers, Leir married one to Henninus, Duke of Cornewale, and the other to Maglanus, Duke of Albania. When he had asked Cordella how much she loved him, she replied that as a child should love a father, and as he deserved, so much she loved him. Leir disinherited Cordella; but Aganippus, one of the twelve kings of France, had heard of her beauty and goodness, and he now sends a proposition for her hand, notwithstanding Leir's refusal to give her a dowry. Leir divided his kingdom between the Dukes of Cornewale and Albania, one-half to become theirs then, the remainder at his death. But they, becoming tired of doing without their inheritance, soon reduced Leir to such dire distress that he fled to Gaul, stung by the unkindness of his daughters more than by the wicked treatment of his sons-in-law. Cordella, hearing of his coming, sent him money and servants, so that he might come to the French court as became a king. She and Aganippus received him cordially, raised an army, and passed over to Britain in a great navy. A battle is fought in which the Dukes of Cornewale and Albania are slain. Leir is replaced on his throne and rules for two years. At his death Cordella ascends the throne, and reigns for five years, when her sisters' sons rise and drive her from the throne. She is captured and imprisoned. Being a woman of manly courage, she commits suicide.

The story of Gloucester follows the episode in Sidney's *Arcadia* until we come to the part where Edgar deceives his father about the cliff. In the original, Leonatus refuses to lead his father to the cliff at all, and, unlike Shakespeare's version, the unfortunate father is restored to happiness and power. The wicked son is overthrown, and the blind king again takes possession of his throne.

6. The characterization, the combination of circumstances, the tone of exalted passion, and the aim of the play are the work of Shakespeare's master mind. That he sought his materials for this grand structure in an outside work, cannot be doubted. Mr. Dowden has very properly said that Shakespeare was not remarkable for his invention of incidents, but *Lear* was not adapted in the sense that *Henry VI.* Part I. was. Holinshed furnished the suggestions, and *occasioned*, but did not *cause*, this masterpiece of passion.

---

7. I. i. 99. "Return *those* duties back *as* are right fit."

Mr. Abbott gives this as an instance of an ellipsis in the latter of two clauses connected by a relative or conjunction. The Elizabethan authors preferred clearness to grammatical correctness, and brevity to both clearness and grammatical correctness. They were especially averse to the repetition now considered necessary in the latter of two conjunctional clauses. Some one has said that *as* is here used for *which*, and cites "with *that* ceremonious affection *as* you were

wont," as a parallel instance. But Mr. Abbott reads, "Return those duties back as (they are) right fit (to be returned)." See below, line 178. —
"And on the sixth (we do allot thee) to turn thy hated back."

And IV. ii. 11. —
"What most he should dislike seems pleasant to him.
What (most he should) like (seems) offensive."

In V. iii. 120. —
"and (I ask) why you answer
This present summons?"

I. iv. 63. "With *that* ceremonious affection *as* you were wont."

As is here loosely used for *which*. *Such* (A.-S. *swulc, suilc, suilch, swich*) was the natural antecedent of *which:* hence its use as an antecedent to other relatives. Since *as* was used in a sense varying between a conjunction and a relative, it shared in the confusion which arose from this use of *such*, for, by analogy, *that* soon came to be used as an antecedent, and in the unsettled state of the language *which* was replaced by *as*.

8. I. i. 153. "*Answer* my life my judgement."

Answer is here a subjunctive used optatively or imperatively. The construction is common in Latin, as well as in O. E. In A.-S. the moods were distinguished by inflection. In the destruction of inflections, during the Elizabethan era, all kinds of tentative experiments were tried; some inflections were lost and their power retained, some were retained and their power lost, and some were retained with their power, which we have discarded. *Answer* is an example of an inflection lost but the power retained. Compare Hamlet I. i. 70. —

"Good now *sit* down and tell me *he* that knows."

And also I. i. 33.—

"Well, *sit we* down."

Also V. ii. 410.—

"The soldier's music and the rites of war
Speak loudly for him."

9. I. i. 163. "Thou *swear'st* thy gods in vain." Shakespeare frequently omits the preposition where the verb can be easily regarded as transitive. The construction is common when a person is the object, but very unusual in calling upon the gods to witness an action. Compare Macbeth I. v. 17.—

"I do *fear* thy nature."

Hamlet I. iii. 51.—

"O, fear me not."

Macbeth II. ii. 29.—

"*Listening* their fear, I could not say 'Amen.'"

In the present play we have, V. iii. 181.—

"*List* a brief tale."

Lear IV. ii. 31.—

"I *fear* your disposition."

Othello II. i. 219.—

—— "*list* me."

Hamlet I. iii. 30.—

"If with too credent ear you *list* his songs."

10. I. i. 194. "*Hath* rivall'd for our daughter." An instance of the inflection of the third person in a verb agreeing with a relative whose antecedent is in the second person.

The Elizabethans were probably led to this use by the fact that the relative does not signify, by any inflection, its agreement with its antecedent. Compare:

 Lear II. iv. 277. —
  "If it be you that *stirs* these daughters' hearts."

11. I. i. 207. "And *stranger'd* with our oath." In the Elizabethan age, the addition of *en* was sufficient to change any monosyllabic noun or adjective into a verb, usually with an active signification. In the general destruction of inflections this *en* was particularly discarded, but its converting power was retained. See Macbeth II. iv. 4. —

  "Hath *trifled* former knowings."

 Hamlet I. v. 90. —
  "And 'gins to *pale* his uneffectual fire."

The addition of *ed* gave these curtailed verbs a passive meaning, and from this formation arose a curious use of passive verbs. The distinction seems to be that verbs formed from nouns mean "endowed with (the noun)"; formed from adjectives they mean "made (the adjective)." *Strangered* is an exception to this rule, as is also "He *childed* as I *fathered*" in this play. As an instance of the regular construction, see Othello I. iii. 373. —

  "My cause is hearted."

12. I. i. 223. "That *monsters* it."
An instance of a verb formed from a noun. Compare:

 Lear I. i. 194. —
  "Hath *rivall'd* for our daughter."

 Lear II. ii. 128. —
  "That *worthied* him."

Also III. vi. 40. —
> "*Bench* by his side."

Hamlet I. i. 72. —
> "So nightly *toils* the subject of the land."

13. I. i. 227. "*If for* I want that glib and oily art."

Abbott gives this as an example of ellipsis from a desire for brevity, and reads: "If (it is) for (because) I want." — He cites: "Return those duties back as are right fit," as a parallel case.

14. I. i. 234. "A *still*-soliciting eye."

Still, constantly, which meaning the word gets from the derivation "quiet," "unmoved." Compare:

> Hamlet II. ii. 42. —
> "Thou *still* hast been the father of good news."

> King Lear II. iv. 108. —
> "Infirmity doth *still* neglect all office."

The present signification of the word, referring to a period of time reaching through the past and embracing the present, is easily traced to the derivation.

15. I. i. 251. "*Since that* respects of fortune are his love."

Just as *so* and *as* were added to give a relative meaning to words which were originally interrogative, so *that* was frequently added as a conjunctional affix. Compare:

> Macbeth IV. iii. 106. —
> "*Since that* the truest issue of thy throne."

And Othello II. iii. 234. —
> "*For that* I heard the clink and fall of swords."

And again, Othello II. iii. 321. —

"*For that* he hath devoted and given up himself."

16. I. ii. 43. "The contents are *to blame*."

Mr. Abbott gives this as an instance of the retention of the strong meaning of addition in the word *to*. We have this meaning only in *too*. I think that *to blame* here is an active infinitive used for the passive, and that the construction is similar to Macbeth V. vii. 28.

"And little is *to do*," equal to "And little is left to be done." In the present case there is an ellipsis of "fit," "worthy," and the sentence means,

"The contents are worthy of blame or censure."

17. I. ii. 106 and 125. "I pray *you* . . . It shall lose *thee* nothing."

Thou was the pronoun of affection towards friends, of good-humored superiority to servants, of contempt to strangers, and of solemn address. The change of feeling here is sufficient to justify the change from *you* to *thee*. When Gloucester says *you*, he is making a request; when he says *thee*, he is making a promise to Edmund. Where there are exceptions to the rule, they can always be explained by change of feeling, or by euphonic reasons, especially where the change is made in speaking to the same person.

18. I. iii. 1. "For *chiding of* his fool."

In A.-S. there was a verbal noun in *ung*, a present participle in *inde*, and a gerund in *enne*. In the changes which took place in the early and middle English periods, these three forms became confused; as a result the Elizabethans had *ing*, which they used indiscriminately, sometimes giving it a verbal, sometimes a noun signification, and frequently both the verb and noun idea. The verbal noun and the gerund became so far confused as to admit of an object, and yet be qualified by an adjective, or limited by an article. Compare :

> Macbeth II. iii. 2.—
>> "He should have *old turning the key*."
>
> Macbeth I. iv. 7–8.—
>> ——"nothing in his life
>> Became him like *the leaving it*."
>
> King Lear IV. iv. 9.—
>> "In *the restoring his bereaved sense*."

19. I. iv. 40. "Not *so* young, sir, *to* love a woman for singing."

Just as in relative clauses sometimes the relative, sometimes the antecedent, was omitted, so also in relatival constructions we should expect "*as* to love a woman." Compare :

> King Lear II. iv. 278.—
>> ——"fool me not *so* much
>> To bear it tamely."

Also

> King Lear III. i. 35, 36.—
>> "If on my credit you dare build *so* far
>> To make your speed to Dover."
>
> Macbeth IV. iii. 74.—
>> "*That* vulture in you *to* devour so many."
>
> Macbeth II. iii. 55.—
>> "I'll make *so* bold *to* call."

20. I. iv. 112. "*An* thou *canst* not smile."

Horne Tooke derived this *an* from the imperative mood

of *unnan*=to grant. Mr. Abbott thinks this a very plausible but false derivation, because *and* is found in E. E. in the sense of *if*, and this is, of course, the original of the Elizabethan *an*. *Canst* is the indicative frequently found with *if* when no futurity or doubt, but merely a condition, is implied. The indicative conveys rather the idea of inevitability. We have a similar construction in the logical condition in Latin.

21. I. iv. 204. " I would not be *thee*, nuncle."

Thee is found after the verb *to be* not only in the Fool's mouth. The explanation is that *thee* was referred to as a person about whom something was predicated, and not as the person spoken to. It was formed on the analogy of *he* and *she*, meaning man and woman.

22. I. iv. 221. " But *other* of your insolent retinue."

All, each, every, and *other* were interchanged and used in senses different from present usage. But *other* is here only a substitute for the old plural *othere*. In Chaucer the plural of adjectives is formed by adding *e* to the singular. See *Prologue*, line 104. —

"A shef of pocok arwes *brighte* and *kene*."

Also line 10. —

" And *smale* fowles maken melodie."

In the destruction of inflections this *e* was lost. Its power was retained, however.

23. I. iv. 225. " *To have found* a safe redress."

This use of the completed infinitive is not found in modern English, except in " I would have done it " and the like. To the Elizabethan the completed present expressed something that was past and finished which ought to have been done but was not. See Hamlet V. i. 267. —

"I hoped thou shouldst have been my Hamlet's wife;
I thought thy bride-bed to have decked, sweet maid,
And not have strew'd thy grave."

24. I. iv. 306. "Her *brow of youth.*"
Nouns connected by *of* were regarded by Shakespeare as a compound noun, and a qualifying word which really belonged only to the last was put before the compound. Compare:

Macbeth V. viii. 18. —
"For it hath cowed *my better part of man.*"

Sometimes the second noun can be explained as being a kind of genitive limiting the first, and hence its adjective signification. Compare:

Hamlet I. iv. 40. —
"Be thou a spirit of health."

Also Hamlet III. ii. 350. —
— "what is *your cause of distemper?*"

Again, Hamlet IV. vi. 20. —
"They have dealt with me like *thieves of mercy.*"

King Lear III. v. 22. —
"I will persevere in *my course of loyalty.*"

And Shakespeare *passim*.

25. II. iv. 277. "If it be you that *stirs*[1] these daughters' hearts."
The relative does not show by any inflection its agreement with its antecedent. Hence a verb agreeing with it may be in a different person and number from the antece-

---

[1] *Cf.* Abbott's *Shakespearian Grammar*, § 247. W. T. T.

dent according to Elizabethan usage. See above, "Hath rivall'd."

26. I. i. 125. "And thought *to set my rest.*"
Set my rest is a term from the game of primero. Metaphorically it means "to stake my all." In the game it means "to stand on the cards in one's hand."

27. I. ii. 4.
——"and permit
The *curiosity* of nations to deprive."

Curiosity in the sense of nice or critical distinction. The reference is to the custom of primogeniture in England, where the real estate passes to the oldest son.

28. I. ii. 149. "*Fa, sol, la, mi.*"
This has been given as conclusive evidence that Shakespeare was acquainted with the property of these syllables in solmization. Just as a combination of these notes makes a discordant sound, so Edmund was describing the confusion which resulted from "*these divisions*" by comparing it to this sound. But, with Mr. Wright, we think that he is only singing to pretend that he does not see his brother's approach.

29. I. iv. 18. "*And to eat no fish.*"
In the Elizabethan reign the distinction was clearly marked and the opposition determined and persistent between the Puritans and the Papists. The Papists were considered no good subjects of Elizabeth; and since they were compelled by their religion to eat only fish on certain occasions, the eating of fish from necessity became a mark of contempt.

30. I. iv. 282.
" More hideous when thou show'st *thee* in a child
Than the *sea-monster.*"

Thee is here used for *thyself*, as it often is in Shakespeare.

The *sea-monster* has been thought to refer to the hippopotamus, as that animal is the hieroglyphical symbol of impiety and ingratitude. But why should Shakespeare call a river-animal a sea-monster? Some one has suggested the whale. Hudson thinks that the story of the serpents of Troy furnished the suggestion, and when we think of Laocoön writhing in inextricable folds, it is not improbable that Shakespeare would compare the fruitless struggles of the old king to the death-agony of the Trojan. But did Shakespeare know of these serpents? I should rather think that the reference is to the monster, mentioned by Wright, "which ravisheth its dam."

31. I. v. 2. "These *letters*."
7. "Your *letter*." How is letter used?

Probably *letters* was used in the plural when only one was meant, like the Latin *litteræ* and *epistolæ*. But why change from *letters* to *letter* in the same speech? We have I. iv. 357.—

"What, have you writ *that letter* to my sister?"

And again, in II. ii. 38.—

"You come with *letters* against the king."

In both these cases *letters* may have been used in its ordinary sense; for it is reasonable to suppose that Lear was not driven from his throne without much opposition by his adherents, even in his daughters' households, and without preconcerted plans with those who concurred in the unjust treatment of the abdicating king. *These letters* may refer to other communications besides *the* letters delivered to Kent, while "letters against the king" does not necessarily refer only to "that letter" which Goneril had spoken to Oswald about (I. iv. 357).

32. ii. 16–20. "*Three-suited, worsted-stocking, lily-livered, one-trunk-inheriting.*"

These are all compounds expressing contempt. When Edgar mentions having had "three suits to his back" as an evidence of former pride, he is probably referring to the foppish love of dress, which led him to take the full allowance of that article in a *servant's* position. He has already called himself in III. iv. 87. —

"A serving man proud in heart and mind";

and Ben Jonson mentions a woman who asked her henpecked husband, "Who furnished him his clothes and gave him three suits?" Three suits were probably included in the stipulation for the salary of a serving man, and the mention of it here conveys the idea that Kent regarded Oswald's base character more suitable to the station of a servant too proud for his position, than for the knightly service supposed to be required of a ladies' "gentleman."

At a time when no one but servants and the lower class of society wore woollen stockings, those articles became a mark of inferior rank.

Our ancestors regarded the passions as originating in the humours of the body. The liver was believed to be the seat of courage, and hence a coward was called white-livered. We have a reference to the same belief in Macbeth V. iii. 15.—

"Go prick thy face, and over-red thy fear,
Thou lily-livered boy."

One-trunk-inheriting. *Trunk* can hardly mean trunk hose here, but rather the modern receptacle for clothing.

Kent means to say that Oswald is so poor that he can put all he has in one trunk. *Inherit* is used, as it often is in Shakespeare, in the sense of *possess*.

33. II. ii. 84. "Turn their *halcyon beaks*."

The halcyon is the king-fisher. The reference is to the belief that when that bird was hung up by the neck, its breast and beak would always be against the wind. "Halcyon days" received their name from the belief that the bird has some agency in bringing about the calm weather about the time it is brooding.

34. II. ii. 90. "I'ld drive ye cackling home to *Camelot*."

Camelot was Arthur's capital, to which, according to the Arthurian legends, the Knights of the Round Table sent those whom they had conquered, to be disposed of by Arthur. The reference is most probably to this legend, though possibly Kent means to compare Oswald to the geese with which the country around Camelot or Cadbury abounds.

35. III. ii. 10. "*Court holy-water* in a dry house."

A proverbial expression for flattery.

36. III. vi. 78. "Poor Tom, *thy horn is dry*."

It has been said that Edgar speaks this in a low tone, and means that he can no longer keep up the part he is acting. But there is another and more obvious meaning when we know that these "Abraham men" carried a horn which they wound when they came to a house, and then had the milk which was given them poured into it. But after all, I think the first explanation the more plausible one, for Edgar is in the habit of expressing his feelings aside. See IV. i. 53.—

"I cannot daub it further."

And III. vi. 63.—

"My tears begin to take his part so much,
They'll mar my counterfeiting."

Again, IV. i. 27–30. —
> "O gods! Who is't can say, 'I am at the worst'?
> I am worse than e'er I was ";

and
> "And worse I may be yet: the worst is not
> So long as we can say, 'This is the worst.'"

The words can convey both ideas; perhaps Shakespeare intended that they should.

37. $\begin{cases} \text{IV. v. 29.} & \text{"Take this } \textit{note.}\text{"} \quad \textit{Cf.} \text{ IV. v. 33.} \\ \text{V. iii. 27.} & \text{"Take thou this } \textit{note.}\text{"} \quad \textit{Cf.} \text{ V. iii. 245.} \end{cases}$

Undoubtedly, *note* in V. iii. 27 refers to a paper giving instructions for the murder of Lear and Cordelia.

> "As this instructs thee"

(l. 29) and l. 37
> "Carry it so as I have set it down"

would be convincing testimony even were it not that we have positive evidence in V. iii. 245. —

> —— "for my writ
> Is on the life of Lear and on Cordelia."

In IV v. 29 the reference must be to a letter, for Regan says, "give him this" (IV. v. 33). And in IV. vi. 254 we have

> "And give the *letters* which thou find'st about me
> To Edmund earl of Gloucester."

Again, in IV. vi. 261. —
> —— "the *letters* that he speaks of
> May be my friends."

Edgar says "papers" until he has selected Goneril's letter from the rest, and then he says "paper" (IV. vi. 283).

The evidence is good, though not conclusive that Oswald had a letter given him by Regan, and that "letters," "papers," etc., are used in the ordinary sense of more than one.

38. IV. vi. 187. "This a good *block*."

One theory is that Lear takes off his hat to preach to Gloucester, and that the capital idea of shoeing a troop of horse with felt is suggested by the soft hat. Another conjecture is that Lear mounts a stump to speak, and the idea occurs independently. When we think of the facility with which Lear's mind passed from one thing to another, and remember that he was a king, and that the stratagem was one which would probably have been considered good by him in his sane moments; when we think of the proneness of his mind to recur to a means for regaining his kingdom, we see no need of a tangible object to suggest the stratagem to him; and, notwithstanding the fact that block was the name of the fashion of the hat in Shakespeare's time, we must decide against the hat in favor of the substitute for a stage.

39. IV. vii. 17. "*Child-changed* father."

Changed by his children, and not to a child, for childishness is an attribute of old age, and not of insanity. Shakespeare could never have thought of calling this fierce Titan of passion "childish."

40. IV. vii. 80. "To make him *even o'er* the time."

Even may here be either an adjective or a verb. In either case the doctor is warning Cordelia against the danger of making her father recall the trouble which had overthrown his reason. It was not the mental exertion that he feared so much, though that too was to be guarded against. I think it is a verb.

41. I. i. 126. "Hence, and avoid my sight."
Rowe thinks that this command evidently refers to Cordelia. Heath argues that it is given to Kent. Wright says that it of course refers to Cordelia, although she does not obey, which Lear would be apt to forget in his excitement. He thinks that Kent has already received an implied pardon for his interruption in the sentence, " Come not between the dragon and his wrath "; and, moreover, Lear is explaining to Kent the cause of his wrath, and would not offer an explanation to a man whom he was ordering from his presence. I believe the command to be addressed to Kent, for Lear has referred to Cordelia in the third person, both before and after it. Lear knows Kent's character for upholding calm, even-handed justice; perhaps he is aware of Kent's respect and love for Cordelia, and anticipates remonstrance from him. Lear is in a passion, and unreasonable, and the mere fact of Kent's interruption would be sufficient to call down the king's wrath. Lear is speaking, thinking of Cordelia; hence he would not forget so flagrant a change from her usually quiet yet implicit obedience. Cordelia could have no object in remaining, since her presence only increased the fury of her father. At first, firm adherence to truth and reluctance to add to her father's unreasonable desire for flattery was a sufficient excuse for her seemingly obstinate behavior. Now her only purpose can be to try to retrieve what she has evidently lost. The supposition is not in keeping with her character. I cannot imagine the tender, shrinking Cordelia obstinately disobeying her father when she has resolved to sacrifice all rather than swerve from duty. On the other hand, Kent prefers to remain " the true blank " of Lear's eye, and his rash disobedience when Lear says, " Out

of my sight!" shows plainly that Lear wanted Kent and not Cordelia away. Lear at once sends for France and Burgundy in order that he may offer Cordelia dowerless, and with his "displeasure pieced," to their "quest of love." He expected her to remain until the interview with her suitors.

42. I. i. 151. "Reverse thy doom" (Q). "Reserve thy state" (F). Best reading, and why?

Johnson thinks that Shakespeare wrote "Reverse thy doom" first as being more apposite to the present occasion, and afterwards changed it to "Reserve thy state" as conducing more to the progress of the play. The argument generally urged against "Reverse thy doom" is, that it could only refer to Cordelia's fate, while Kent's subsequent talk and action prove that it was Lear's interest he was watching. I see nothing in either reading which would be incompatible with Kent's having Lear's good in view. If he said, "Reverse thy doom,". it was because he saw that if Lear disinherited Cordelia and gave his power and state to the sisters, there was no hope for any other fate than the one which actually befell him. It is absurd to think that the far-seeing Kent had lived in Lear's court ignorant of the cold, calculating selfishness, the malignant power, and atrocious cruelty of Goneril and Regan, even though they had blinded their father with flattery. He has read Cordelia, and with her he resolves to lose all in the endeavor to check the tide of his master's folly.

I think "Reserve thy state" the better reading, inasmuch as the speech follows the announcement that Léar's power, pre-eminence, and all the large effects that troop with majesty, were given into the hands of the wicked daughters. Kent appeals to his master's generosity and fatherly affection only when he finds that no regard for, or perception of, his true interest can "check this hideous rashness" in the irate old king.

When he finds that Lear no longer distinguishes between the uprightness to which he may trust power and wealth, and the designing wickedness which will "sweep him from its sight and bid its will avouch it" when it has the power,— when Lear has lost sight of dutiful affection and bows to flattery,— when Kent perceives this, then, and not till then, he says (below, l. 167) : —

> "Revoke thy doom,
> Or, whilst I can vent clamour from my throat,
> I'll tell thee thou dost evil."

It is no longer "Reserve thy state"; from those who will soon prove the emptiness of their protestations; but "'Revoke thy doom,' for thou art violating a holy trust."

Evidently Kent said "Reserve thy state "; else why should Gloucester say in III. iv. 167.—

> "His daughters seek his death: ah, that good Kent!
> He said it would be thus, poor banished man."

43. I. ii. 104, 105. "To his father that so tenderly and entirely loves him."

The speech is not in keeping with the character of Gloucester, if we regard it as an expression of the real feelings of the man. His first appearance and talk about Edmund prove his lack of true parental affection for *him*, and he says (I. i. 19).—

"But I have, sir, a son by order of law, some year elder than this, who yet is no dearer in my account."

Now Edmund has "been out nine years, and away he shall again." He has had no opportunity to form the tie by which association strengthens natural affection; moreover, the shame of acknowledging him is stronger than the father's love. If Edgar is no dearer than this son, the relationship between him and his father does not deserve the epithets "tender" and "entire." I do not think that a nature so credulous and superstitious, so wanting in all that goes to make up a strong, noble character, would be capable of loving tenderly and entirely. But his selfishness would be calculated to suggest such an expression. He felt that he had been injured by Edgar's treachery, and the greater the affection he expressed, the greater the injury would appear. But Gloucester was honest in the assertion that he loved Edgar. He mistook his grief and disappointment, in that he had been outwitted, for sorrow at the unworthiness of the object of his affection.

44. II. iv. 213, 214. —

"To be a comrade with the wolf and howl
Necessity's sharp pinch";

or —

"To be a comrade with the wolf and owl —
Necessity's sharp pinch."

Best reading? I think the first reading preferable.

Roofs are to be abjured, war is to be waged with the elements, companionship with the very wolves, where misery is so complete that nature howls out its unsupplied necessities, is preferable to the humiliation of obeying those who have trampled duty, love, and honor under foot, in the mad rush for power. If it be objected that "to howl a pinch" is a violent metaphor, we can only say that it is not more so than "take arms against a sea of troubles," and other like expressions which no one denies are evidently Shakespearian.

There is nothing frightful in a companionship with the owl, and it sounds tame after the strong expressions preceding it, while to make "Necessity's sharp pinch" explanatory of Lear's proposed action would spoil the whole thing by dragging on after the first wild burst was over.

45. IV. ii. 62. "Thou changed and *self-covered*."

Some one has said that "*self-covered* thing" means that Goneril has taken upon herself the semblance of a fiend. But I think such a notion not in accordance with the general impression of Goneril's character. Her conduct throughout this play, as well as in the old play and Holinshed's account, can only be explained by supposing her in possession, from the first, of a strong impulse of malignity and deceit. Albany says (IV. ii. 60): —

"Proper deformity seems not in the fiend
So horrid as in woman."

Proper in the sense of "own," "peculiar," is not singular in Shakespeare. When Albany says, "See *thyself* devil," he means Goneril as she *is*. "A woman's shape doth shield thee" (IV. ii. 67) shows that Albany regards the sex which she is supposed to represent dishonored by the untold wickedness which a woman's shape has concealed and protected, howe'er she was a fiend. *Self-covered* cannot mean deceiving by a false appearance *now*, for Goneril — no longer restrained by the necessity of humoring her father's whims in order to advance her own interests — has thrown off her covering of deceit and appears in her true character. Albany says, "Bemonster not thy feature" (IV. ii. 63). This must refer to the distorted face of Goneril as she writhed with passion and conscious guilt, with the effort to retain her assumed superiority and to conceal the acknowledgment of the justice of the accusation, for even Goneril must have shrunk from such a scathing and unexpected rebuke. I think *changed* and *self-covered* refer to this, and Mr. Crosby's derivation of "feature," in the next line, from the Latin "facere," seems to favor the interpretation.

46. Spedding was dissatisfied with the want of time and importance given to the battle which decided the fate of Lear and of Cordelia (V. ii.); moreover, he thought that the interest was allowed to flag in the long scenes which followed the crisis. He says that just as we were expecting the wave, which has come dashing on and paused and crested, to break in thunder on the beach, it subsides into an insignificant murmur, and leaves us disappointed, to wade through a monotonous gathering up of lost threads. At least, this is the way I understand him, and such is the impression which the play produces on me. The first act closes with Lear's burst of anger and his final renunciation of Goneril; the second closes with the driving out of the old king into the storm; the third leaves him raving in the terrific scene of the mock-trial where the inspired babbling of the Fool, the jargon of Poor Tom, the howlings of the storm without, and the mighty upheaval of the moral world within, make the most sublime picture which pen ever drew. The horror is increased by the blinding of Gloucester in another direction; vague rumors are afloat of a French army, and we are left in fearful suspense. Making Act IV. close a scene and a half further on, the interest reaches its climax at the end of the fourth act. The rumors begun in Act III. have grown into certainties; Lear's affairs are not hopeless. The French army has landed; the powers of the kingdom approach apace, and the arbitrament is like to be bloody. Spedding would have Act IV. to close with the exit of Edgar (V. ii. 4). This gives time for the battle, the imagination fills, and the remainder of the play is less

monotonous. *King Lear* was not divided into acts and scenes at first, and hence it is probable that the present arrangement was not intended by Shakespeare.

47. V. iii. 305. "And my *poor fool* is hanged."

Yes; throughout that part of the play in which the Fool appears Lear speaks of and treats him with an indulgent regard that is touching. He had been connected with Cordelia in all Lear's domestic relations, for it was to them that the king looked for amusement and watchful kindness, for sympathy and prompt obedience. When Lear is told, " Since my lady's going into France, sir, the Fool hath much pined away," he says ('I. iv. 81) :—

"No more of that ; I have noted it well."

The Fool was with Lear when the storm broke over his head and Lear felt the throb of sympathetic woe which shook that sensitive frame, and all the tenderness of his nature welled up in the expression —

"How dost, my boy ?
Art cold ? I am cold myself."

Lear knows of the Fool's attachment to Cordelia, and the silent sympathy of these two strong natures suffering under a common woe, formed a bond too strong to be broken by the unsettling of Lear's wits. In the last moments, when the light shines dimly upon his darkened intellect, when the influences that have moulded his life come trooping up like faint shadows from the past and mingle with the imperfectly comprehended things of the present, it is no wonder that the lost link in the chain of memory should take the semblance of that with which its past connection served as a present reminder, and that Cordelia embodies all that he had found in both. It is not necessary to conclude that the Fool was hanged, for Lear is still "far wide," and hanging was impressed on his mind. *Fool* was a term of endearment in Shakespeare's time, but Lear does not so use it elsewhere, and there is a delicate touch of feeling in thus gathering up the lost threads which is wholly lost if *Fool* applies only to Cordelia.

48. Act III. vi. 21-91. King Lear has lost control of his thoughts; they come and go with the speed of lightning, and the least circumstance serves as a link of association in the chain of ideas. Age and grief and the violent physical shock which he has just received would render optical illusion very probable; and in the uncertain light of the house Lear may have mistaken any object for his daughter. But when he looked attentively at her, in the act of describing how the wickedness of her heart showed itself in her face, he perceived his mistake; but so confused are his ideas and so active his conception, that he thinks the disappearance of the image is the escape of his daughter. Naturally he flies into a passion. The fabrications of an intellect, bounding to fearful heights and depths, in the absence of restraining reason, become intense realities; the thronging rush of incongruous images through his brain works up to white heat the already excited nervous system. Hence it is that while the physical condition in part causes the aberrations of mind, the mental excitement reacts on the body, and Lear perhaps sees everything around him in a violent state of commotion.

49. III. vii. In Shakespeare's time there were none of the modern "improvements" on the stage. The elevated chair in the centre which had served Lear as a throne, when he had divided his kingdom is the one to which Gloucester is bound. This chair was situated on a stage a little higher

than the main stage, from which it was separated by pillars and a curtain. Thus Gloucester, sitting in this chair with his back to the spectators, and surrounded in part by the servants holding the chair, was imperfectly seen through the pillars and half-drawn curtains and in the general confusion. Thus placed, the scene would not be more horrible than the smothering of Desdemona or the sacrifice of Iphigenia, and not half so dreadful as the suspense and fear of Macbeth when he murders Duncan. Coleridge says Shakespeare has urged the tragic element in this play to its farthest limits and to the *ne plus ultra* of the dramatic. But Hudson thinks that some such scene is necessary in a play where passion and suffering reach such an immense height. Breadth of basis is necessary to sustain the vast structure. The physical sufferings of Gloucester become insignificant when compared to the intense mental anguish of Lear. We lose our interest in the former when we come face to face with the latter, and the horror, by which Shakespeare has prepared us for the convulsion of the moral world, for this convention of agonies, is lost in the sympathetic woe which fills the imagination to aching. Then, too, the demands of justice are satisfied (to the uttermost, I admit), while the presence of a sympathizing servant relieves the horror by redeeming the scene from the utter depravity which would otherwise characterize it.

The blinding of Gloucester is in perfect accordance with dramatic art, nor does it exceed the cruelty of actions which may have come under our own observation.

ÆSTHETIC.

50. Our estimate of King Lear depends very much on the view we take of the Fool. Superficially considered, his presence is a blemish in the work; but a close analysis of the characters proves that he is necessary to the full development and right understanding of all the principal characters. The intense passion of Lear would be wanting in pathos were it not for the silent sympathy which exists between him and this soul of pathos. Shakespeare endears him to us when he introduces him pining for the embodiment of womanly purity. We know at once that his soul reverences truth and seeks with a tender, clinging love for the loyalty whose " low sound reverbs no hollowness." Endowed with a peculiarly sensitive nature, his tongue ever struggles with a jest and his cheek dimples with a smile to relieve the eye of a burden under which it is reeling. Courageous enough to dare Goneril in the angry words —

> " A fox, when one has caught her,
> And such a daughter,
> Should sure to the slaughter,
> If my cap would buy a halter." — I. iv. 340.

there is yet a "shrinking, velvet-footed delicacy in the Fool's antics" which binds him still closer to the pathos of the play. A privileged character, he everywhere turns his privileges into charities. Highly intellectual, he uses his wit in urging his master to resume the shape he has cast off; and so pointed and earnest are his reproaches, so acute is his perception of the wrongs done to Cordelia, and which his master persists in doing to himself, that we cannot believe that he is "altogether fool" in any speech. Even after the attempt to goad Lear into a reasonable course has been given up, we find the Fool laboring to out-jest the "heart-struck injuries" of the insane king. But we do not need a second confirmation of the bond between this tenderest, truest of natures and the obstinate, persistent, remorseful Lear when we hear —

"No more of that; I have noted it well."

This common suffering, too strong for expression — the Fool mourning a loss and deploring a cause for which he can only reproach the rashness of his master, Lear drinking the bitter cup which wounded pride holds to his lips — makes the Fool one of the most important personages of the play. And when we know that he has been slowly but surely dying as his heartstrings broke one after another under the weight of another's woe, the exclamation (III. vi. 92) —

"And I'll go to bed at noon"

becomes one of the most touching in all Shakespeare; and as the Fool disappears tottering under the burden of his master, when "oppressed nature sleeps," our parting words must be with Hudson, "Truly thou art the soul of pathos in a sort of comic masquerade."

There are many reasons for believing that he was a boy. His mourning for the loss of Cordelia; Lear's speaking of him as "my pretty knave," and again, his saying, "How dost, my boy?"; his sensitiveness to cold in the cry, "This cold night will turn us all to fools and madmen"; his fright at Poor Tom in the hovel; and his dying of grief, would seem to indicate a delicate, boyish sensitiveness and a physical nature incapable of enduring the intense mental anguish through which he passes. Such is, I believe, the opinion of the majority of the best critics; but Mr. Furness thinks that he was one of the shrewdest, tenderest of *men* — shrewd from his experience of the world's deceitfulness, tender from participation in the woes to which his position was incident. I see nothing incompatible with this shrewdness in the active, discerning intellect of a boy; and an intensely sympathetic nature is always tender. "The truest are the tenderest, the loving are the daring." The Fool has, in the space of a few months, passed through the vicissitudes of a lifetime. These trials develop in him loving, whole-souled boyhood, the qualities which Mr. Furness claims for the "man" only.

51. From this and her subsequent action in the play we decide that firm adherence to duty and tender, watchful, self-sacrificing love were Cordelia's characteristic traits. She had observed her father's proneness to yield to flattery — the morbid desire for outward manifestations of love becoming a disease, so completely had it taken possession of the springs of his action. She has already read the selfish, unscrupulous hearts of her sisters, and feels that she must strive to counteract their influence. Then, too, she is indignant at the idea of the holiest, most unselfish feelings being dragged forth to gratify a whim, to stand as a measure for worldly interest. Following the impulse of her heart (though she "cannot heave her heart into her mouth," for the simple reason that she has so much of it), and doing what she thinks to be her duty, Cordelia displays a degree of daring and firmness which almost amounts to reckless obstinacy. But there are other considerations which — if they do not explain the refusal to sacrifice truth to interest — serve to soften the appearance of undue strictness in the performance of filial duty. There is a lack of forethought in all her actions, but here we cannot believe that

her calm resistance to her father's will was without hope in the future, should the worst come to the worst. France had won even Lear's respect (see I. i. 212) by his noble behavior, and it is not strange that Cordelia had learned to trust him. Endowed with an organization which rather felt than perceived the innate peculiarities of those with whom she was associated, no doubt she has long since made choice between France and Burgundy, and given to France the esteem which the pure accord to the pure. She places herself in circumstances beneath which so delicate a nature would have succumbed had there been nothing to sustain it but the trust in its own truth. France's faith in her is so firmly rooted that to believe her guilty of any heinous sin

"Must be a faith that reason without miracle
Could never plant in me." — I. i. 225.

And I. i. 261, —

"Not all the dukes of waterish Burgundy
Can buy this *unprized precious* maid of me."

I think Cordelia must have reciprocated this trust. She does not foresee the dethronement of her father, but thinks (I. i. 283) —

"Time shall unfold what plaited cunning hides.
Who cover faults, at last shame them derides."

She only fears their influence on his mind. Her surprise at the contents of Kent's letter (IV. iii. 26–30) carries us back to this scene, and we can interpret her action only in one way; "half her love" was already given to France. Although in this case it was

"Love, dear love and our aged father's right"

that prompted her action as well as in IV. iv. 28, we must think that her persistence was due, in a measure, to the fact that she *believed* — though she may not have known — that France loved her and would remain true.

52. The picture that presents itself to my mind is that of a tall, strong-looking woman, with bold black eyes, and a firm, scornful expression in the cast of the features; of a woman whose movements are quick and decided, but skilful, whose appearance indicates a man's power of endurance, a man's will, and a man's feeling of superiority, with a woman's power to hide her feelings, and to gain her ends by stratagem. Mr. Hudson does not seem to accord to her the wisdom necessary to form complicated plots. The play leaves quite a different impression on me. Her close observation and cunning, her prompt action, and Albany's reluctance to come to an open issue with her, seem to me to indicate a peculiarly active intellect — not inventive, it is true, nor imaginative, but prompt to obey the impulses of a wicked heart. Morally, Goneril's character possesses scarcely a redeeming feature. Formed for all evil, nourished in the deceitful atmosphere of a court, deprived of the holy influence of a mother, partaking of the nature and following the example of a father whose only rule of action was his own passion, — what good could we expect from such a woman?

53. The scene of this play was laid in a time when the peculiarities of men were less subjected to the stamp of a common impression than now. Eight hundred years before the Christian era, human nature was allowed to develop in all its elements. Less restrained than now by religious influences, the prevailing tendency must have been towards crime. With little or no parental training and under such circumstances did Goneril and Regan form their characters. Perhaps they will seem rather monstrosities than women in

the combination of all evils. But we are not to crush art down to the level of every-day experience. Its business is to teach us moral truths, and we must take them as they *are*. Besides, the wickedness, which seems to us so horrid, is not peculiar to art. The existence of the words "fratricide," "matricide," "patricide," and "suicide" is a sufficient indication of actual crimes which they represent. These things are of daily occurrence, and such atrocities as are attributed to these women come under most people's observation. Within my limited experience I have known a *mother* driven from a son's door when she was begging for food and shelter for the night. Goneril and Regan have, no doubt, often been annoyed by the passionate exactions of old Lear; they have restrained their inclination to an outbreak on account of their worldly interest, and when, by Lear's abdication of the throne, the power passes into their hands, they begin to use "checks as hindrances" to his unreasonable conduct. Lear resists; they increase their demands until they exceed the limits of justice and of Lear's patience. Lear flies into a passion, and then comes the throwing off of the assumed kindness. The daughters, who have "hit together" in the beginning to restrain their father, have but one step to make before they reach a state of depravity in which they will protect themselves against the blind fury of that father by exposing his white head to the rage of a storm. They do not *murder* him. Perhaps *they* would shrink from that. I cannot think that Goneril actually concurred in the writ for Lear's execution, though Edmund knew that her sense of right was not strong enough to make her countermand his order. The murder of a sister is not unknown to civilization, and the firm conviction that even a beautiful, accomplished and, in other respects, lady-like woman is capable of murdering her husband, is illustrated by the case of Mary Stuart. Shakespeare does not exceed the natural. Endowed with strong, natural impulses, actuated by desire for power, incited by an unholy love, and provoked to envy and hatred, these women do nothing for which we cannot find a parallel in our own day. Art is founded on actual life.

54. When we first see Lear, he is not a lunatic, although in his lack of judgment, in the excitability of his nerves, and in his unmanly yielding to passion, we discover a decided predisposition to insanity. As Dr. Bucknill says, if we regard this trial of his daughters as a fabrication of a sane mind, we must admit that the play is founded on a gross improbability, and the action of Lear in the subsequent scenes is inexplicable.

It is true that improbabilities of circumstance are not of infrequent occurrence in Shakespeare. We have a ghost in *Hamlet*, fairies in *A Midsummer Night's Dream*, and witches in *Macbeth*, than which no fabrications of the brain can be more improbable. But we never have the systematic development of strength from weakness. As in the after-part of the play we stand before the vast ruin of Lear's mind, — immethodized from the ordinary pursuits of life, but sublime in the heights and depths which it reaches, — it is wonderful, impossible that such power and vigor, such energy and unrest, should be traced to a weak love of flattery in a mind whose normal state was little more than idiocy. No; Lear is already far on the way to that unsound state of mind to which "not alone the imperfections of long en-graffed condition, but therewithal the unruly waywardness that infirm and choleric years bring with them," have been urging him. We perceive that the kingdom has been already divided. The trial, then, was but a trick to entrap his daughters into a profession of attachment to him.

Cordelia's opposition was wholly unexpected. Tottering reason is overwhelmed in the tide of passion, and woe betide the man who tries to stem the current. "Our nature nor our place can bear" opposition even to a whim, and "This hideous rashness" is only the beginning of a series to which the end is the wild race through the fields when Cordelia finds that he is "As mad as the vex'd sea." Cordelia is his favorite child. See I. i. 125. —

> "I loved her most, and thought to set my rest
> On her kind nursery."

Again, I. i. 217. —

> — "she that even but now was your best object,
> The argument of your praise, balm of your age,
> Most best, most dearest."

Lear's subsequent recognition of the folly of his course only proves more clearly his inability to control his wandering faculties in this scene. See I. v. 25, where the sad "I did her wrong" steals a sense of woe into the stoutest heart, and again, IV. vii. 71-75. —

> "If you have poison for me, I will drink it.
> I know you do not love me, for your sisters
> Have, as I do remember, done me wrong:
> You have some cause, they have not."

In this scene the case is one of emotional insanity; it is not until the king receives a violent physical shock that he becomes a lunatic.

The remarkable power of passion in the resurgence of the faculties which age had quietly inurned, in the development of that fierce Titan of mental strength with clear insight into purposes, with sublime power of moral reasoning, and with unlimited reach of imagination, is shown in the vast convulsion of mind, in the volcanic explosions of passion, in the wild tumult of thought where matter and impertinency are mixed.

King Lear's actions send the mind back to the time when a vigorous, comprehensive intellect was held in strict subjection to the noble impulses of an upright heart. We see him gradually yielding to the influences to which nature and political station have subjected him, until all the nobler qualities — generosity, sympathy, disinterested affection, all that makes a man lovable — have degenerated into mere selfishness. Through all faith in filial piety controls his action. When that faith is lost and anarchy sets in, the elements which have been before buried, are thrown up again in the wild convulsion. Lear's trust in filial piety is justified by the event, though his judgment, as to the proper person to whom it should be given, was wrong. Lear's purposes were right, but he lacked the judgment and the strength of will to carry them out.

55. Cordelia appears only at the first and the last of the play, and occupies only about one hundred lines. She is absent from nearly all the impressive scenes, and yet when we lay down the book, we feel that she has ever been present; a peculiar, pervading influence has gone out from her and directed the good in their labor of love and restrained the evil in their power. The youngest and the least of Lear's daughters, modest and retiring, we must know her long to know her well, but we love her when we know her. A sweet, tender picture of perfect womanhood — unalloyed by the frivolous ideas and disgusting manners which we are apt to associate with a pretty, petted child — is the one

which comes to us when we think of Lear's doting love, of France's manly affection, of Kent's dignified respect, and of the Fool's pining attachment. We do not wonder that the sisters envied her. But there is a delectable smack of her father's "quality" in the way she switches off her higgling suitor, I. i. 250. —

"Peace be with Burgundy;
Since that respects of fortune are his love,
I shall not be his wife."

Then, too, there is a lack of forethought in all her actions. But in strict performance of duty and courageous daring of fate to the worst, Cordelia commands the admiration due to the purest and strongest of Shakespeare's characters. Although she nowhere says anything very intelligent, she leaves the impression upon us that she possesses a penetrating, vigorous mind. But her intellect is so bound up with her feelings — kept in perfect solution, as it were, and never falling down into a sediment — that she cannot express her judgments. There is always so much more meant than is said, that even those who are present with her find themselves drawn and controlled by a word, a gesture. Mrs. Jameson defines Cordelia's power to be —

"a tardiness in nature
Which often leaves the history unspoke
That it intends to do."

There is the peculiar recurrence of longing which comes with a note of music when —

"The music in my heart I bore
Long after it was heard no more."

Lear has had no conscious reasons for his preference for Cordelia, and therefore he cannot reason it away; the Fool pines away when she goes to France, and he cannot tell why, only he was happy when she was by, he is miserable now; the gentleman sent by Kent with letters to her, returns mad with admiration and eloquence, although he has heard nothing but sighs and broken sentences. The sisters are glad to be rid of the restraint which her presence puts upon them. Cordelia's influence upon our estimate of the other characters is as little capable of measurement as is the aroma-like spirit of goodness which she diffuses about her. Through her, woman is redeemed from the "proper deformity" which seems not in the fiend so horrid as in woman. Through her, Lear's life is redeemed from utter futility; and following her example, Kent and the Fool are ennobled by their loyalty to duty, while Goneril and Regan, made doubly wicked by the contrast with her purity, are redeemed from deserving the title of Gorgons, since they are only at the other extreme of human nature from herself. She is modest, yet daring in the cause of truth; active, yet quiet in the performance of duty; firm, loving, and tender, yet scorning the weakness which leads her father to rashness. Perhaps Schlegel was right when he said, "Of Cordelia's heavenly purity I do not dare to speak."

56. The scene of *King Lear* was laid in an age antecedent to any historical record of England. Eight hundred years before Christ, manners were in a crude state. Christianity, with its civilizing influence, has done much to guide men in their duties to one another. The principle of force then ruled men, and absolute power was one of the rights of the king or chief of a nation. Superstition took the place of religion, and the brightest minds were dimmed by its baleful

influence. The innate peculiarities of men found ample room to develop in the exercise of the functions which belonged to the *individual*. Climatic and other natural influences made our ancestors a daring, liberty-loving people; consequently we find woman occupying a position in which she is honored and protected. In *King Lear* we have every phase of political and religious life, from the despotic old Lear to the dependent on Gloucester, from positive skepticism to the utmost faith in divine supervision. The mistakes of the highest political authority, the extent to which absolute power may counteract benign influences and the idea of justice which dwells naturally in the mind of man, and the instability of a government convulsed by civil strife, have their causes traced and their development outlined in the disastrous effects of Lear's unreasonable course. In religion we may find particular examples of the forces which, to-day, are building or destroying, in the moral world, the beliefs arising from different apprehensions of the truth, the evil overwhelming the good and producing fruit after its kind. Heathenism prevailed, and man worshipped his ideal type of nature, or, contemning the weakness of man's grandest efforts or ideas, turned in disgust from the creations of his intellect. We have Edgar firm and loyal in the course which he has marked out for himself, sustained by his faith that "the gods are just, and of our pleasant vices make instruments to plague us"; Gloucester shrinking from the ominous combination of circumstances which opened up the fate superstitiously accepted by himself; Kent striking right and left for the truth, which comes to him only by instinct; Edmund, with his keen, penetrating intellect, spurning the vile trust in Gloucester's capricious deity and turning in disgust from the apparently crushed truth of the nobler characters; Goneril and Regan daring fate to the worst; Albany exemplifying patient endurance; while Lear exemplifies parental affection and trust, and Cordelia embodies filial piety. We have here duty clashing with interest, selfishness with disinterested love, ingratitude with trust, evil with good. In the end, it would seem as if the evil conquered and as if the struggle had been useless. The great mystery of life remains unsolved, and Shakespeare, writing in a Christian age under Christian influences, leaves us to infer the moral in a Christian spirit.

57. Shakespeare sets life before us in all its phases, working free from restraint, and leaves us to estimate the truth as it *is*. When we ask the question: Where shall the love, the fidelity, and the courage which have closed the breaches in the moral world find their recompense? there can be but one answer: "Only in the life to come and in the consciousness that the struggle has borne valuable, if bitter, fruit in this life." Again, shall justice be content with the defeat and death of the instigators of this vast rebellion in nature? The moral points to a harder, more enduring punishment. The old Roman idea of virtue consisting of courage, honesty, patriotism, and energy was very good; but Shakespeare sees something higher and nobler in the Christian principles,— self-sacrifice, forgiveness of injuries, loving of enemies, faith, and charity. Engrafting these principles upon a blind idolatry, Shakespeare has endeavored to show us what life would be if man were free from the restraints which education — in the modern sense of that term — and Christianity put upon him, to show how, left to himself, he would develop the active powers of his nature, and the consequences of the free expansion of intellect, sensibility, and will. He has demonstrated the problem of life with mathematical precision; but he leaves us to examine ourselves and the people and things

around us for the application of the proposition which he sets before us. We must find the lemmas and corollaries; and last, but not least, he leaves us to make for ourselves the deduction of the great life principle, which forms the axiom of life's comedies and tragedies. With the lesson of life before us in Cordelia, silently, lovingly, reverently pausing before its great mystery, but taking it firmly for better or for worse, would we spurn it because the event *seems* to be barren of result, nay, is even fraught with sorrow? Would we follow Lear, flapping like a caged bird against the world, which is too narrow for his unlimited desires? We turn shudderingly from his awful fate. Then, shall we seek in Edmund's course the happiness which the restless soul demands? No; there is more hope in Kent's farewell, —

"I have a journey, sir, shortly to go;
My master calls me, I must not say no" —

than in the death agony of Edmund's last words, —

"The wheel is come full circle; I am here."

If it be true that "All friends shall taste the wages of their virtue, and all foes the cup of their deservings," we find in the lives of Edgar and of Albany the earliest fruition of "the hope that is in us."

This play is the one which, from the difficulties of the subject and the skill and power of its handling, best illustrates the strength, energy, and versatility of the author's genius. It is worked out in the spirit of the Gothic art, where no rule governs but that each of the parts be perfect and in mutual relation. The more the design is varied and the more magnificent the parts, the grander will be the structure. Hence it is that when the tragedy is ended, and we come back from life as seen by Shakespeare to life as it is before us, we feel that —

> "The oldest have borne most: we that are young
> Shall never see so much, nor live so long."

I have received no aid on this examination.

MAGGIE WILLIAMS.

SHAKESPEARE EXAMINATION:

OTHELLO.

MISS FANNY E. RAGLAND,
OF HALIFAX COUNTY, VIRGINIA.

HOLLINS INSTITUTE, VA.

1884.

SHAKESPEARE PRIZE EXAMINATION IN OTHELLO.[1]

June, 1884.

TEXTUAL.

1. When was the play of *Othello* published, and how?
2. When was *Othello* probably written? Dowden's opinion of it as falling into what period of Shakespeare's literary development?
3. Source of the play, and how modified by Shakespeare?

Explain the Shakespearian use of the following words and constructions :—

4. I. i. 75.—
   "Do, with like *timorous* accent and dire yell
   As when by night, etc."
5. I. i. 95. "*The worser* welcome."
6. I. i. 126.—
   "Transported with no worse nor better guard
   But with a knave of common hire, a gondolier."
7. I. i. 172.—
   "*Is there not charms*
   By which the property of youth and maidhood
   May be abused?"
8. I. iii. 91.—
   "I will a round unvarnished tale deliver
   Of my whole course of love."

---

[1] References to the *Globe Shakespeare.*

9. I. iii. 96.—
    "Of spirit so still and quiet, that her motion
    Blushed at *herself.*"
10. I. iii. 284.—
    "With such things else of quality and respect
    As doth import you."
11. I. iii. 322. "'Tis in *ourselves* that we are thus or thus."
12. I. iii. 390.—
    "For I mine own gained knowledge should profane,
    If I *would* time expend with such a snipe."
13. II. i. 7. "If it hath *ruffian'd* so upon the sea."
14. II. i. 156. }—
    II. i. 229. }
    "She that in wisdom never was so frail
    To change the cod's head for the salmon's tail."
    "And what delight shall she have *to look* on the devil?"
15. II. iii. 49. "I'll do't: *but it dislikes me.*"
16. II. iii. 188. "How comes it, Michael, *you are thus forgot?*"
17. III. i. 45.—
    "I am sorry
    For *your* displeasure."
18. III. iii. 384. "I think my wife *be* honest and think she *is* not."
19. IV. i. 188. "I would have him nine years *a-killing.*"
20. V. ii. 4.—
    "I'll not shed her blood;
    Nor scar that whiter skin of hers than snow."
21. V. ii. 161. "*Peace, you were best.*"

———◆———

PHILOLOGICAL.

22. I. i. 126.—
    "Transported with no worse nor better guard
    But with a knave of common hire, *a gondolier.*"
    What is the force of Roderigo's remark here?

23. I. iii. 143–5. What about the credibility of these lines?—
"And of the *Cannibals*, that each other eat,
The Anthropophagi, and men whose heads
Do grow beneath their shoulders."

24. I. iii. 162, 163. How to be understood?—
"She wished that heaven had made her such a man."

25. III. iii. 23. "*I'll watch him tame* and talk him out of patience."

26. III. iii. 260–263.—
"If I do prove her *haggard*,
Though that her *jesses* were my dear heart-strings,
I'ld whistle her off and let her down the wind
To prey at fortune."

27. III. iv. 74.—
"It was dyed in *mummy* which the skilful
Conserved of maidens' hearts."

28. IV. i. 40, 41. "Nature would not invest herself in such *shadowing* passion without some instruction."

29. IV. ii. 54, 55.—
"A *fixed figure for the time of scorn*
To *point his slow unmoving* finger at."

30. V. ii. 109–111.—
"It is the very *error* of the moon;
She comes more nearer earth than she was wont,
And makes men mad."

31. V. ii. 190–192.—
"Villany, villany, villany!
I think upon't, I think: I smell't: O villany!—
I thought so then:—"

ÆSTHETIC.

32. Shakespeare's Iago as compared with the original of the character?

33. Character and motives of Iago — is the character a logical and self-consistent one in its developments?

34. Do you agree with Schlegel's view that Othello is of the African type?

35. Your estimate of his character?

36. What is the constraining motive with Othello in killing Desdemona?

37. How do you explain the ascendency which Iago obtains over Othello in III. iii.?

38. Is there anything beyond the natural order of events in the affection between Desdemona and Othello, as is asserted by Brabantio and insinuated by Iago?

39. Character of Desdemona, and rank among Shakespeare's women?

40. How do you reconcile Desdemona's character as described by Brabantio and as shown in the handkerchief scene, with her elopement and her bold stand before the Duke's council?

41. Do we excuse or condemn Desdemona's dying assertion that she killed herself?

42. How does Othello's suicide affect us as a matter of morals, and as to the dramatic necessities of the play?

43. What seems to be the relation between Iago and Emilia?

44. What change does Iago produce in the character of Roderigo which enables him to maintain his control over him up to the very end?

45. Illustrate by the roles of Roderigo and Emilia the importance to his plays of Shakespeare's secondary characters.

46. Show from this and other of Shakespeare's important plays the relation of the introductory scenes to the whole play.

47. The play of *Othello* as a whole; its rank among Shakespeare's plays; its lessons?

1. *Othello* was published first in quarto form in 1622, being the only play published in quarto during the time between the poet's death in 1616 and the publication of the folio edition in 1623. It was again published in quarto in 1630 and in folio in 1632: these editions differ among themselves to a certain extent — the folio having about 168 lines not found in the quarto of 1622, and the quarto containing some lines not found in the folio, while the quarto and folio following are edited from these, — but, on the whole, the play has reached us in a pretty fair condition. "Othello the Moor of Venice" was entered at the Stationers', "under the hand of Sir George Buck and the Wardens" on the 6th of October, 1622, by Thomas Walkley.

2. There is a great diversity of opinion among commentators as to the date of *Othello*, but it was probably written about 1604. Mr. Hudson says that until the last fifty years it was placed among the latest of Shakespeare's plays, but that the forgeries of Collier and Cunningham, maintaining that it was written as early as 1602 and 1604, gained some credit for the time. They were afterwards proved to be without authority. Stokes says that *Othello* was written before 1606, when the Act of Parliament was passed forbidding the taking of God's name in vain upon the stage, since we have "'sblood," etc., occurring in the play.

In Act III. Sc. iv., ll. 46, 47, occurs the following: —

> "The hearts of old gave hands;
> But our new heraldry is hands, not hearts;"

which seems to refer to the new order of Baronets created by James in 1611. This passage, however, may be an interpolation, or Shakespeare may have written it without reference to any such event.

Dowden thinks that *Othello* belongs to that period in which *Lear, Hamlet,* and *Macbeth* were written; that is to say, in the third of the four periods into which he divides the twenty years preceding the poet's death. Dowden designates the four periods as follows: The period of apprenticeship, or "In the Workshop"; "In the World," when he wrote his "joyous comedies" and "historical plays"; "Out of the Depths," in which he wrote great tragedies and "bitter comedies"; "On the Heights," in which he wrote his romantic plays, *The Tempest, Winter's Tale,* etc. The period, "Out of the Depths," extending from 1601-1608, embraces the great tragedies of "crime and passion," while the fourth period contains those serious yet glad plays which finally end in peace and reconciliation; and that *Othello* should be placed among the former rather than among the latter. Dowden also says that the general style of the play, the "versification, the psychological grain, and imaginative turn" all point to a period of Shakespeare's "maturity," but he thinks it ought to come before *The Tempest, Winter's Tale,* etc.

3. Shakespeare drew the source of this play from Cinthio's *Hecatomithi*, an Italian story, which he probably read in the original, as there was no English translation of the story at that time. The story is exceedingly bare and rude: A valiant Moor in the service of the Venetian state marries the daughter of a Venetian senator much against her father's pleasure. The Moor is ordered to Cyprus, and goes, accompanied by his wife. The Moor's Ancient and his wife, of whom Desdemona is very fond, go also. The Ancient falls in love with Desdemona, but his attentions being rejected, his love turns to bitter hatred, and in a most cunning and skilful manner he incites the Moor to suspect her of

being false to him on account of his "lieutenant," a very handsome man. Desdemona has a handkerchief of great beauty which the Moor has given her, and while at the Ancient's house playing with his little girl, he steals the handkerchief and leaves it with the lieutenant, who, thinking to return it, goes to Desdemona's lodging; here he is met by the Moor, with whom he is in disgrace, so he runs away. Finally the Moor and the Ancient kill Desdemona with "a stocking filled with sand"; the Moor is called to trial, tortured, and banished, and finally killed by his wife's relatives. The Ancient returns to Venice, and finally suffers death for his many crimes. So we see that Shakespeare got only a bare outline of the plot, one name, and *very* few hints as to characterization from Cinthio. Some one has said that the "character, poetry, passion, and pathos" are entirely Shakespeare's.

Explain the Shakespearian use of the following words and constructions : —

4. I. i. 75. —

"Do with like *timorous* accent and dire yell
As when, by night and negligence, the fire
Is spied in populous cities."

This illustrates the indifferent use of active and passive adjectives in Shakespeare's time ; especially the adjectives in *ful, ble, ive, ous*, etc., were used now with a passive signification, now with an active signification.

Here, *timorous* — causing timor or fear (act.). With us *timorous* — full of fear, fearing (pas.).

Macbeth I. vii. 21. —

"And pity like a naked new-born babe,
Striding the blast, or heaven's cherubim, horsed

> Upon the *sightless* (pas.) couriers of the air
> Shall blow the horrid deed in every eye,
> That tears shall drown the wind."

Othello III. iv. 140. —

> "Something sure, of state,
> Either from Venice, or some unhatched practice
> Made *demonstrable* (pas.) hire in Cyprus
> Hath puddled his clear spirit."

So we find *mortal*—both active and passive,—*inexpressive, intrenchant, sensible,* etc.

5. I. i. 95. "*The worser welcome.*"

The in this case represents the instrumental case of the Old English relative and demonstrative, — E. E. *thi, thy,*— and is used to denote the measure of excess or difference.

Macbeth III. i. 26. —

> "Go not my horse *the* better,
> I must become a borrower of the night,
> For a dark hour or twain."

Worser illustrates the Shakespearian use of double comparatives. The old inflections were rapidly breaking down and being discarded, but in some cases the inflections were retained but destitute of their former force; hence when the poet wished to form a comparative of *bad* or *good*, for instance, he wrote *worser* and *more better*. We see the same thing in the case of the double superlative, *most unkindest*.

6. I. i. 126. —

> "Transported, with no worse nor better guard
> *But* with a knave of common hire, etc."

But in the sense of *except* is often used after a negative comparative where we use *than*.

Macbeth V. viii. 41.—
"The which no sooner had his powers confirmed,
But like a man he died."

Hamlet I. i. 108.—
"I think it be in other *but* e'en so."

But (E. E. and modern N. E. *bout*) is formed of *bi* + *utan* = by + out, formed like *without*. From this sense of of "out-take" we get *except*, = *than* here. Desdemona had no worse nor better guard, "*out-take*" a "gondolier." From the exceptive sense of *but* we get the adversative sense, because an *exception* to a rule is opposed, adverse to the rule, "contrary to it." From the different shades of meaning between *but* in the sense of *except* (1), and *but* where the negative is omitted (2), we get the various shades of meaning which *but* may convey.

7. I. i. 172.—
"*Is there not charms*
By which the property of youth and maidhood
May be abused?"

An example of the *quasi*-singular verb preceding a plural noun, which we often find in Shakespeare. Abbott says that when the subject is future, as it were, and as yet unsettled, the verb may be regarded as the normal inflection, the result of the northern plural, E. E., in *s*.

Hamlet III. iii. 14.—
"Upon whose weal *depends*[1] and *rests*[1]
The *lives* of many."

Lear III. iv. 65.—
"What; *has*[1] his *daughters* brought him to this pass?"

---

[1] These are the readings given by Abbott in *Shaks. Gram.* W. T. T.

8. I. iii. 90. —
"I will a round unvarnished tale deliver
Of my whole course of love."

The two nouns *course* and *love* connected by *of* were considered as one word, so that often the pronominal adjective is placed before the former of the two nouns, while we would place it before the latter.

Macbeth V. viii. 18. —
"My better part of man."

So in *Hamlet*, "Your sovereignty of reason"; and in *Lear*, "Your brow of youth."

9. I. iii. 96. —
"A maiden never bold:
Of spirit so still and quiet that her *motion*
Blushed at *herself.*"

Herself, = *itself. It* and *its* had not come fully into use in Shakespeare's time, so we find that he often used the other pronouns for *it.*

10. I. iii. 284. —
"With such things else of quality and respect
As doth import you."

Owing to the fact that the relative had no inflection to show its agreement with its antecedent in person and number, we often find the verb in the relative clause (1) in the singular or plural where it should have been the opposite, or (2) an irregularity in the person of the verb.

Here the poet has no inflection to show that the antecedent is plural.

Hamlet II. iii. 26. —
"Your visitation shall receive such *thanks*
As *fits* a king's remembrance."

Othello IV. i. 125.—
"They laugh that *wins.*"

11. I. iii. 322. "'Tis in *ourselves* that we are thus or thus."

This *self* (A.-S. *se, swa,* + *lf* = German *leib*) was first an adjective meaning *same*. It was not always used, but sometimes to denote emphasis and to connect the second pronoun with the subject; as, "He did it himself." The *self* is both emphatic and serves also to connect the *him* with the *he*. In "He hine selfne band," *self* is the adjective declined and agreeing with *hine*. "He did it himself"—*himself* is adverbial, a contraction of a prepositional phrase, "*of himself*," "*by himself*," or something of the kind. In Shakespeare's time the *self* began to be considered as a noun; "Tarquin's self," and the *our, by, him,* etc., as adjectives agreeing with the noun *self*.

12. I. iii. 390.—
"I mine own gain'd knowledge should profane
If I *would* time expend with such a snipe
But for my sport and profit."

This *would* is sometimes considered as used for *should* but in reality it "would be willing." It contains the idea of "willing," "desiring," "wishing."

13. II. i. 7.—
"If it hath *ruffian'd* so upon the sea,
What ribs of oak, when mountains melt on them,
Can hold the mortise?"

Almost any word may be changed to a verb by the suffix *en* (A.-S. infinitive termination *an*), but with Shakespeare this use of *en* was discarded, owing to the general tendency to do away with inflections; but the power of converting other words into verbs remained and was greatly exercised. See *pale* in *Hamlet,* and *trifle* in *Macbeth.* For the form of the participle here, see *fathered, childed* in *Lear,* also *balmed,* and *womaned,* in the present play.

Here *ruffianed* = "played the ruffian."

14. II. i. 156, also 229.—

> "She that in wisdom never was so frail
> To *change* the cod's head for the salmon's tail."

Also,—

> "And what delight shall she have *to look* on the devil?"

These are illustrations of the loose or indefinite infinitive construction. Formerly the simple infinitive ended in *en,* and *to* was used only with the *gerund,* like *ad* and the Latin gerund to denote purpose. But as the *n* and finally the *e* of the simple infinitive were lost, the *to* came to be used in a more indefinite and varied sense, with the simple infinitive. Sometimes in the sense of *by, with, as regards,* etc.

> "What delight shall she have *in* looking on the devil."

Macbeth IV. ii. 70.—

> "To fright you thus, methinks I am too savage."

15. II. iii. 49. "I'll do't; *but it dislikes me.*"

The impersonal construction, which marks an early stage in a language when man has not reached that stage of development in which he feels bold enough to attribute his own words and deeds to himself as agent. There were more impersonal verbs in E. E. than in Shakespeare's time, and more then than now. We would say "I disliked." We find *methinks* and many other impersonal forms in Shakespeare.

16. II. iii. 188. "How comes it, Michael, *you are thus forgot?*"

The division of labor between *is* and *has* had not taken place fully in Shakespeare's time, and *is* and *has* were used indifferently. "*Is* is now almost superseded by *has* except in the passive of transitive verbs." We would say, "How comes it, Michael, that you have thus forgotten yourself?" In this same play we have —

"I am declined into the vale of years."

17. III. i. 45. "I am sorry for *your* displeasure."
Your is here the objective genitive. We could not use *your* in this sense now. With us "your displeasure" = the displeasure which you feel toward some one else; here it = the displeasure which Othello feels toward *you*.

18. III. iii. 84. "I think my wife *be* honest and think she *is* not."

In the first case the *be*, the subjunctive, expresses an agonized doubt. Othello *wishes* to believe Desdemona honest, but cannot. In the second place, the *is*, the indicative, expresses the conviction of Othello's mind that his wife's guilt is a *fact*.

19. IV. i. 188. "I would have him nine years *a-killing*."
A = older *in*, which by rapidity of pronunciation lost the *n*. *A-killing* = in the act of killing. This *ing* here is the result of the three older forms *ung*, of the abstract noun, the *nde* of the participle present, and the *enne* of the gerund.

Othello III. iii. 71. —

"Michael Cassio, that came *a-wooing* with you."

Macbeth III. iv. 34. —

"The feast is sold
That is not often vouch'd, while 'tis *a-making*."

Lear III. iv. 59. —
"Tom's a-cold" = in a chill.

20. V. ii. 4. —
"Yet I'll not shed her blood
Nor scar *that whiter skin of hers than snow.*"

When the adjective was not a mere epithet, but denoted something essential, it was placed after the noun; but when that adjective was itself modified by a phrase, it was feared that the adjective would be drawn too closely to the phrase, and lose something of its importance to the noun, so the adjective was placed before the noun and the modifying phrase after, and the noun not being emphatic did not seriously interfere between the two.

Macbeth V. viii. 7. —
"Thou bloodier villain
Than terms can give thee out."

Of hers, of yours, etc., generally implies a class, or number, either real or imaginary. As Desdemona has but one skin, we would not now say, unless colloquially, "skin of hers."

21. V. ii. 161. "Peace, *you were* best."

Instead of "I had rather," the E. E. said, "(To) me (it) were liefer"; but there gradually arose a confusion of these two expressions, partly because "me were liefer" seemed to be ungrammatical. The proper construction here = "To you it were best." After this construction the *to* before the infinitive was often omitted, perhaps because there was here a confusion of two constructions too, the imperative and infinitive.

"Peace [imp.], it were best for you."
"It were best for you to keep peace."

Explain the following expressions : —

22. I. i. 126. "A gondolier," etc. What is the force of Roderigo's remark here?

A gondolier was the conveyer of persons only, and of great wealth at Venice. They were thus conversant with the intrigues, the secrets and plans of the Venetians, and were constantly subject to the temptation of revealing all they knew. Brabantio might well feel alarmed at the idea of Desdemona's being —

> "Transported with no worse nor better guard,
> But with a knave of common hire — a gondolier."

23. I. iii. 143-145. What about the credibility of these lines in Shakespeare's time?

These reports, and others still more wonderful, were circulated in Shakespeare's time, and were really believed. New lands had been discovered, and society was rife with the reports of these which adventurers had brought back. And Mrs. Jameson says that this picture described here was drawn from the actual life of the day; that there was no surer way of wooing than by appealing to the feminine imagination.

24. I. iii. 162, 163. "She wished that heaven had made her such a man." Explain. It may mean one of two things, — she wished that heaven had made for her a man like Othello, or, that heaven had made *her* (acc.) such a man.

Some commentators think that the former interpretation would be detrimental to Desdemona's modesty, but Hudson says that "Desdemona is too modest to be prudish." *I* think that Desdemona might have meant the former, *i.e.*, "She wished heaven had made such a man for her," and still have been perfectly unconscious of the fact that she was giving Othello the "hint whereon he should speak." We can imagine the innocent, childlike girl wishing that heaven had made her such a man, without even thinking that Othello might be that man. But if she did say it, and *mean* it too, there seems no harm in that. She saw that Othello, feeling his inferiority in rank, would never speak until she gave the "hint."

25. III. iii. 23. "I'll watch him tame and talk him out of patience."

This is a metaphor taken from hawking. A hawk was tamed by keeping him awake, and thus tiring him out.

26. III. iii. 260-263. —

> "If I do prove her haggard,
> Though that her jesses were my dear heart-strings,
> I'ld whistle her off and let her down the wind,
> To prey at fortune."

Another metaphor from hawking. *Haggard* = wild, unreclaimed, wanton. *Jesses* = the cords or straps by which the hawk was attached to the hand. The sportsman let fly the hawk *against* the wind; for if she flew with the wind, she would not return, but go off "To prey at fortune."

So if Othello prove Desdemona wanton, though the links between them be his very heart-strings, he will cast her from that heart and let her "prey at fortune."

27. III. iv. 74. "And it was dyed in mummy which the skilful conserved of maiden's hearts."

The liquor which exuded from mummies was thought to have great medicinal virtue. And it was also much prized by painters as being a transparent brown, which threw a kind of warmth over the shadows of a picture. In *Macbeth* we find an allusion to it.

28. IV. i. 40, 41. "Nature would not invest herself in such *shadowing* passion without instruction."

Shadowing may mean passion coming over Othello like a dense cloud which enshrouds with terrible darkness his whole being, or it may mean full of "shapes and images," referring to all the proofs which have been adduced by Iago, and which are all present to his mind at once.

29. IV. ii. 54, 55. —

> "A fixed figure for the time of scorn
> To point his slow unmoving finger at."

The *fixed figure* is Othello himself. *Time of scorn* = the scornful world. *Slow unmoving finger* is the finger moving slowly *with* but never *from* the "fixed figure."

Some one reads, "A fixed figure *of* the time *for* scorn," etc., which seems to be a good change. But the reading "slow and moving" for "slow unmoving" does not seem a good one to me.

30. V. ii. 109–111. "It is the very *error* of the moon."

This passage refers to the belief in astrology which was so common in Shakespeare's time, and to which he so often alludes. Othello says in the next line that the moon wandering near the earth hath made him mad.

21. V. ii. 190–192. —

> "Villany, villany, villany!
> * * * * *
> I thought so then ... I'll kill myself for grief."

I thought so then, that is, after Othello's cruelty toward Desdemona. Perhaps she was going on to say, "but I never dreamed that it was my husband." Emilia's surprise and reiteration of the words "my husband," when Othello tells her of what has happened, seem to me convincing proofs that she did not even suspect Iago. If she had not been ignorant, would not her love for Desdemona have urged her to reveal Iago's treachery, though he was her husband? She is low and mean, but not criminal to this degree, I think.

ÆSTHETIC.

32. Cinthio's Iago is merely the cunning villain which one may meet with not unfrequently in every-day experience. Shakespeare's Iago is the impersonation of an *almost* superhuman intellect unrestrained by any moral law. The latter is an infinitely higher type of creative genius.

33. Iago is the perfect villain. He neither respects moral beauty as seen in Desdemona, nor the grand nobleness of the mighty-souled Othello. All things pure and noble in their nature are looked upon as far beneath his "learned spirit." As Mr. Hudson says, Iago is "severely introversive," and is only satisfied by dipping what is good into his own vileness and bringing it forth reeking in the filth of his own evil nature. The purest of all sentiments is, in his mind, a mere "lust of the blood and a permission of the will." It is utterly foreign to his nature; indeed, we cannot even conceive of Iago's *loving* anything. As in *Macbeth*, we may, perhaps, regard the "Weird Sisters" as the personification of the evil existing in Macbeth's mind, so Iago may be regarded as the personification of *all* evil, the superlative degree of evil, of which the Witches are merely the positive. To Iago and in an intensified sense, "Fair is foul, and foul is fair." The very quintessence of his nature is the consummate power which he possesses of reversing the order of good and evil so as to make the good appear the evil, as when he

turns Desdemona's generous solicitations in behalf of Cassio into solicitations for her own destruction, as it finally proves to be; and the evil into good as, *i.e.*, in his own mind when, after urging Cassio to entreat readmission through Desdemona, he says:—

"And what's he, then, that says I play the villain?
When this advice is free I give and honest,
Probal to thinking, and, indeed, the course
To win the Moor again."

With the other characters of the play his villainous intellect sports and trifles at will. Roderigo is the instrument with which he works his diabolic plan. In the reunion scene (II. i. 3), where the happiness of husband and wife seems almost too exquisite, we find Iago glorying and exulting in the sad havoc he is soon to make within their Eden; he here appears more cruel than Milton's Satan, who feels some pity and remorse on seeing the happiness which he is about to destroy.

The consummate skill with which he links together in one continuous chain his many plans for evil is a striking mark of Iago's genius.

Another thing to be remembered is, that the poet has not made Iago an old man, hardened by disappointments and contact with this rough world; we would generally suppose this to be the case, but Iago tells us himself that he is only twenty-seven, a young man, and hence his innate, inveterate, instinctive vileness seems more horrible. We can almost forgive a man hardened and changed by the unrelenting hand of Fate, but we feel the deepest repulsion for the naturally and instinctively mean man.

As to Iago's motives, much has been said. He says that the Moor and Cassio have wronged him. So report goes; but we see from his conduct afterwards that he does not really believe this report; besides, this would be no adequate *cause* for the terrible *effect* which he brings about. Coleridge speaks of Iago's alleged motives as "the motive-hunting of a motiveless malignity." So *revenge* is not his motive. I am inclined to agree with Hudson, Dowden, and others on this point, when they say that Iago had no *motives* in the real sense of the word, but that his intellect, spurning all law, motive, influence from without, was unto itself all in all; and that he did evil simply because he had the power and liked to exercise it. Yet there is another thing to be considered in this respect; *i.e.*, Iago says: —

> " Cassio hath a daily beauty in his life,
> That makes me ugly."

Perhaps I should say, then, that *envy* has a strong influence over his mind. The two things envy and conscious power, are then his motives, I think.

Yes, Iago's character is a logical and self-consistent one in its developments. His position, as shown by his own words in the first scene of the play, seems but the first link in the chain which ends with the characteristic words: —

> " Demand me nothing.
> What you know you know:
> From this time forth I never will speak word."

From his words, "I am not what I am," we see his conduct of duplicity with the Moor in III. iii. Starting out with the assertion that he is one who has "some soul," he closes with defiance and sullen silence. Since he feels that lying, cheating, and deceiving will no longer avail, he gives up everything and is silent, but neither remorseful nor repentant. Yet we do not feel at the end that Iago has conquered, but that he has failed, miserably failed. Having no real motives in the beginning for his conduct, Iago cannot change as these motives change, but steadily and closely works out little by little his diabolical plans. Some one has said that the absence of all passion in Iago enables him to assume at any moment the feeling or passion which best suits that particular place and circumstance: thus we see him affecting the greatest friendship for Cassio, in order that he may effect his own ends thereby.

34. No; Othello is not of the African type, I think, either mentally or morally or physically. He is distinctly spoken of all through the play as a "Moor," and the Moors differed widely from the mere negroes in both intellect and color. Roderigo calls Othello " *thick lips,*" but we must remember that he speaks as an unsuccessful rival. Othello is several times spoken of as " black," but then as now " black " was often used of a dark complexion in contradistinction to a fair one. The Venetians had much intercourse with the Moors, but little with the negroes : Iago says that Othello is going to Mauritania. Besides, there is something repulsive to my mind in the idea of the beautiful Venetian girl falling in love with an African prince; and Shakespeare would hardly have made Othello a prince if he had intended him for a negro. So we conclude that Othello was a Moor and not a negro.

Schlegel thinks that Othello's love, jealousy, and killing of Desdemona were the animal passions and violent deeds of an African savage; whereas his love is pure and elevated, his jealousy is that passion to which we are all more or less subject, intensified by the convincing proofs drawn from the circumstances and words which an apparently " honest " and loving friend produces, and the death of Desdemona is rather a sacrifice to his honor than a jealous murder. Schlegel's view is entirely wrong, it seems to me.

In order to comprehend fully Othello's conduct here, we must try to put ourselves in Othello's position. He is too noble and true himself to dream for an instant that what Iago says is an untruth; if he did suspect, he would lose something of his purity, for the mere fact of suspecting would imply that he himself was not entirely free from the guile which he sees in other people. We must imagine that Desdemona is really false, as indeed she is to the mind of Othello who has been brought to see things through the light of Iago's words. To Othello the proofs of Desdemona's guilt are indubitable; there does not cross his mind the least shadow of suspicion as to the falsity of these alleged proofs. After a hard-fought battle with himself he goes calmly and sadly to the fulfilment of the saddest of all sad duties. Could we conceive of the savage, passionate African acting thus?

35. Othello is a type of moral grandeur, of heroic courage, of a brave warrior. He is the "Lion of the desert," powerful in his pride, virtue, innocence, veracity, and free from the guile and deceit by which he is surrounded; yea, so free from it himself that he cannot see it in others. It seems a striking fact to me, that Shakespeare should have put Othello's praise in the mouth of Iago, his bitter enemy; even villainy cannot fail to mark some of Othello's nobleness.

Othello's character is drawn out in all its beauty by being brought into such close contrast with Iago's villainy.

Othello seems to be the embodiment of the highest degree of bravery and heroism, and of all the tenderness and gentleness of the most refined woman. How we pity him when we see him being bound slowly but surely by the arch-fiend Iago. Perhaps Othello is the most heroic of all Shakespeare's heroes, for in him are combined in the highest degree both moral and physical heroism.

36. Honor—not jealousy, surely; for would the *merely* jealous husband give vent to such feelings as Othello does in V, ii.? "It is the cause, it is the cause, my soul," seems to be the cry of a soul moved rather by love, pity, and the feeling of justice, than the cry of an enraged husband. Othello distinctly says that "Justice" bears the "sword" (V. ii. 17). Whatever hold that stormy passion of jealousy may have had over Othello before, we feel convinced that the calm, sorrowful, but determined feeling of justice reigns supreme, and love must yield to honor and justice. Here we see that "calmness of intensity" which is such a striking feature in Othello's character.

37. In III. iii. we see cold, evil intellect brought in contact with innocence and simplicity. The subtlety and cunning, the insight into Othello's mind here seem almost supernatural. Iago urges Othello on by suggesting to his mind what he wishes him to believe.

Here, too, we see Iago's power of making the good seem evil.

We must remember that were we in Othello's place we would probably feel and act as he does. He has never had any reason to suspect the honesty and faithfulness of Iago; he is too innocent to suspect guile; the proofs all seem indisputable. Iago, by his subtle power of intellect, forces Othello's mind to move in the channel which he has prepared. He attacks and destroys him through his virtues, which tends to enhance his villainy; he destroys Othello's happiness, and finally his life, by turning his grandest virtues, his love for

Desdemona, his heroism, his grand innocence and simplicity, into instruments of torture: so he proceeds in the case of Desdemona. Elsewhere he works upon the faults and weaknesses of his victims.

38. No; I think not. It seems perfectly natural that a woman like Desdemona, gentle, pliant, loving, susceptible to impressions from without, feeling almost unconsciously that the wealth of sterner qualities in Othello were entirely wanting in her own composition, should revere these qualities in a man like Othello. This union seems to be a verification of the old proverb, "extremes meet"; yet there is between the two one thing in common, a gentle, loving heart, in the one case concealed beneath a beautiful and winning exterior, in the other, beneath the rough, unprepossessing exterior of the hardened warrior. It is, as it were, "deep calling unto deep."

39. The predominant feature of Desdemona's character, Mrs. Jameson thinks, is her extreme gentleness, amounting almost to passiveness, incapable of resenting and resisting. She possesses, as Dowden says, mind, but in the general harmony of her whole being the intellectual or mental activity does not appear by itself. She has a kind of "soft credulity," a proneness to superstition, a susceptibility to impression, extreme sensibility. Mrs. Jameson thinks that Desdemona is not *weak*, for the negative only is weak; and since Desdemona possesses affection and a deeply religious sentiment, she cannot be weak. Desdemona displays at times a transient energy, as when she by "direct violence and storm of fortune" leaves the parental roof for her valiant Moor. What strikes me most is Desdemona's extreme purity and innocence; she cannot even fully take in the meaning of the foul words of Emilia, nor the gross jests of

Iago. She has also what Mrs. Jameson calls the instinctive "address" of her sex, as seen in her reply to her father and in urging her suit for Cassio's return. Desdemona reminds me much of Elaine. She is the pure lily over whose first day of existence comes the scorching sun of Iago's villainy.

Mr. Taine says that Desdemona is a fair type of Shakespeare's women, that they are all creatures of passion and impulse, unreasonable and unreasoning, having the beauty, the prettiness, and merry chatter of birds. Yet it seems to me that Desdemona's tragic fate has thrown a halo around her which none of the rest of Shakespeare's women possess to such a degree. In Ophelia we do feel that there is a certain weakness, a negativeness, which is wanting here. Hermione calls forth our respect for the sorrow she has borne; Desdemona calls forth *pity*. She has not that coolness in the trying hour that characterizes Lady Macbeth. She possesses a wealth of constancy foreign to Gertrude's nature.

40. This is a strength born of her great love for Othello. Here the gentle, timid girl is transformed into the still gentle but *firm* woman. It would seem that some of Othello's bravery has entered her own breast. Indeed, one of the most striking points in the play seems to me to be the notion of man's influence and man's individual influence over the individuality, the life and mind and soul of those around him.

Some one has suggested that Brabantio had been too strict with Desdemona, and that here we see the natural rebound of her nature from its bondage. But this energy is only transient, and she sinks back into her former cowardice — if that be not too strong a word — when the present pressure is removed, and is driven into the falsehood about the handkerchief.

41. I think we excuse it rather; for if ever untruth were told with pure motives, this is a time. And if ever falsehood were *pious*, it is here, when the dying wife sees the agony of her husband, feels that he loves her perhaps better at this moment, when he feels that the "fair rose" is withering fast, and thinks to shield him, even for a moment though it be, from the external consequences of his deed. "He that loveth much to him much shall be forgiven."

42. As a matter of morals, Othello's suicide strikes us as being *wrong* since "the Everlasting has fixed His canon against self-slaughter": "Thou shalt not kill." And yet, looking at it from another standpoint, Othello's suicide seems but a just retribution for the death of Desdemona. The play would lose much of its interest for us were Othello to live after losing honor, love, and the pure being who had been as the inspiration of his life; and certainly our great admiration for Othello's sense of honor would be diminished. We would feel a kind of indignation, a kind of resentment, as it were, for the death of Desdemona, for there is in us an instinctive feeling or idea of justice and reparation, and Othello's death is the reparation which Fate requires at his hand for the innocent death of Desdemona.

As Othello has lived like a hero, he will not forfeit his claim to that title in his death. His last two acts were perhaps the most heroic of his life. He sacrifices his wife, his love, all that makes life worth living to his sense of honor, and then finding that this very sacrifice has brought not honor but dishonor, as he is now a "murderer," he sacrifices himself to his honor, and dies by his own hand.

There is a gentleness, a respect for the feelings of others, that those who, like Schlegel, make Othello a half-tamed savage, cannot explain. See his gentleness and respect to

Brabantio, even when the old man heaps accusations and insults upon him. See his tenderness for Desdemona, even when he is about to put her to death.

43. There certainly is not that strong and equal tie of love which we would expect to find existing between man and wife. Iago uses Emilia as his tool; she is cared for only in so far as she is of use to him. Iago has neither the desire nor the ability to love anything or anybody.

Emilia seems to love Iago with a kind of passionate devotion. Her sole aim seems to be to do his will, as is seen by her theft of the handkerchief, and her words at the time are:—

> "I'll have the work ta'en out,
> And give't Iago: what he will do with it
> Heaven knows, not I;
> I nothing but to please his fantasy."

This great love, even though its object be unworthy, is a redeeming trait in Emilia's character, which raises her morally far above Iago. Indeed, we can look back on Emilia in her girlhood, free from the tarnish, the smut, with which Iago has begrimed her. Can we not find almost a touch of sadness for this change in her words: "The ills we do, their ills (husbands') instruct us so"?

Emilia's love for Desdemona is perhaps the purest of her feelings. The bond, then, between Iago and Emilia is the bond of evil, in the one case instinctive, in the other acquired.

44. "Evil communications corrupt good *morals*." By constantly being brought in contact with Iago, Roderigo cannot but be blackened by the soot which cleaves to him. At first we find Roderigo not evil, perhaps, though destitute of virtue; his intention then has nothing criminal in it;

here is merely the disappointment of a rejected lover together with the desire, called into life by Iago, of finding and separating Desdemona and the Moor before they are married. But urged still further by Iago, he becomes so much indued with Iagoism that he follows Desdemona to Cyprus. Even here his conscience hurts him; he repents, and wants to return, but Iago's power grows too strong, and he becomes more and more like "his cause," if we may call Iago such. Finally, this evil reaches a height that is almost worthy of Iago. Iago maintains his ascendency by assimilating Roderigo more and more to himself, by filling his mind and soul with evil.

45. The rôles of Roderigo and Emilia illustrate well the importance of the secondary characters in Shakespeare's plays. They are not superfluities, but necessities, as without the rough iron chisel the sculptor could not mould the delicate and beautiful statue. Much of Iago's villainy is exercised upon Roderigo. Emilia serves as a strong contrast to Desdemona, and serves to draw out her innate purity by contrast with her own low, base character. So Roderigo's dulness makes Iago's intellectual capacity seem more powerful.

They each have a lesson to teach, too. Roderigo's example teaches the insignificance of money when compared with intellect; Emilia's, the punishment following the infringement of truth and honesty.

46. The first scenes are of the greatest importance as furnishing a key by which we read and understand the whole play and its characters; for instance, a mere superficial view of the first scene of *Othello* gives us the idea that Iago's motive for his abominable work is *revenge;* a closer view dispels the illusion. It gives us the first hint of

Othello's character. In Hamlet, Act I. i. 111-126, we see, as it were, the great tragedy to follow looming up in the distance.

Romeo and Juliet, as well as *Othello*, opens with an upheaval of society, a fit prelude to the after tragic scenes.

In *Macbeth*, the very headings of the first scene : "*A desert place. Thunder and lightning. Enter three witches*" — are symbolical of the whole tragedy.

47. As in *Lear* the play turns upon the breaking of the tie which binds father and children, in *Macbeth*, the tie which binds subject and sovereign, so in *Othello* we have the breaking of the tie between husband and wife, — of the most sacred of all sacred ties. There is also the breaking of the tie between father and daughter.

Hudson, I believe, says that *Othello* is the "*best organized*" of all Shakespeare's plays; that as a dramatic structure it is splendid. Johnson says that, had the play been opened in Cyprus and the events of the first act been narrated occasionally, "little had been wanting to a drama of the most exact and perfect regularity." " But this would have destroyed the regularity of the substance." (Rolfe or Hudson said this.)

Macaulay thinks that *Othello* is "perhaps the greatest work in the world "; Wordsworth, that it is one of the most pathetic. Mr. Hudson says it has not " the impressions and elements of moral terror " found in *Macbeth*, the variety and breadth of characterization of *Lear*, the compass and reach of thought of *Hamlet*, but it has this interest, that its scene is laid in domestic life, and it therefore appeals to the sympathies of all.

Its lessons seem to be summed up in the few and simple words : " Thou shalt not *lie* " ; " To thine own self be true."

Every character in the play who suffers in that final scene of agony is but paying the penalty due to injured moral laws. Look at Iago — at Othello's story of the charmed handkerchief — Desdemona's untruth about the same — Emilia's countless evils. Intellect untempered by moral obligations, sentiment unaccompanied by sense of moral law — indeed, nowhere can there be perfectness and harmony without moral ideas.

I have received no assistance in this examination.

FANNY E. RAGLAND.

SHAKESPEARE EXAMINATION:

THE MERCHANT OF VENICE.

MISS BESSIE PORTER MILLER,
Of Montgomery County, Maryland.

HOLLINS INSTITUTE, VA.

1886.

SHAKESPEARE PRIZE EXAMINATION ON THE MERCHANT OF VENICE.[1]

JUNE, 1886.

1. When was *Merchant of Venice* written, and when printed?
2. Is the present form the original, or probably a revised one?
3. How are the upward and downward limits of the date of the play fixed?
4. State briefly the method of determining the chronological order of Shakespeare's plays. Its value?
5. And where, according to this scheme, does the *Merchant of Venice* come?
6. With what earlier play is it compared in some particulars, on which play it is an advance?
7. Where did Shakespeare probably find the plot of the *Merchant of Venice?*
8. What are those main sources of the plot most resembling the story of *Merchant of Venice?*
9. What additional hints for his plot do the *Clarendon Press* editors think Shakespeare may have gotten elsewhere?
10. Wherein is Shakespeare's originality in the play? Can you illustrate from any other great author whom you have read?

Explain fully the *grammatical* usages in the following passages : —

11. I. i. 35. —
". . . *but even now* worth this, .
And now worth nothing." — III. ii. 169-171.

---

[1] References to the *Globe Shakespeare.*

12. I. i. 93. "As *who* should say, 'I am Sir Oracle.'" I. ii. 45. (*Macb.* 14.)[1]

13. I. i. 126. "Nor do I now make moan *to be abridged.*" I. i. 154. IV. i. 431. (*Macb.* 29; *K. L.* 19; *Oth.* 14.)

14. I. i. 148. "To shoot another arrow that *self* way." (*Oth.* 11.)

15. I. ii. 100. "You *should* refuse to perform your father's will if you *should* refuse to accept him." (*Oth.* 12.)

16. I. iii. 4. "For *the which* Antonio shall be bound."

17. I. iii. 7. "*May* you stead me?"

18. I. iii. 146. —
"Seal me there
Your single bond." (*Oth.* 17.)

19. I. iii. 163. "Whose own hard *dealings teaches* them suspect." (*Macb.* 22; *Oth.* 7.)

20. II. ii. 124. "Put the liveries *to making.*" (*Macb.* 13; *K. L.* 18.)

21. II. iv. 13. —
"Whiter than the paper it *writ* on
Is the fair hand that *writ.*"

22. II. v. 52. "Perhaps I *will* return immediately."

23. II. viii. 33. "*You were best to tell* Antonio." (*Oth.* 21.)

24. III. ii. 224. "If *that* the youth of my new interest." III. iii. 30. (*K. L.* 15.)

25. III. ii. 230. "My purpose was not *to have seen* you here." V. i. 204. (*K. L.* 23.)

26. III. ii. 247. "Contents in yon same paper *that steals.*" (*Oth.* 19.)

27. IV. i. 283. —
". . . a wife
Which is as dear to me as life itself."

28. V. i. 200. "Or half *her* worthiness *that* gave the ring."

29. V. i. 201. "Or your own honor *to contain* the ring." (*Macb.* 29; *K. L.* 19.)

(*a*) Give other illustrations if you can, and show by the meaning of

---

[1] These cross-references to the other examinations have been added to encourage and facilitate comparison. *Macb.* 14. refers to the number of the question in the *Macbeth* examination.

contain the position of Latin derivatives in Elizabethan English as compared with Modern English.

(*b*) Causes of the great influx of Latin words during that period.

(*c*) Light thrown by the discussion upon Shakespeare's learning as a Latin scholar.

(*d*) Any other instance of a great author's use of words said to be *un*-English at a transition period of the language.

Explain in the following passages the Shakespearian meanings or usages unfamiliar or changed in Modern English; also any other matters : —

30. I. i. 11. "Or as it were the *pageants* of the sea."
31. I. i. 78–82. —
 "Let me play the *fool:*
 With mirth and laughter let old wrinkles come,
 And let my *liver* rather heat with wine
 Than my *heart cool* with *mortifying* groans."
 — III. ii. 86.

32. ⎰ I. ii. 142–143. —"the *condition* of a saint and the *complexion* of a devil."
 ⎱ III. i. 32. —"it is the *complexion* of them all to leave the dam."

33. I. iii. 42. "How like a *fawning publican* he looks."
34. I. iii. 113. "And spit upon my Jewish *gaberdine*."
35. II. ii. 110. "I have *set up my rest* to run away."
36. II. ii. 167. "Well, if any man in Italy have a *fairer table*."
37. II. v. 43. "Will be worth a *Jewess' eye*."
38. III. i. 93. "Would she were *hearsed* at my foot."
39. III. i. 126. "It was my *turquoise;* I had it of Leah when I was a bachelor."
40. III. ii. 63. "Tell me where is *fancy* bred." Probable meaning of the song.
41. III. ii. 242. "That *royal merchant*, good Antonio."
42. IV. i. 50–51. "*Affection*, mistress of *passion*, sways it to the mood."
43. IV. i. 180. "You stand within his *danger*, do you not?"

44. IV. i. 254. "'Nearest his heart': those are the very words." I. iii. 152.
45. IV. i. 324–331. Explain this speech of Portia.
46. IV. i. 380–390. Explain this speech of Antonio.
47. V. i. 59. "Is thick inlaid with *patines* of bright gold," — or *patterns?*
48. V. i. 61. "But in his *motion* like an angel sings."
49. V. i. 109. "The *moon sleeps* with *Endymion*." Whence so many classical allusions in Shakespeare as compared with modern writers?
50. V. i. 199. "If you *had known* the *virtue* of the ring."

ÆSTHETIC.

51. As its name suggests, what is the material, so to speak, of *The Merchant of Venice* as compared with some others of Shakespeare's plays?
52. Antonio's character and his part in the play?
53. Development of character in Bassanio?
54. Launcelot in himself and in his relation to others? The Launcelot element in *Hamlet*, in *Macbeth*, in *King Lear?*
55. Shylock in the early scenes of the play?
56. Is Shylock's love for his religion and his "sacred nation" a genuine one as compared with Antonio's philanthropy? See his talk with Tubal and Tubal's apparent feeling for him. Compare him briefly with Nathan the Wise.
57. Does Shylock already look forward to compassing Antonio's death when he proposes the pound of flesh forfeiture? Your reasons.
58. Compare Shylock and Macbeth as to the progression of their natures.
59. What is it in the characters themselves that enables Shakespeare to satisfy our ideas of retributive justice while permitting Othello and Lear and Hamlet to perish and yet letting Shylock and Iago live?
60. Jessica's character and conduct, particularly with reference to Shylock's influence and training; — in contrast with Portia's home-influence?

61. Compare the character-progression in Portia with Lady Macbeth; with Goneril; with Imogen.

62. Is Portia's intellect masculine in its grasp? How is it that she beats Shylock in their contest?

63. Is the fifth act necessary dramatically or not, and its relation to the rest of the play?

64. The fifth act as showing the working out of the principles of good and evil? Why does Antonio appear in it and Shylock not?

65. Compare the fifth act with the fifth acts of *Cymbeline, Lear,* and *Hamlet,* so as to show how good could triumph positively in *The Merchant of Venice* and *Cymbeline,* and only negatively in *King Lear* and *Hamlet.* Compare with final result in Tennyson's *Enid.*

66. How does Shakespeare set about delineating his chief characters as compared with other authors? Importance of his secondary personages in this particular?

67. What do you think of Shakespeare as an artist? Illustrate by his groupings of characters in *Merchant of Venice;* in *King Lear.*

68. By single scenes and by contrast of scenes in *Merchant of Venice;* in *Macbeth.*

69. And by contrast of plots and of incidents in *Merchant of Venice,* in *King Lear.*

70. What seems to you Shakespeare's value as a moralist, — and do you regard him as having moral teaching distinctly in view in his works?

71. What is the ethical import, the life lesson of *The Merchant of Venice?*

72. Shakespeare's last plays as showing his general and personal view of life. His last years compared with Bacon's and Milton's.

73. What do you think of Shakespeare the man, and his own character-progression as shown in his works? Compare Mrs. Cowden-Clarke, Taine, and others.

---

1. *The Merchant of Venice* was written some time before 1598, probably about 1596. It was first printed in 1600. Two quarto editions were then issued, one by Roberts, the other by Heyes. It was not printed again until the publication of the first folio, in 1623.

2. There are some reasons for thinking that the play, as we now have it, was a revised copy of one Shakespeare had written some years previously. Some features of the style, such as the numerous classical allusions, the frequent rhymes, and the occasional doggerel, would seem to connect it with the period of his earlier plays; while, on the other hand, the great advancement in the delineation of character would seem to indicate as clearly that it was written at a later date, when Shakespeare had acquired a more thorough control over his material. The theory of a revision of an earlier play seems to account for these discrepancies in style, as well as for several trifling disagreements which appear in the play; — for instance, the announcement of the departure of only four of Portia's suitors, when six of them had already been mentioned.

3. As to the upward limit of the play, it is hard to come to any definite decision. Under the date of 1594, Philip Henslowe makes mention in his Diary of "The Venesyon Comodey"; but as dramatists of the day were fond of laying their scenes in Italy, it is doubtful if the comedy alluded to is *The Merchant of Venice*. In 1598 *The Merchant of Venice* was entered at the Stationers' Hall by J. Roberts; and mention was made of it and eleven more of Shakespeare's plays in the same year by Francis Meres, in his *Wit's Treasury*. These facts serve to establish 1598 as the downward limit, at least of the first copy of the play; and the publication of the play in 1600, in its present form, fixes that date as the downward limit of the supposed revision.

4. The evidence as to the date of Shakespeare's plays is of three kinds. 1st, Evidence wholly external; such as the date of the registration or publication of a particular play, a mention of the plays by other and contemporary authors,

the quotation by other authors of a passage known to occur in Shakespeare (though doubt may exist as to whether the borrowing did not occur in the reverse order), and the date of the license of a dramatic company known to have performed certain plays. 2d, Evidence partly external, partly internal; such as mention made in the plays of some historical event of recent occurrence, and the quotation by Shakespeare of a passage occurring in the works of some other author. 3d, Evidence wholly internal, upon which more or less dependence can be placed. Under this head may be mentioned Shakespeare's growth in taste and judgment; his advance in style and diction; his increasing freedom in the grouping of his figures; the wonderful advance in characterization, in his entire reflective power, in the employment of his vast imagination, in his sympathy with human passion, in the application of his humor, in his deepening pathos, and finally, in moral reach, charity, true justice, and self-control. Besides evidence of this description, we have the so-called Verse-Tests, of which the first is his employment of rhyme. It may be laid down as a general rule that his early plays are to be distinguished from his later ones by the occurrence of frequent rhymes, though of course the extent to which they were used varied somewhat with the nature of the materials upon which he worked. Then as a rule, in his earlier plays the punctuation falls at the end of the line; while in the later ones, "run-on" verse predominates. In the later plays, too, weak endings (*i.e.*, where the line closes with some unemphatic word, such as *and*, *he*, *her*, etc.) and double or feminine endings abound; whereas they are comparatively seldom found in his earlier works. All these methods are more or less valuable in helping to determine the relative chronological order of Shakespeare's plays, though in comparatively few instances can we fix upon the precise date.

5. Taking all the evidence into consideration, the date of *The Merchant of Venice* may, as before stated, be placed at about 1596, falling, according to Dowden, in Shakespeare's second period, " In the World." It would come later than *The Comedy of Errors, The Two Gentlemen of Verona, Love's Labour's Lost, Romeo and Juliet,* but before *Measure for Measure, Much Ado about Nothing,* and others of the third group of comedies. In Dowden's classification of the plays, *The Merchant of Venice* constitutes a group to itself,— that of Middle Comedy.

6. In several particulars there is a resemblance between *The Merchant of Venice* and the *Two Gentlemen of Verona.* Launcelot, in the former, resembles Launce, in the latter, even in name; though his joking and buffoonery is decidedly less boisterous and unrefined. The conversation between Julia and Lucetta in the *Two Gentlemen of Verona* is also very much like the first conversation between Portia and Nerissa in *The Merchant of Venice.* In each case, mistress and maid are discussing the merits of the various suitors for the hand of the lady; though in the first instance it is the maid, in the second, the mistress, who assumes the office of critic. The friendship of Valentine and Proteus reminds us forcibly of that existing between Antonio and Bassanio, though at the same time presenting a striking contrast to it.

7. It seems probable that in this, as in many other instances, Shakespeare found his plot in some older play. Under the date of 1579 we have mentioned by Gosson, in his *School of Abuse,* a play called *The Jew,* which represented "the greediness of worldly chusers and bloudy

mindes of usurers." This coincides so well with the significance of the two chief stories woven together in the plot of *The Merchant of Venice* as to leave little doubt that Shakespeare made use of the older play in the construction of his comedy.

8. The incidents both of the caskets and of the pound of flesh are found in various guises before Shakespeare put them into their present garb. The most direct source of the story of the caskets seem to have been a collection of tales known as the *Gesta Romanorum*. The story is briefly this: Ancelmus, Emperor of Rome, has at length a son born to him. The sovereign of Naples proposes that an end shall be put to hostilities by the marriage of his daughter with the Roman heir. To this Ancelmus agrees; and in due time the maiden embarks for Rome. But a terrible storm arises, the ship and all on board are swallowed by a whale, and the princess alone survives. She contrives to wound the whale, which retires to the shore to die; and she makes her escape. Arrived at last in Rome, she is forced by the emperor to prove her worth by choosing among three caskets. The caskets are of gold, silver, and lead, and bear the following inscriptions : " Thei that chese me shulle fynde in me that thei seruyde." — " Thei that chesithe me shulle fynde in me that nature and Kynde desirithe." — " Thei that chese me shulle fynde in me that God disposid." The resemblance between this story and that presented in *The Merchant of Venice* is apparent, especially in the inscriptions for the caskets.

The form of the story of the pound of flesh, from which that in the play seems to have been immediately drawn, is found in a collection of Italian tales, called *Il Pecorone*, written by Ser Giovanni, a notary of Florence, about 1378.

In the tale, as there related, it is the lady concerned who plays the part of judge; the lady's estate is known as Belmont; and it is in this version alone that the incident of the rings, upon which Shakespeare founds his fifth act, appears.

9. The *Clarendon Press* editors think Shakespeare may have gotten the idea of Shylock's speech in court from the 95th "Oration" of Alexander Silvayn, which was translated from the French in 1596, and which purported to be the speech of a Jew who demanded a pound of flesh from a merchant in recompense for a debt unpaid. The idea of Shylock's whetting his knife may also have been gotten by Shakespeare from a ballad called *Gernutus the Jew*, in which the Jew is represented as standing "with whetted blade in hand."

10. In this, as in all other plays in which Shakespeare has borrowed, he got only the bare outlines of the plot from his predecessors. The characterization was his alone; and it is in this direction that his originality appears. The delineation of character, and not merely the successful exposition of a plot, is his great object. Instead of making the plot his chief care, and sacrificing the characters to its requirements, he only uses the plot as a background, to bring into stronger and clearer relief their distinguishing traits. In the same way Sir Walter Scott drew the plots for his great historical novels from facts as recorded by prosaic historians, but the characters as he presents them to us are creations of his own originality nevertheless. The same may perhaps be said of Bulwer's *Last Days of Pompeii*, and of Tennyson's *Idylls of the King*.

GRAMMATICAL.

11. I. i. 35.—
"... *but even now* worth this,
And now worth nothing."

But even now used here to mean *only a moment ago*. *Even* is used by us in such a connection as this to show that an action has been going on for some time, including the present. It is used by Shakespeare in the same way, but also to signify the actions as occurring just now; hence, scarcely longer ago than the present: hence, the moment previous to the present; in which sense it is here used. In III. ii. 169, we have *but now*, used in this latter sense; while two lines lower, *even now, but now* is used as indicating the present moment.

12. I. i. 93. "As *who* should say, 'I am Sir Oracle.'"

Who is here used indefinitely, in the sense of *any one*. Even in Anglo-Saxon the corresponding form *hwa* was used in a similar manner. I suppose its use in this sense arose from the fact that an interrogative was by nature indefinite. So in I. ii. 45, "as *who* should say, 'If you will not have me, choose.'"

13. I. i. 126. "Nor do I make moan *to be abridged.*"

An instance of the surviving influence of the old gerundial infinitive, which was formed in Anglo-Saxon by adding *enne* to the verbal stem, and which was governed by *to*. Like the Latin gerund with *ad*, it was at first used only to express purpose; but later, as the infinitive came to be almost universally preceded by *to*, and as the application of the old gerundial became more extended, forms arose partaking of the nature of both, and expressing various relations which we now express by means of participial constructions. In this instance, we would probably say, "Nor do I now make moan *at being abridged.*" Similar constructions are: I. i. 154, "*to wind* about my love with circumstance"; and IV. i. 431, "I will not shame myself *to give you this.*"

14. I. i. 148. "To shoot another arrow that *self* way."

Self, meaning, by derivation, *so*, *like*, or *same*, was in Anglo-Saxon an ordinary adjective, and was so used; of which usage the present instance is an example. We seldom use it as an adjective except compounded with *same*. As we ordinarily use it now, it is compounded with some form of the personal pronoun to form a reflexive. In Anglo-Saxon, the simple form of the personal pronoun was generally used as the reflexive, though sometimes it was used in connection with *self*. When this was the case, *self* was inflected like any other adjective. But even thus early, we find an oblique case of the pronoun used when the reflexive is to agree with the subject of the sentence, while the accusative case is regularly used when it is to agree with the object of the sentence. This arose from the fact that in the former case the reflexive might be taken as governed by some proposition; as, "He did it himself" = "he did it *by* himself." For some time the idea seems to have remained that *self* was an adjective agreeing with the pronoun; but gradually the feeling arose that *self* was a noun, and the reflexives were inflected accordingly. So that, in the modern forms, *myself*, *thyself*, *himself*, *my*, *thy*, and *him* represent by derivation inflected cases of the pronouns; and *my* and *thy* are not necessarily genitives, as we are apt to consider them, any more than *him*.

15. I. ii. 100. "You *should* refuse to perform your father's will if you *should* refuse to accept him."

From the derivation of *should*,—meaning *ought, must, it is destined,*—obligation is implied; and though, in the time of Shakespeare, both *will* and *shall* were used as futures, there was more or less of volition implied in the one, and of obligation in the other. Hence arose a courteous disinclination, much more strongly marked now than in Shakespeare's time, to use *shall* or *should* in the second person. In a conditional clause, however, where there can be no suggestion of obligation, *should* is still retained. Consequently the modern English version of the sentence would be, "You *would* refuse to perform your father's will, if you *should* refuse to accept him."

16. I. iii. 4. "For *the which* Antonio shall be bound."

Which, when extended from an interrogative to a relative use, was frequently preceded by *the*. This was partly the result of its adjectival force, partly of the fact that in many instances there were two or more possible antecedents between which there was a desire to distinguish.

17. I. iii. 7. "*May* you stead me?"

In modern English, *can* (original meaning, to *know*, to *know how to*, hence, *to be able*) has appropriated this meaning of *may;* so that *can* is now used to indicate physical, while *may* is restricted to moral possibility. The same distinction exists between the modern German *können* and *mögen*.

18. I. iii. 146.—

"Seal me there
Your single bond."

That is, the bond *of you*, and of you alone;—a survival of the genuine old genitive of the personal pronoun. In most cases of the so-called possessive case of the pronouns, it is rather a descendant of the old possessive adjective than of the genitive case of the pronoun.

19. I. iii. 163. "Whose own hard *dealings teaches* them suspect."

One of the comparatively few instances where Shakespeare uses the old Northern plural of the present indicative in *es*. One of the chief distinctions between the three great English dialects of two centuries previous had been that the Northern had its present plural indicative in *es*, the Middle in *en*, the Southern in *eth*. The Midlanders soon dropped their *en*, and the consequent shortened form is the one used by us, and generally used by Shakespeare, though in his time the other two forms were sometimes used. We have an instance of the same use in III. ii. 17, 18. —

"O these naughty times
Puts bars between the owners and their rights";

though in this case, as in many others, modern editors have struck off the final *s*. In King Lear V. iii. 234.—

"Which very *manners urges*."

20. II. ii. 124. "Put the liveries *to making*."

Probably *to making* is here a corruption of the old gerundial infinitive in *enne*. At the period in the history of the language when terminations were being largely abandoned, there was a great confusion between the final *ung* of Anglo-Saxon feminine abstract nouns, the *nde* of present participles, the *enne* of the gerundial infinitive, and sometimes even of the *en* of the past participle.

21. II. iv. 13. —

"Whiter than the paper it *writ* on
Is the fair hand that *writ*."

In many of the Anglo-Saxon strong verbs there was a difference of vowel in the preterite singular and plural; and after the abandonment of inflections, and during the settlement upon definite forms, the vowel sometimes of the singular, sometimes of the plural, was used. In the case of *write*, Shakespeare uses the form of the preterite plural, while the modern form is derived from the preterite singular. The choice of the preterite singular in this class of verbs was determined by the fact that the past participle retained the final *en*, while the preterite plural dropped it, thus destroying the similarity between the two forms, which caused the choice of the vowel of the preterite plural in the case of another class of verbs, such as *bind, bound, bound*.

22. II. v. 52. " Perhaps I *will* return immediately."

Will was used by Shakespeare to denote futurity, though it almost always implied volition as well. Here the meaning seems to be: my desire is to return immediately, if circumstances will permit.

23. II. viii. 33. "*You were best to tell* Antonio."

We have here a trace of the old impersonal construction. A literal translation of an Anglo-Saxon phrase corresponding to this in meaning would probably be " It were best to you to tell Antonio "; but in the time of Shakespeare, though the form of the construction was retained to some extent, and also the power, both were in process of decay. *You* is in all probability in the dative by derivation; though Shakespeare almost certainly considered it as a nominative. Other instances of the old construction are " (to) me (it) were liever "; and " it likes me not."

24. { III. ii. 224. "If *that* the youth of my new interest."
III. iii. 30. "Since *that* the trade and profit of the city."

That was frequently added to *when, where*, and other interrogatives to give them a relative force; and hence was by analogy added to various other particles, such as *if, since*, etc. By derivation it is sometimes more distinctively demonstrative, sometimes relative in nature. In such a phrase as the A.-S. *for thaem the, because*, since the demonstrative *thaem* is more emphatic, it is the demonstrative *thaem* and not the relative *the* which survives in the Shakespearian *for that*. On the contrary, in the A.-S. *siththan the, since*, it is the relative *the* and not the demonstrative *than* which has survived in the Shakespearian *since that;* since it is the relative alone which remains separate and distinct. So as a general rule we may say that *that*, when found added to prepositional conjunctions, is by derivation demonstrative; while *that*, added to conjunctions not prepositional, is by derivation relative. *That*, in such cases as those above quoted, is often inserted, but is as often omitted. King Lear V. iii. 142.—

> "But, *since* thy outside looks so fair and warlike,
> And *that* thy tongue some say of breeding breathes."

Othello III. iii. 263.—
> "Haply *for (that)* I am black."

25. III. ii. 230. "My purpose was not *to have seen* you here."

In modern English a construction similar to this would be considered a grave offence; but in Shakespeare's time it was customary after verbs of *wishing, intending*, etc., implying a wish or desire which was, notwithstanding, unfulfilled, to use the complete infinitive. Here the intention is expressed in the noun *purpose*. A similar use of the complete infinitive is to be found in V. i. 204.—

> "If you had pleased *to have defended* it."

26. III. ii. 247.—
> "There are some shrewd contents in yon same paper
> *That steals* the colour from Bassanio's cheek."

Frequently it is found to be the case in Shakespeare that even when the antecedent is plural, or when it is in the first or second person, the verb agreeing with the relative is put in the third person singular. This arises from the fact that a relative, from its very nature, does not in itself denote the person or number of the thing or things to which it relates; hence the normal inflection of its verb would be the third person singular.

27. IV. i. 283. "A wife *which* is as dear to me as life itself."

The relative *which* retains somewhat of its old demonstrative adjective force, and means "a wife *of such a kind that she* is as dear to me as life itself." *What* is used in a similar manner in King Lear V. iii. 125.—

> "*What's* he that speaks for Edmund Earl of Gloucester?"

Hamlet I. i. 46.—
> "*What* art thou that usurp'st this time of night?"

28. V. i. 200. "Or half *her* worthiness *that* gave the ring."

There was still sufficient idea that *her* and similar forms were really the genitives of personal pronouns, and hence a sufficient idea of the *personality* expressed in them to allow them to be used as the antecedents of relatives. So in King Lear V. iii. 2, 3.—

> "Until *their* greater pleasures first be known
> *That* are to censure them."

29. V. i. 201. "Or your own honor *to contain* the ring."

(*a*) In Hamlet I. i. 154, "the *extravagant* and erring spirit," we have *extravagant* used in its literal Latin signification of "wandering beyond bounds." So Shakespeare uses *exorbitant* as meaning *beyond limits* of any kind, whereas in modern English it is only used in connection with business demands which are beyond the limits of reason. So, in this play, *continent* is used in exact conformity with its Latin derivation; whereas in modern English its meaning is restricted to immense bodies of land kept in, or held in, as it were, by the seas. These illustrations and many others that might be given, go to prove that, as was perfectly natural, the Latin words which were being introduced in such numbers in the time of Shakespeare were used in their exact Latin sense. In fact, some time would have to elapse before their secondary or derived meanings, such as we have in modern English, could be developed. (*b*) The age of Shakespeare was one of intense activity in every respect. National affairs were in a more prosperous condition than they had been for years, business flourished in every department, and mental growth kept pace. To express the multitude of new thoughts that surged in the brains of men, the need of further powers of expression was felt; and new words, phrases, and constructions, chiefly from Romance sources, were appropriated wholesale. (*c*) Taking these facts into consideration, it would seem entirely superfluous to suppose Shakespeare to have been a great Latin scholar, as some would assume. He used the Latin words brought into the language in their directly derived meanings, simply because they were the only meanings known to him. The uses to which we put the same words are the results of a long process of development, which was only just begun in the time of Shakespeare. (*d*) In a somewhat similar way, Chaucer is often accused of introducing an unnecessary number of French derivatives into his English; but he only made use of the words current in the spoken language of his time. French was, for many years after the Conquest, the language of culture in England; and in the struggle which ensued between the two languages, French and English, though the works of Chaucer finally gave the latter supremacy, it was not until long after his day that the influence of French ceased to be felt. So, bearing in mind these facts, we would rather conclude that his language was *not* un-English, but was English in its widest national sense.

30. I. i. 11. "Or as it were the *pageants* of the sea."

The word *pageant* was first applied to huge stages or platforms upon which plays or shows were given; then it was transferred in application to the plays performed upon the stages; and finally, it was used to signify any great show or spectacle. Shakespeare probably gained the idea of "pageants of the sea" from the gorgeous pageants which were displayed upon the Thames. *Pageant* is probably derived from the low Latin *pagina*, the final *t* being merely a euphonic addition, like the final *t* of *ancient*.

31. I. i. 78-82. The *fool* was a regularly employed character in the old Moralities, in which the various actors were personifications of as many virtues and vices, with, in the time just preceding Shakespeare, an occasional historical character distinguished by some one trait. It was a prevalent belief in the Elizabethan Age that the liver was the seat of the courage; the heart, of the emotions. A white liver was considered a sign of cowardice; while sighs or groans were thought to drain the blood from the heart.

See III. ii. 86.—

"How many cowards . . . have livers white as milk."

And M. N. D. III. ii. 97. —
"With sighs of love that cost the fresh blood dear."

Also Macbeth V. iii. 15. —
"Thou lily-livered boy."

A similar use of the word *mortify* is made in Macbeth, V. ii. 5, "the mortified man"; both instances serving as illustrations of the greater exactness as to the meanings of Latin derivations in the days of Shakespeare than in our own time.

32. { I. ii. 142-3. "the *condition* of a saint and the *complexion* of a devil."
III. i. 32. "it is the *complexion* of them all to leave the dam."

Condition as here used means character. *Complexion* is used in the first instance in about its present signification, with reference to the skin of Morocco, the "tawny Moor"; while in the second case it has the meaning which Shakespeare usually gives it; that of *nature* or general temperament.

33. I. iii. 42. "How like a *fawning publican* he looks."

It would seem that Shakespeare made a mistake in the use of his adjective, since the publicans, or Roman tax-collectors, were much more likely to maintain an attitude of contempt than of flattery toward the Jews. Still, he may have only remembered that in the Bible publicans and sinners are classed together as objects of contempt to the Pharisees.

34. I. iii. 113. "And spit upon my Jewish *gaberdine*."

A gaberdine, — or gavardina, as it was sometimes called, — was a short coat or cloak of some coarse material.

35. II. ii. 110. "I have *set up my rest* to run away."

An expression for which Shakespeare seems to have had a fondness, and which he borrowed from the then fashionable game of primero. The term was used to denote the determination to depend wholly, hence to stake one's all, upon the cards in hand.

36. II. ii. 167. "Well, if any man in Italy have a *fairer table.*"
Launcelot is referring to the old method of fortune-telling by means of the lines in the palm of the hand. In this connection, the palm might easily be termed a *table* upon which his fate was engraved.

37. II. v. 43. "Will be worth a *Jewess' eye.*"
This seems to have been a proverbial expression from the time when it was customary to extort large sums from the Jews by submitting them to torture.

38. III. i. 93. "Would she were *hearsed* at my foot."
Hearsed, prepared for burial. I do not think the term is applied by us until the body has been consigned to the vehicle which is to transfer it to the place of burial.

39. III. i. 126. "It was my *turquoise,*" etc.
The turquoise is, I believe, the customary *gage d'amour* among the Germans to this day, its color being a token of the constancy of affection. It was supposed to have the property of warning its owner, in some mysterious way, of approaching danger. It was also supposed to become deeper or paler in color, according as its owner was well or ill.

40. III. ii. 63. "Tell me where is *fancy* bred."
The word seems to be here used as we use it in speaking of a passing fancy; to signify a sort of transient liking, caused more by the senses than by the understanding. The song was probably intended as a warning to Bassanio, not to judge solely by external appearances, which were apt to be deceptive.

41. III. ii. 242. "That *royal merchant*, good Antonio."

Royal merchant was a complimentary term applied in England to merchants possessed of exceeding great wealth. Sir Thomas Gresham was called the "royal merchant" because he transacted business for Elizabeth. The merchant and other guilds were of such power and renown in the centuries preceding the Elizabethan Age that we often find nobles, and sometimes the sovereigns themselves, enrolled as members. Edward I. was, I think, a member of the Armorers' Guild; and Edward IV. was styled "the merchant prince" because of the traffic he carried on in his own behalf with other countries.

42. IV. i. 50, 51. "*Affection*, mistress of *passion*, sways it to the mood."

Affection, as distinguished from *passion*, seems here to indicate the emotions aroused by external objects through the senses. Hence, since it was in a certain sense the precursor of passion, it might easily be called the mistress of passion as well.

43. IV. i. 180. "You stand within his *danger*, do you not?"

A phrase similar in form and meaning to our "within his power." *Danger* is derived from the Old Fr. *daunger*, which was, in its turn, from the Latin *domigerium*, the power of inflicting a *damnum*, or fine for trespass.

44. IV. i. 254. "'Nearest his heart': those are the very words."

In the conversation between Shylock, Bassanio, and Antonio preliminary to the drawing up of the bond, the only stipulation as to the position of the pound of flesh is to be found in Shylock's words, I. iii. 151-153. —

fo1
"— an equal pound
Of your fair flesh, to be cut off and taken
In what part of your body pleaseth me;" —

to which Antonio replies, "Content i' faith : I'll seal to such a bond." But when the words, "Nearest his heart," are quoted by Shylock directly from the bond, we must infer that before it was drawn up in its final form, he had specified from just what part of the merchant's body it pleased him to take the flesh.

45. IV. i. 324-331. In Portia's speech is found a decided climax, her indignation leading her to explain in more and more emphatic terms the difficulty in which the Jew has involved himself. First she states merely that he must shed no blood, and must cut an exact pound of flesh; next, that it must be no more nor less than an exact pound of flesh; then, that it must weigh neither more nor less by even so much as the division of the twentieth part of a scruple; and finally, if it weighs too much or too little, even by the estimation of a hair, his life and goods are confiscate.

46. IV. i. 380-390. The Duke has already stated that of the Jew's confiscated wealth one-half belongs to Antonio, the other half to the state, though humbleness on Shylock's part may cause the state's share to be reduced to a fine only. But Antonio has a still further modification of this plan to propose, and still further leniency to show toward the Jew. He accordingly proposes that Shylock shall retain half his property without even the subtraction of a fine; that he, Antonio, shall keep the other half in trust until Shylock's death, and shall then render it up to Lorenzo and Jessica; that Shylock shall become a Christian, and shall sign a deed, giving all of which he may die possessed to his daughter and her husband.

47. V. i. 59. "Is thick inlaid with *patines* of bright gold."

Patines were the plates used in the Eucharist, and were

often very costly and of elaborate design; so it was probably this word that was intended, and not the commonplace *patterns*.

48. V. i. 61. "But in his *motion* like an angel sings."

One of Shakespeare's many allusions to the "heavenly music of the spheres," the grand harmony of the universe, every atom in creation, even the smallest, doing its part toward swelling the chorus of praise to the Creator.

49. V. i. 109. "The *moon sleeps* with *Endymion*."

An allusion to the old story of the love for Endymion felt by Diana, goddess of the moon, who nevertheless retained her title and dignity as the virgin goddess. As was stated before, this was an age of great mental activity; and literary work was carried rapidly forward in every department. The field of the classics was in particular thoroughly explored; and in the old mythological stories was found an abundance of romantic material, which was freely employed. In his earlier writings, Shakespeare over-burdened his plays with classic lore; but he soon learned self-control in this as in other respects.

50. V. i. 199. "If you had known the *virtue* of the ring."

Virtue was constantly used by Shakespeare in the sense of *property* or *quality*. Portia had already declared most emphatically the *virtue* of the ring when she said (III. ii. 174-176): —

> "Which when you part from, lose, or give away,
> Let it presage the ruin of your love
> And be my vantage to exclaim on you."

To which Bassanio had replied (III. ii. 186-188): —

> —— "when this ring
> Parts from this finger, then parts life from hence:
> O, then be bold to say Bassanio's dead."

In the present instance, however, Portia wished to imply that in spite of all his vows, Bassanio had *not* understood the "virtue of the ring"; though this was far from being the expression of her real feelings on the subject.

ÆSTHETIC.

51. In others of his plays, such as *Macbeth*, *Romeo and Juliet*, and *Othello*, Shakespeare uses as his chief material human traits and passions, and the development and transformation of character caused by their growth and action in individuals. Thus in *Macbeth* we have an exposition of the power and evil of undue ambition; in *Romeo and Juliet*, of the nature and power of love; in *Othello*, of jealousy. But in the *Merchant of Venice* there is an additional element in the material upon which he works. Here he treats of human beings with a view not only to their relative attitudes with regard to human emotions, but also with regard to what is a less elevated, but nevertheless an indisputable and necessary connecting force in civilized human society, — worldly possession. Employing this twofold material, then, of passion and property, we would naturally expect, as is the case, to find in this play more lessons applicable to the every-day affairs of life than in almost any other of Shakespeare's plays.

52. As to Antonio's character, we learn as much from what is said about him as from what he says himself. As is natural for one of his rank and wealth, he is surrounded by friends; but, in spite of the opinion of Gervinus, I can see no reason for regarding any one of them as merely a fawning parasite. They never speak of him except in terms of warmest love and esteem, as when Salanio says, "The good Anto-

nio, the honest Antonio, — O that I had a title good enough to keep his name company!" And when the news of the bad fortune of his ventures reaches them, they all express genuine sorrow; but on his account, not their own. Judging by the light given us in the play, he seems to have been a man somewhat advanced in years, with no immediate family, but with a nature craving affection. In this position he has taken to his heart his young kinsman, Bassanio, for whom he cherishes a love as tender as ever father bore for son, or an older for a younger brother. In the opening words of the play he confesses to a sadness for which he will give no reason; and on further inquiry, the only discoverable cause lies in the fact that he will have to resign his position as first in Bassanio's affections, since the latter is about to commence his suit for the hand of some unknown fair one. Yet he shows himself thoroughly unselfish in his devotion, and is even willing to violate all business principles and borrow money at interest, in order to lend Bassanio the money wherewith to purchase his outfit. Antonio shows not a little pride and belief in his own independent strength in the calm indifference with which he treats the dangerous condition inserted in the bond by the Jew; and his imprudence in this particular, combined with his former harsh treatment of Shylock, came near resulting in his utter destruction. Indeed, it is hard to reconcile his harshness toward Shylock with his general disposition and deportment. Still, there are extenuating reasons for his feelings of hostility. In the time in which he was supposed to live, the Jews were looked upon universally with abhorrence and contempt; the taking of interest was regarded as being in direct opposition with all Christian principles; and the individual character of Shylock was such as to arouse aversion in even the most tolerant.

Still, the treatment he received from Antonio was unjustifiable; and Antonio had to suffer for it. But in spite of this grave blemish, the merchant, with his grave kindliness, constancy, and unselfishness, is one who exacts admiration and esteem from all.

Considering the play as an organized whole, Antonio occupies the central position: hence the title of the play. As an individual, or as a dramatic personage, he excites far less interest than either Shylock or Portia; but it is nevertheless he who furnishes the ground for the meeting and contest of these two great forces in the play. It has well been said that Shakespeare has made this character verge on the neutral, else his overpowering hold upon our sympathies would have prevented us from duly appreciating the other influences at work in the play. But though he is thus the centre of the organic structure, his presence in the play is not due solely to a dramatic necessity. Through his instrumentality Shakespeare teaches us one of the gravest of lessons — the beauty, durability, and power of true friendship.

53. Bassanio is an example of a type of young manhood to be found almost every day. Handsome, clever, pleasure-loving, and pleasure-seeking, but still with many noble traits, it is not until some sudden crisis occurs in his life that he discovers his own littleness, or that his friends realize how much there is in him that is truly manly and noble. His first act in the play is to borrow money — not for the first time — from Antonio in order to purchase a suitable outfit in which to woo a lady of great wealth whom he believes to be already prepossessed in his favor. He confesses to a feeling of great admiration for the lady, which is, in one of his temperament, probably his leading motive in seeking her, though he declares to Antonio, to spare the feelings of the cousin who had done

so much for him, that his chief object is to gain money with which to pay his debts. But shortly after his arrival at Belmont, his feelings undergo a sudden and unexpected revulsion. The utter truth and candor of the beautiful Portia, her implicit trust in his equally good faith, and her unreserved surrender of herself and all her fortune into his keeping, strip him of all his customary polite pleasantries, and leave him "bereft of all words"; but by the loss of the ornamental and self-admired flourishes, the manhood within him, already clearly discerned by the keener eyes of Antonio and Portia, is revealed to himself and to others more plainly than ever before. He recognizes at once how utterly despicable had been all mercenary motives, and rallies all his innate nobility to enable him to cope with the matchless creature who would, with a generous simplicity that was almost sublime, entrust him with her all-in-all. With all his nobler energies thus suddenly aroused, the knowledge that Antonio's life is endangered through his fault, and the action incumbent upon him in consequence, are just the forces needed to continue and confirm the beneficial change already produced in his character. His conduct throughout the trial-scene testifies to the development going on within him, and gains the entire approval of the ever-watchful eyes of the youthful judge; so that in the fifth act, when complete harmony is at last restored, we feel that Bassanio, purified and elevated by her influence, though he may not be her equal, is yet worthy of his Portia.

54. Though some may cavil at the presence of Launcelot as being a marring feature, yet he is, in himself, a character worthy of introduction. He is throughout irresistibly ludicrous; and in his constant attempts to grasp at something witty, and in his equally constant failures to do so, he

forms an element that could be ill spared. He serves to present to us much more clearly the character of Jessica, and also to point out some of the finer details in that of Shylock. In *Hamlet*, the ludicrous element appears in the grave-diggers, whose grim humor serves to give a deeper intensity to the interest of the scene. In *Macbeth*, the same element is introduced in the person of the porter, whose drunken jests serve to heighten, and at the same time to relieve the horror of, the preceding scene, and to prepare the mind for the nervous tension of the one to follow. In the Fool, in *King Lear*, there is a mingling of the humorous and the pathetic that touches the heart indescribably, forming from the rudest materials one of the most striking examples of the exceeding delicacy and refinement of the working of Shakespeare's genius.

55. In the first two scenes in which Shylock appears, he is as hard, as cold, and as keen as glittering steel. Throughout the play the effects of his intensely active intellect are to be seen; for every word he utters hits the mark with a suddenness and an unerring precision that is at once startling and terrifying. But in these early scenes, before his passions are roused to activity, he is shown as the shrewd business man ready and willing to sacrifice anything for the sake of his idol, — money. In each one of the sudden moves he makes in I. iii., — in his rapid, but sure calculation of the relative value of mercantile ventures, in his quick perception of his advantage over the Christian who would borrow of him, in his shrewd defence of his use of the interest system, in the wily and plausible way in which he drives the proud merchant into the snare he has set for him, — the acuteness of intellect and promptness of action which came so near making him the victor over Antonio are apparent. So in I.

v., the mean littlenesses into which avarice will betray a man are clearly shown, giving an additional hideousness to a picture already repulsive.

56. I do not think Shylock had a genuine love for anything but his gold. But beyond that, probably the nearest approach to affection of which he was capable was his feeling towards his nation. Even in the intensity of his antagonism to the rest of the world, he found himself inevitably associated with the other members of his tribe; and a position of partisanship being thus forced upon him, his intense pride caused him to assimilate as far as possible an emotion of loyalty naturally foreign to his nature. On the other hand, Antonio's philanthropy grows out of his own generous, kindly nature, the tendencies of his age alone preventing it from extending as far as the Jew himself. Shylock and Nathan the Wise stand at the opposite poles of national character; — Shylock embracing all that is most repulsive, Nathan all that is most noble among Jewish traits and Jewish characteristics. While Shylock's egotistical one-sidedness can only be forced under protest to espouse the cause of his tribe, Nathan's large-heartedness causes him to admit the whole world into his brotherhood.

57. I think not. As Shylock himself stated, Antonio had already hindered him from gaining half a million; and, prompted by business motives, his great object in exempting Antonio from the payment of interest was to place him under an obligation and so get him in his power. The condition of a pound of flesh was, I think, little more than a sudden thought, prompted by his animosity toward the Christian as affording possibly, but not probably, a chance of feeding fat the ancient grudge he bore him. It was quite natural that he should, as Jessica declared, often express his

desire for revenge upon his business enemy without having the least belief that his opportunity for revenge would ever come. As it seems to me, the most cogent necessity for the presence of Jessica in the play is that her flight with a Christian lover may arouse the fiend within her father to the pitch requisite for the prosecution of Antonio.

58. In Macbeth, we have the history of the debasement and ruin of a soul which was at first, as human beings go, a noble one. In the case of Shylock, the debasement had already proceeded to a considerable extent; but the completing steps in that process, and his final ruin, were yet to be accomplished. The suggestion of a great crime comes to Macbeth and is allowed to linger there. It is received, not only with toleration, but with strong encouragement by his wife, the person who has the most influence upon him; and with her aid and active co-operation, the irrevocable deed is committed. But though the deed is outwardly completed, its inward impress is a plague-spot — which increases and spreads until the man's whole soul is black, and his spiritual peace forever destroyed. Crime after crime is perpetrated, one hallowed affection after another is weakened and dissolved, until finally, when he hears that his wife, goaded on by anguish and remorse, is dead, his only expression is one of selfish regret that it had not come hereafter. The depth of his degradation has been reached; and he shortly after gives up the ghost, filled to the last with savage rage and disappointment, and utterly hopeless as to the life to come.

Shylock lacks much of the natural nobility of Macbeth, and many steps in his downward progress have already been taken before the opening of the play; but there is nevertheless a strong similarity in the progression which takes place in the two characters. In an evil moment, the thought comes to him of inserting within the bond between himself and the Christian the condition relative to the pound of flesh. Prepared by his former yielding to evil promptings, he has not even a thought of resistance; and by a few cleverly turned sentences he gains the easy acquiescence of Antonio. The thought of the forfeiture constantly recurs to him, and his nature grows more in harmony with it with every recurrence. His daughter's flight with one of Antonio's friends gives an added impulse to the purpose already shaping itself within him; and he becomes in mind, as he sought to become in deed, a murderer. It is true that the completion of the deed is not allowed to become a reality; but his spiritual ruin is nevertheless final and complete.

59. The activity or inactivity of conscience, the distinguishing glory of Man. Its active working in Othello, Hamlet, and Lear causes them to realize and to repent bitterly the wrong done by them, thus forming in itself the sharpest punishment which could be inflicted. So that, while it is in full accordance with retributive justice that they should perish, yet the mercy which is ever granted to those that truly repent is shown in the fact that death was the thing most desirable to them. Desdemona has met with her death at Othello's own hands; Cordelia has perished in the attempt to aid her father; and Ophelia has been brought to an untimely grave chiefly through Hamlet's treatment of her. Any one of these three men, to find happiness, must find it in the life hereafter; and in view of their deep repentance, it is the very refinement of retributive justice to keep them no longer in this world of suffering and sorrow. With Shylock and Iago the case is widely different. In the pride of individual strength and intellect, they have with malice afore-

thought committed crimes the most heinous against their fellow-men; nor even after their downfall does that same pride permit them to acknowledge or to strive to redress the evil which they have done. So that it becomes the truest justice and the most efficacious punishment to humble and to mock them before the eyes of all mankind, and to leave them to drag out a miserable existence in all the wretchedness and humiliation of conscious impotency.

60. Jessica had in her all the rudiments of a very lovely womanhood; but a deal of cultivation was needed to develop them to anything like perfection. It is highly improbable that Shylock had ever consciously given her any training whatever, save such as might be conveyed to her through numerous injunctions to "fast bind" in order that she might "fast find." Though his evil influence had failed to injure to a really dangerous extent her innate truth and purity, yet it had had such an effect upon her character as to make it perfectly easy and natural to her to deceive and desert her unloving father, who made her home a hell, and to cling in preference to her Christian lover. True to the precepts which had been dinged in her ears through her whole life, she did not make her escape without a fair supply of the needful gold. But though this general principle has been imparted to her by Shylock, she has failed to learn the lesson of the value of money; and she spends his hard-earned ducats with a freedom and recklessness that is positive torture to her grasping father. To me, one of the most pitiful evidences of Jessica's lack of proper home training is the way in which she speaks of her father after her arrival at Belmont. That she should have lost all respect and love for him, and that she should have voluntarily deserted him without apparently feeling the slightest com-

punction, is perhaps no more than natural; but when she listens to, and even joins in, the accusations of wickedness and cruelty made against him, we cannot but deplore the blemish which ignorance of the good and the beautiful has left upon her character. Had she had the refining influences thrown around her which Portia enjoyed in her home life, though she might never have been the force which the latter was, she might have been, as she doubtless afterwards became, as true, beautiful, and loyal as her instincts would direct.

61. In both Imogen and Portia, the one absorbing love of a lifetime, acting in conjunction with the nobler tendencies of their natures, forms an elevating and ennobling force in the higher development of their characters. But Lady Macbeth allowed her love for her husband to act in unison with the promptings of her lower nature; and the result was the destruction of her peace of mind and the loss of all she most valued in the world. In Goneril the progression in character is that of a nature constitutionally selfish and unloving from an attitude of cold indifference to one of most cruel activity, which must of necessity end in final overthrow. Through the action of the passion of love in its nobler aspects, Portia and Imogen advance unfalteringly to womanhood the fullest and truest. Through the action of the same passion in its lower aspects, Lady Macbeth progresses as surely to womanhood the most perverted and pitiful. Through the utter absence of that passion in any recognizable form, Goneril presents a picture of womanhood the most degraded and shameless. Portia's character is developed by defending others,— Imogen's, by defending herself,— from the attacks of evil. Lady Macbeth yields to the power of evil; Goneril connives with it.

62. Let us hope there are few women who do not look forward to such a future for their sex as would enable them to answer the first half of this question with a most decided negative. Of what avail is the struggle which has been going on for the past half-century as to the higher education of woman if, as soon as she gives evidence of the calm judgment, unbiassed opinions, and firm self-control, which it is to be hoped will result from that higher education, she is to be branded as *masculine?* Intellect is not necessarily a distinguishing trait of either sex as compared with the other; and it seems to me that in Portia Shakespeare has given us a glorious example of what woman may and ought to become. She is "strong-minded" in the best and grandest sense of the word. She has a heart loving and noble enough to prove a fitting guide for her splendid intellect; and it needs the two combined to make her the power that she is. It is indisputably true that in the female sex the heart predominates, in the masculine the intellect; but it is not necessarily in the distinctively emotional woman nor yet in the distinctively intellectual man that the highest perfection of either sex appears. The human soul, be it masculine or feminine, to assume its most perfect form needs equal cultivation of its two essential elements, heart and mind; and it is only in the development of the finer details of each that sex should appear. A lesson that girls of the nineteenth century are sadly in need of learning is that the possession and use of intellect makes them not less, but more womanly; and there is no better way of proving it to them than by referring them to Portia.

In the contest between Portia and Shylock, where Portia was the personification of the principle of good, and Shylock of the principle of evil, the opposing forces were evenly matched, and the result would have been doubtful, had not Evil overrated his strength, and gone a little too far in the very start. In the very point where Shylock thought he was exercising his intellect most acutely,— in imposing the condition of the pound of flesh,— he made his one mistake; and when her cousin Bellario had once showed Portia the weak link in the chain by which the Jew held Antonio bound, her equally acute intellect followed up the advantage thus gained by Right with the quickness and precision which were characteristic of her.

63. Dramatic interest reaches its highest pitch in the trial-scene, but the fifth act is nevertheless a dramatic necessity. As has been often observed, to preserve the nature of a comedy, the tragic element had been carried to its utmost extreme in the preceding act; and after the pomp and stir and excitement of the trial-scene, the calm moonlight scene in Portia's garden, the lyric sweetness of the lovers' dialogue, and the final restoration of harmony among the home-comers, are needed to reduce the mind to the state of gentle interest and pleasure which it is the object of the comedy to excite. Then, too, without it the plot is left with numerous unfinished ends. Those of us who have not such a strong predilection for artistic effect as to wish that Shakespeare had stopped short when he completed the masterly picture contained in IV. i., think it only natural and proper that we should witness the reunion of Bassanio and Portia, the meeting between Antonio and Bassanio's wife, and the effect produced upon all parties by the announcement that it was Portia who had acted so successfully the part of judge. It is not without pleasure, too, that we have a parting glimpse of Lorenzo and Jessica, safely harbored in the peaceful domain of Belmont, and of

Gratiano and Nerissa, with their half-comical, wholly serious imitation of their lord and lady. Few things could be more exquisite than is this fifth act, in its way; and without it one of the great charms of *The Merchant of Venice* would, to me, be lost.

64. It is to the fifth act that we naturally look for the harvest, both of good and of evil, to result from the sowing done in the preceding scenes. With regard to Jessica, I suppose it may be said that justice is finally done her, though through rather a doubtful medium, by placing her in a position where the beneficial influences of which she stands so sadly in need will at last be thrown around her. Lorenzo, too, meets with his reward after a fashion, in the fact that the virtue of his deed in removing Jessica from a baneful to a healthful atmosphere at least serves to cancel its unlawfulness. Portia has restored to her her husband, who has, as she herself can testify, passed victoriously through the trials brought upon him by his youthful imprudence, and who, largely through her own endeavors, returns to her, purified and ennobled. Antonio, who, through his harshness in one direction and his unhesitating generosity in all others, has unsuspectingly jeopardized his life, hâs that life restored to him, and receives the news that his property is safe, by the hand of Portia, who, as he had before thought, had deprived him of his place in the affections of his dearest friend, Bassanio. Antonio, as the person most sinned against in consequence of the least sin, deserves a prominent place in the closing act, and a fair share of the blessings held in the right hand of Justice. But Shylock, whose sin was woven into the very fibre of his being, had received his fitting reward, and had voluntarily taken his departure. Justice had already done her work there, and

there was no need for the further introduction of the disturbing element.

65. In the characters espousing the cause of the right in *The Merchant of Venice* and *Cymbeline*, good predominates largely, and in some cases, such as Portia and Imogen, would seem to exist exclusively; so that in these two plays we might expect for good a triumph positive and complete. To Antonio, Bassanio, and Portia in the one, and to Posthumous and Imogen in the other, is granted continued life and prosperity for their fidelity to what is to them the highest truth. In the closing acts of *King Lear* and *Hamlet*, however, through the faults and passions of Lear in the one, and the hesitation and weakness of Hamlet in the other, though good does at last triumph, it seems to us, who are prone to look upon death as defeat, to gain but a negative victory at best. In order to compass its entire object, Cordelia had to be sacrificed, though her death for her father's sake is even more glorious and triumphant than her longer life could have been. And Lear, doomed by his own actions, and losing in her all that could make life endurable, must pass on to the next world, where "whatever is, is right." So with Hamlet: after many struggles and retreats, his mission was at last accomplished; but before the final achievement of the duty laid upon him, he had made so many mistakes and given evil so much the advantage that his own death was an inevitable result. In *Enid*, good gains another grand positive triumph. The patient endurance and unconquerable fidelity of the wife at last vanquish the rough impatience and causeless jealousy of the husband, and from the good deeds which proceed from the afterglow of happy reunion, the people call her " Enid the Good."

66. The distinguishing feature of Shakespeare's delineation of character is the utter absence of all formal and deliberate effort to assist us in gaining an insight into the minds of his creatures. Little by little the whole tissue of their minds is revealed to a carefully observant eye; but it is all done in the natural course of conversation and events, and without the slightest consciousness on the part of the reader of an intentional discussion of character by Shakespeare. With most other authors the case is different. Take George Eliot for an example. Her character-portrayals are marvellously powerful, but her method is the exact opposite of Shakespeare's. After every trifling incident she dissects and analyzes each sensation and emotion of her characters with a carefulness and minuteness of detail due to her very excess of mental grasp; and so far as the characters themselves are concerned, she requires little mental action on the part of her readers save the following out of her own train of thought. Though Shakespeare's transcendent genius enabled him to surpass, in the opinion of most, all other men of all nations in the delineation of character, yet for the average literary talent, and taking into consideration the mental ability of the average reader, George Eliot's method is probably the safer.

It is easy to see, in pursuing his method, of what great value Shakespeare's secondary characters would be to him. By means of casual remarks or involuntary displays of emotion on the part of chance-acquaintances or of more intimate friends, many of the finer touches are added, almost without our being conscious of it, to the images which shape themselves in our minds as we read, but which would have instantly jarred upon us had they come to us from the lips of the chief characters themselves.

67. As a dramatic artist, Shakespeare stands, so far as I know, and in the opinion of many wise, learned, and talented men and women, not only unexcelled, but unequalled. In his middle and later plays, formal grouping and contrast of characters was avoided; but his work became only more effective on this account. It is not what lies on the surface, but what has to be sought out by each one for himself, that stimulates and satisfies the human soul. Take the female characters in *The Merchant of Venice*,— Jessica, full of a delicate sweetness and sensibility,— Nerissa, of homely common sense, yet both lacking in cultivation and refinement, and both serving as a contrast with Portia, with her perfect development of both sense and sensibility. Among the male characters, Antonio, the grave, earnest, discerning friend; Bassanio, the gay, pleasure-loving youth who needs the assistance of all his friends to show him the good that is in him; Shylock, the opponent of all mankind, who twines the arms of his affection around his money alone; Gratiano, the unconventional and loquacious giber, whose sayings yet contain a deal of homely wisdom; and the various friends to Antonio, who show the spirit of true gentlemen,— all these form a group where each in turn serves as a contrast to the rest, where all is diversity, and yet where the refinement of artistic harmony exists. In *King Lear*, the contrast between Cordelia and her sisters, Goneril and Regan, though sharp and decided, is not an abrupt one. Lear, weak and at the same time powerful through excess of passion, is a masterpiece in himself which might well make any artist immortal; yet we have grouped with him Gloucester, sinning and sinned against; Edmund the faithless, and Edgar the faithful; Kent, and the Fool, each embodiments, though in widely different forms, of all that is

constant and loyal; and numerous other minor characters of equally marked significance. Every stroke reveals the hand of the master-artist; and to such an overpowering extent that words fail to express the feelings that rise within us.

68. Of course the first single scene in *The Merchant of Venice* that comes to our minds in illustration of Shakespeare's artistic genius is the trial-scene, with its rapid fluctuations of hope and despair, its sudden bursts of eloquence, its fierce flashes of wit, the sharp conflict of good and evil, and the final grand victory of good. Equally fine in its way is the single scene of the fifth act; and I know of no better illustration of contrast in the play than between these two scenes, the second scene of the fourth act being insufficient to make a noticeable break between them.

In *Macbeth*, the opening scene is one of wonderful power, as are the majority of those in which the Witches appear. The murder-scene, that in which the discovery of the murder takes place, and the sleep-walking scene, are also possessed of a magic influence over the minds of spectators or readers; while the contrast between the porter-scene and those immediately before and after it is striking and salutary. The scene embracing the murder of Lady Macduff and her little son is also worthy of special attention as to its artistic merits.

69. I think Shakespeare is about the only dramatic writer who has succeeded in combining two decided, almost distinct plots into a single play. In *The Merchant of Venice*, the love-story of Jessica and Lorenzo has a little plot of its own, proceeding out of, yet distinct from, that in which Portia is the heroine, and, I suppose I may say in a certain sense, Bassanio is the hero. Yet, though not necessarily at the expense of either plot, our attention remains undivided

throughout; and the light, almost ethereal beauty and grace of the one, and the grave, tender depth and earnestness of the other, give a charm of contrast we would each of us be sorry to lose. It has often been remarked, as it seems to me, with truth, that in the two chief incidents of *The Merchant of Venice* — those of the caskets and of the pound of flesh — the improbability of the one serves as a counterbalance to the improbability of the other. The presence of each seems to justify the presence of the other, without allowing the mind to dwell unduly upon either one.

The same general effect of the double plot is produced in *King Lear* by the stories of Lear and his daughters, and of Gloucester and his sons. The two are woven together with a dexterity that makes them almost inseparable; yet there is no interference of the one with the other, and at the same time no apparent avoidance of it. The similarities and diversities of the two give an added intensity, just as views of the same mountain taken from different standpoints give a heightened idea of its loftiness and grandeur.

70. A more unpretending, and at the same time a sounder or a more efficient moralist than Shakespeare, it would be hard to find. He never "preaches," — never says directly or indirectly what we are to approve of, or what we are to disapprove of; but he so expresses himself as never to leave a doubt in our minds as to what he himself approves or disapproves of, or as to the dividing line of right and wrong; and he distributes his punishments and rewards with an even-handed justice that cannot fail to command our admiration and emulation. I do not think he ever set out with the definite or indefinite intention of writing one of his plays in illustration of some moral maxim, but it was as impossible for him to write without introducing moral

teaching as to live without breathing the air. Morality is the essential element in the truth of human nature; and since Shakespeare possessed a keener insight into the true inward life of the human soul, and a greater ability in representing its phases to the children of men than any other man who ever lived, it necessarily follows that his acknowledgment and appreciation of the power and value of morality must have been proportionately great.

71. As stated in the answer to the preceding question, I do not think we can put our fingers upon any one thing in *The Merchant of Venice* and say, "It was to teach us this that Shakespeare wrote the play." But at the same time, as a result of the unity of thought in the structure, the ethical teaching must assume some more or less definite shape. In *The Merchant of Venice*, owing to the diversity of interests and materials incorporated into it, it is difficult to say what is the *life-lesson* conveyed by it; it would be far easier to say what are the *life-lessons* which it teaches. As well as I can express what is to me the greatest teaching of the play, it is the duty and importance of proper self-development, self-control, and self-devotion, expanding the life of each one of us, in our relations to each other as individuals of a common race and of the great mass of human society, to its utmost limits of roundness and beauty. Some portion of this great truth is brought home to us by each one of the characters; and the fragments as thus presented are all in themselves "pearls of great price." Without attempting to mention the offerings brought by each one, willingly or unwillingly, to the shrine of truth, it may still not be out of place to mention Portia's sublime plea for the mercy which should temper our justice in adjusting the affairs of this life; Bassanio's warning, of the truth of which he himself proved an example:—

"So may the outward shows be least themselves";

and Portia's words, again:—

"How far that little candle throws his beams!
So shines a good deed in a naughty world."
"I never did repent for doing good."

72. The spirit of peaceful repose and quiet enjoyment which breathes from Shakespeare's last plays, such as *The Tempest* and *The Winter's Tale*, is one that might be expected to proceed from a great soul which has passed through the preparatory stages of early hardship and struggle, literary fame, and worldly prosperity, with a succeeding period of bitter disappointment and weariness; which has fought the fight bravely, and has at last reached the pinnacle of calm self-control, from which to view, with philosophic enjoyment, the affairs of life both retrospectively and prophetically. So that we naturally look to these plays to discover to us the general view of life of the matured Shakespeare. The opinion is held by some that in *The Tempest*, Shakespeare consciously drew an allegorical parallel with his own life, Prospero, possessed of magic power over created things of every region, being thought to represent himself and the magic power of his matchless genius. The Epilogue is, I believe, especially regarded as being of a personal import, and is considered as a formal renunciation of the sceptre with which he had so long ruled the hearts of men. The parallel is an interesting one; but, though I do not pretend to have made the matter a subject of much thought, much less of anything like study, I am very much inclined to doubt whether Shakespeare himself attached any such significance to this wonderful fairy-tale, the self-imposed task of his ripest years.

The latter years of Shakespeare's life may be not inaptly compared with those of Bacon and Milton. Bacon, after a long season of brilliant worldly success, met with a sudden but well-deserved downfall; but he recovered, though he did not regain his footing, and enjoyed years of peace and calm in which some of his best work was accomplished. And so Milton, after years of political struggle, and then of deep gloom caused by the loss of his eyesight, acquired a philosophic calm, the result of which was the crowning glory of his life.

73. I think that the very susceptibility of Shakespeare's nature must, in the presence of evil, have made it difficult for him to live up to the ideals which his keen appreciation of the good, the true, and the beautiful created within him. It is not surprising that, considering the influences thrown around him, and his own sensitive temperament, he should sometimes have fallen; but it would have been surprising if, with his intense perception of right and wrong, he should have voluntarily remained in his degraded position. "After all, the truest glory consists, not in never falling, but in rising every time we fall," and this Shakespeare did. His character-progression, as revealed in his works, is indicated briefly and well in the titles given by Dowden to his four periods of workmanship: "In the Workshop," where the pruning and shaping influences are still upon him; "In the World," where successes attend him at every turn, and life, if less beautiful and enchanting than he at first thought, is yet fuller and richer in its significance; "Out of the Depths," when he reaps the bitter harvest of his own shortcomings, and when sin and suffering are revealed with redoubled frequency to his already sorely troubled heart; and at last, "On the Heights," when the final victory over

self is gained, and he can look back upon his past struggles with a quiet smile of pity which has in it not a tinge of regret. The man thus revealed to us is far from being a perfect one, and this very fact makes us feel that his sympathy is the more acceptable and complete. Though Shakespeare bars himself from active participation in his own creations, yet it is impossible to read his works without some perception of the all-pervading influence of his own individuality; and as to the nature of that influence, I think Mrs. Mary Cowden-Clarke is much nearer the truth than Taine. Mrs. Clarke would regard him as a man in whom the nobler qualities of human nature were present in a pre-eminent degree; while in Taine's opinion, his whole inward fibre is such a conglomeration of passions as precludes the possibility of rational self-control, and reduces him to the condition of a slave of impulse, and of rather degraded impulse at that. I can see no reason for regarding Shakespeare as essentially bad because he could create such monsters of wickedness as Shylock, Goneril, and Iago. It is frequently the case that the good can sympathize with and understand the temptations and falls of the weak and wicked; but where was there ever a constitutionally bad person found who could appreciate and comprehend the motives and emotions of the good? Shakespeare was not without outward blemishes, but he was perfectly sound at heart; a confirmed hater of all affectation, and an ardent lover of truth.

I have received no assistance during this examination.

BESSIE PORTER MILLER.

CLASS-ROOM STUDY OF SHAKESPEARE.

CLASS-ROOM STUDY OF SHAKESPEARE.

NO formal discussion will be entered upon here as to whether and why the English Language and Literature should be regarded as incomparably the most important element in the education of American girls. Such it undoubtedly is; and further, it is probably the most valuable thing in their school instruction. Instruction, let it always be remembered, though bringing it about, is not education. Happily the time is come when English is recognized generally as a thing to be taught and studied, though the recognition is far from perfect. Shakespeare, the crowning glory of the English language, has long been studied and read as literature, and now his works are found in the hands of thousands of pupils as text-books. The especial value of his works as text-books for girls will be spoken of incidentally in the following pages.

The manner of using Shakespeare, as the aim of teaching him in the class-room, may vary greatly and through all the intermediary stages, from furnishing pieces to "get by heart" to furnishing illustrations for lectures on versification.

The aim of this paper is to suggest such a method of study as will enable the average girl in our higher schools for girls to get a good idea of Shakespeare's plays. The scope of the paper is therefore practical, and is not intended to be anything else. Its purpose is didactic, but not to develop a theory of didactics. Yet, as certain things too commonly done are plainly wrong for a teacher to do, the writer has thought it best, without assuming to be dogmatic, to warn against those things whosoever will read.

To understand Shakespeare, we must understand his medium of thought, his language, as thoroughly as possible. For this, study is necessary; and one notable advantage of the thorough study of this medium is that the student becomes unconsciously more or less imbued with Shakespeare's turn of thought while observing his turn of phrase. Now, so far as Shakespeare goes, as compared with Scott or Milton or Tennyson, any method of instruction bringing him before the pupil's mind is valuable. But, in so far as the pupil is concerned, the manner and facility of contact with Shakespeare is of great consequence. For, in proportion as he is the deepest, most eloquent, most healthful, most natural of our poets, is misapprehension of his teachings pernicious. And of all our poets, perhaps he is the one to misapprehensions concerning whom people cling most stoutly. Why? Because the mannerisms and comparative singleness of thought and speech of other poets make mistakes more easily avoidable; whereas Shakespeare's complexity of thought and purpose readily suggest errors in judgment; and adequate comprehension of his language can alone prevent such errors. If this be so, there is much reason for choosing for the young the way of contact least liable to wrong going. It is much easier to correct a false estimate of Shakespeare, by showing that it rests on a false basis of word-underpinning, than by dint of any argument how persuasive soever.

For the class-room, then, a non-æsthetic, preliminary study is best. And this may be accomplished in the following way: By studying carefully the Text, — the words themselves and their forms; their philological content, so far as such content is essential to the thought; and the grammatical differences of usage, then and now; by observing accurately the point of view of life (*Weltanschauung*) historically and otherwise, as shown in the text; by taking what may be called the actor's view of the personages of the play; and, finally, by a sober and discriminating æsthetic discussion of the characters, of the principles represented by those characters, and of the play in its parts and as a whole.

I. With regard to the *words themselves* and their *forms:* There is no doubt that Shakespeare's words and word-combinations need constant and careful explanation in order for the pupil to seize the thought accurately or even approximately. Here, as elsewhere, Coleridge's dictum remains true : " In order to get the full sense of a word, we should first present to our minds the visual image that forms its primary meaning." Now, when, — as in the case of *rivals*, *Ham.* I. i. 13; *extravagant*, ibid., 154 (*Ham. Ex.* 36),[1] — the word is shown by Shakespeare in its " primary meaning," the attention of the pupil is all the more powerfully aroused that she has made a mistake about the word, and that the correction of her mistake has involved, not the confession of ignorance so distasteful to all, but the addition of fresh knowledge, or the recalling of half-forgotten associations from the Latin. So, when the meaning of the word as used by Shakespeare is transitional, and, though found in modern English, is not found in the same usage and connection, — as " *approve* our eyes," *Ham.* I. i. 29 ; " the perfume and *suppliance* of a minute," *Ham.* I. iii. 9, — the pupil becomes more interested. She begins, perhaps unconsciously, to take in the notion that Shakespeare's characters, who speak this variable language,

---

[1] These references are to the questions in the Examinations.

are to be judged with a freer, less local, more human judgment than she has been accustomed to use in judging the characters of other writers or the people around her. Such word-study stimulates and feeds at once the mind and makes the pupil curious to go on. And it is an important element in opening the mind of the pupil, this finding that the words will lead her astray. And, if wisely followed up by the teacher, it will quickly so develop as to pass from the close observation of words to the close observation of characters. But not alone the meanings of words, — their *forms*, too, need to be made plain and their equivalents in modern English given; as, "the *mightiest* Julius," *Ham.* I. i. 114; so "*happily* foreknowing," ibid., 134; "the *sensible* and true avouch" (*Ham. Ex.* 17). For with each explanation the pupil's mental horizon grows wider.

II. But this does not exhaust the interest of the words in themselves. They are frequently so full of a particular use and meaning of their own that they have evidently been chosen by Shakespeare on that account, and can only serve fully their purpose of conveying his meaning when themselves comprehended. This opens up to the pupil one of the most interesting aspects of words, — their function of embalming the ideas and habits of a past generation, thus giving little photographic views, as it were, of the course of the national life. Thus, a new element of interest and weird reality is added when we find that "And like a rat *without a tail*" is not stuffed into the witch-speech in *Macbeth* merely for rhyme's sake (*Mac. Ex.* 31). It is doubtful if anything brings so visibly before the mind's eye the age, and therefore the proper point of view, of Shakespeare as the accurate following-out of these implied views of life, these old popular beliefs contained in his picturesque language. They are like illustrations of the thought of which they are themselves a part. And the effect is heightened if the same expression, in the same or even in a different sense, can be traced to the familiar life of to-day. In all this part of the subject, — words, word-forms, *philological content*, — the spoken language of common life as distinguished from the written language of literature is full of Shakespeare's ideas to this day.[1]

Now, valuable as this study is as language-study, and as illustrating as nothing else can Shakespeare's times and their influence upon him, still the most valuable result is the habit engendered in the pupil's mind of following Shakespeare, and the power it cultivates to do so, to perceive the leaps and bounds of his prodigiously active mind. Not knowing and knowing the full meaning of his words is like looking at a cannonade in the day-time and at night. Each shell moves with a train of fire ; you might *know* it in the day, — you *see* it at night. This philological research must not be carried to excess. Within proper limits, like gymnasium exercise, it is invigorating, — beyond, it is exhausting. We must, of course, discriminate. Let the terms used by the witches in *Macbeth* be studied closely, but not so all the witch-terms used by Edgar in *King Lear;* since the precise effect is needed in *Macbeth*, and the general effect is enough in *King Lear*. The pupil will soon acquire the habit of feeling when it is proper for her to think out a metaphor, thereby to determine more exactly the limitations and course of Shakespeare's thought. As, for instance, the image in

"Come, *seeling* night,
Scarf up the tender eye of pitiful day,"

---

[1] Especially is this true, sometimes very amusingly so, of the Negro talk of Virginia, — their speech being largely the spoken tongue of 200 years ago, or more.

in *Macbeth* III. ii. 46, is quite different, with its implied picture of falcon and falconer, to the image of "*scaling night,*" for which a beginner would almost certainly mistake it. The English of Shakespeare deceives pupils just as French deceives the beginners in that language. The words look so much like our words nowadays, and yet are so astonishingly unlike them in meaning. In brief, the word-study should be carried to the extent necessary to give the pupil the definite and clear conception of the poet's meaning, but always be kept subordinate to the conception of that meaning. Words are the means, and this study of them is to make the pupil comprehend that fact thoroughly. Who, on a bright, fresh morning, with the radiant sunlight on the peaks, has failed to feel the gracious beauty of the lines, —

> "Full many a glorious morning have I seen
> Flatter the mountain-tops with sovereign eye,
> Kissing with golden face the meadows green,
> Gilding pale streams with heavenly alchemy " —

(*Sonn.* XXXIII.), and has not felt at the same time the beauty of nature enhanced by the bold personification of the poet's description? Not that it is necessary for a pupil or anybody else to know with a self-conscious, self-complacent knowledge what name the rhetorical people would give this use of the word or combination of words ; but she should so know it as to be able to feel it as fully as she can feel anything. That is the true philological study for Shakespeare pupils. Anything less than that is not enough ; anything more is too much. As to what constitutes the just amount, each teacher must decide for himself; it may vary for each class. And the teacher will usually exercise a wiser continence in illustration and in requirement in proportion as he is himself in possession of Shakespeare knowledge.

To acquire this command of Shakespeare's speech, thought is needful; and for thought, time must be given. Hence, in my opinion, the advantage for the school-class of placing the notes at the end of the volume, — that there must be *some time consumed* in finding the explanation sought. My experience as student and teacher has convinced me in a variety of ways of the bad results of too much help, and never is it more pernicious than when it *anticipates the natural action* of the pupil's mind. While turning over the leaves to find a note, the mind may think of a dozen things, and enjoy perhaps the extreme satisfaction of having hit upon the true explanation by the time the note is reached. Often a lucky guess is so plausible that the student turns back to the text before looking at the note, believes herself in the right, and then goes to the note for corroboration merely. Such a mental habit is what every teacher earnestly desires in his pupils; and foot-notes on the same page certainly do much to hinder its growth. After the true student habit has been acquired, in whatever way, foot-notes are most useful. It is well to use them in reviewing a play already studied in a different edition, when æsthetic considerations are under discussion and the desire is to move rapidly.

But, for a class of boys or girls, I hold that the most effectual and rapid and profitable method of studying Shakespeare is for them to learn one play as thoroughly as their teacher can make them do it. Then they can read other plays with a profit and a pleasure unknown and unknowable without such previous drill and study.

III. Difficulties consisting in the forms of words have been already mentioned; but they constitute in reality only a part, perhaps the least part, of the *grammatical* impediment to our apprehending Shakespeare clearly. There is in him a splendid superiority to what we call grammar which entails upon us more or less of close, critical observation of his word-order, if we would seize the very thought. Thus Lady Macbeth speaks of Macbeth's "flaws and starts" as "impostors *to* true fear" (*Mac. Ex.* 28). Here, if we understand "to" in its ordinary meaning, we lose entirely the fine force of its use by Shakespeare, "*compared to* true fear*,*" and fail to see how subtly Lady Macbeth is trying to persuade Macbeth that there is no cause for fear, that he is not truly "afeard," but merely hysterical and unbalanced; and, failing in that, we fail in part to realize the prodigious nerve and force she was herself displaying, though vainly, for Macbeth's sake. So, too, a few lines farther on, Macbeth's fine saying, "Ere humane statute purged the *gentle* weal," becomes finer when we see that "gentle" means for us "gentled," or "and made it gentle." (*Mac. Ex.* 18; *Ham. Ex.* 29; also *Mac. Ex.* 29.) But for the apprehension of such, to us, unwonted powers in our noble mother tongue, we must study: *work*, that is the word for it. We appreciate Shakespeare, as we do other things: when he has cost us something; and he might say to us, with the gracious Duncan, —

'Herein I teach you
How you shall bid God 'ild me for your pains.
And thank me for your trouble.'

It is very easy to push this kind of study beyond the necessities of the case, as beyond the patience of the pupil. But so long as they are really learning tangible things and feel that they are attaining positive results, they will work and think and profit. This sort of grammatical work should be applied strictly to matters in hand. Outside things, other plays should be noticed only in so far as they furnish quotations for apposite illustration. Particularly should a teacher avoid the pernicious habit of making Shakespeare a stalking-horse for addling youngsters' brains about "*old English.*" Weariness and disgust will be the result.

IV. With such preliminary and coincident study, the pupil prepares herself for that wider sweep of vision called for by the *views of life and of the universe* expressed or implied by the *dramatis personae* themselves. The habit of mind thus acquired enables her to comprehend quickly the notions of God, of life, of creation (*Weltanschauung*) found in ante-protestant times; and she is ready to sympathize with humanity, no matter as to age, or race, or clime. At the Master's bidding, she has learned, literally, to *dis*locate her imagination as to words and constructions, and thence as to the ordering of governments, of religions, of the inner life of man as well; and Pagan Lear is no more foreign to her than Moorish Othello, Catholic Wolsey, Roman Brutus, or that sweet dweller in the island of Nowhere, "admired Miranda." When she has understood clearly, once for all, what Claudius means by telling Laertes 'that, as the star moves not but in his sphere, He could not but by the Queen' (*Ham.* IV. vii. 15), then the pupil is ready always afterwards to accept the Ptolemaic notion of the universe, and to appreciate such expressions in the mouths of other characters. The splendid beauty of Lorenzo's star-lit rapture to Jessica,—

> "There's not the smallest orb which thou beholdest
> But in his motion like an angel sings,
> Still quiring to the young-eyed cherubins,"

(*M. of Ven.* V. i. 60–62), becomes still more exquisite to the pupil realizing the fantastic vision of circling spheres before his mind's eye as Shakespeare wrote the lines. One feels like straining the soul's ear to catch that majestic sphere-music, mightier, more entrancing even than the song of the angel Israfel, —

"Whose heart-strings are a lute."

And if modern science has given us more valuable because more accurate astronomical notions, we are half inclined to be indignant that it has interfered with our poetry.

V. Another prolific source of the realization of Shakespeare's conception is obtained by suggesting the *actor's view* to the pupil. There is much quickening of sympathy in representing to ourselves the look, posture, emphasis of the character who speaks. The same words have a totally different force according as they are pronounced; and it is like a revelation to a pupil sometimes to learn that a speech, or even a word, was uttered *thus* and not *so*. The interest of the play is vastly increased by cultivating this habit of thinking of each character as a "sure enough" person. And it is worth notice that many of those who uphold the madness of Hamlet depend, to a very great extent, upon that "interpretation of the language of gesture" which Poe says, somewhere, is the secret of the dramatic charm of Dickens. Hamlet is mad, those critics tell us, *because* he does or says this or that in a "wild" or "excited" way, or with "uncontrollable fury"; whence it would seem that he would not be mad if he did or said these same things quietly and in a self-controlled way. There is, of course, much liability to wrong conception; but a wrong conception of a character, if strongly entertained, is better than none or a milk-and-waterish one. Mr. Taine has expressed himself so admirably on this point that I quote from him: "Every word pronounced by one of his characters enables us to see, besides the idea which it contains and the emotion which prompted it, ... the mood, physical attitude, bearing, look of the man, all instantaneously, with a clearness and force approached by no one.... We hear the roll of those terrible voices; we see contracted features, glowing eyes, pallid faces; we see the rages, the furious resolutions which mount to the brain with the feverish blood, and descend to the sharp-strung nerves. This property, possessed by every phrase to exhibit a world of sentiments and forms, comes from the fact that the phrase is actually caused by a world of emotions and images. Shakespeare when he wrote, felt all that we feel, and much besides. A word here and there of Hamlet or Othello would need for its explanation three pages of commentaries; each of the half-understood thoughts, which the commentator may have discovered, has left its trace in the turn of the phrase, in the nature of the metaphor, in the order of the words; now-a-days in pursuing these traces we divine the thoughts." (Taine's *English Literature*, Book II., Chap. IV., p. 316.) It is " in pursuing these traces " that we realize most vividly the intensity of Shakespeare's humanity and the mighty force of his genius, — a genius which could enter so thoroughly into the minutest details of half-formed and fleeting emotion and thought without ever losing sight of the true outline of the character or of the character's true place in the play. Faust complains that he has two souls within his breast. We rise from the study of Hamlet with the feeling that not two souls merely, but the multitudinous soul of man, has played before us afresh the old, unending tragedy of life through love and hate up to those portals where 'the rest is silence.'

VI. Now, all this is preliminary work and should lead up to the *æsthetic* appreciation of Shakespeare's characters; and to that end, real conceptions, right or wrong, are essential.

Let it be distinctly understood: all study of words, of grammatical construction, of views of life peculiar to an age past, of bodily posture and gesture, — all are the preparation for the study of the characters themselves; that is, of the play itself; that is, of what Mr. Hudson calls the "Shakespeare of Shakespeare." If the student does not rise to this view of Shakespeare, she had better let Shakespeare alone and go at something else. In studying the lives of such men as Hamlet or Lear, and of such women as Lady Macbeth or Cordelia, it is of the utmost consequence that the attention of the pupil be so directed to their deeds and words, their expression and demonstration of feeling, — to the things, further, which they omit to say or do, — as to make the conception of personality as strong as possible. This is not, and need not be, any "forcing" process; nor need the pupil be made thereby self-conscious and conceited at her own wonderful perspicacity. Such childish superficiality will soon give place to deep interest and close observation; and there will arise in young minds, easily impressed and generous of response to appeal, that profound disgust for evil and that admiration for nobleness which Shakespeare knows so well how to awaken. The permanence of such impression will depend on stability of character. But the impression will be made. In following out closely the outlines of character, the pupil will soon learn to rid herself of the common and false habit of almost all young minds with their hasty judgments, — the fashion, namely, of looking upon Shakespeare's characters as mere types and of expecting them to do the things supposed to be characteristic of those typical natures. Children are apt to take these one-sided views of men and things, to imagine that the person or persons to whom they have attributed certain qualities, or the lack of those qualities, feel and are ready to act as they, the children, suppose them obliged to feel. And this perverse way of thinking is fostered by their periodicals, their cheap novels, their goody-good books. There is no school like Shakespeare for disabusing the young mind of these habitual prepossessions. How strong these prepossessions may be in older minds as well, is seen in the rather stupid stage-villain into whom the actors travesty the shrewd, bold King Claudius of the play of *Hamlet*. A discriminating study of Shakespeare's characters is not surpassed anywhere in its value as teaching the propriety, nay, the duty of taking the objective view of one's self, as of other people.

And yet, Shakespeare does make his characters represent principles, the clash or harmony of which constitutes the external significance of the actors in any particular drama. This is in large measure independent of the internal significance of the actors to themselves and to us; much as the judge's official existence is objective to the man who constitutes, and yet is within himself independent of, the judge. And so we have the twofold existence of the human soul before the pupil's thought — the soul in its strong, conscious freedom to determine well or ill and so to act; and the same soul launched on the tide of life and guided irresistibly by the "great opposeless wills," which will force it to admit, with joy or woe, sooner or later, —

"The wheel is come full circle; I am here."

Thus advancing from the individual to the principle, the pupil must next turn to the whole, — to the result of this play and clash of principles and men, — and give herself some account of what echo is awakened, what deep within her is called upon by the resounding deep within the poet's soul. And whether she reason it out or not, she will hardly escape making some response to the impulse upon her of that strong spirit's creative breath, 'moving upon the face of the waters' within the depth of her being and bringing to light the unknown world there lying hidden. Perhaps the answer had best be left vague; perhaps the soul, especially a young soul, had best not give a strict account at the bar of the understanding of that which the understanding can apprehend but feebly. For the mysteries of the soul dragged into the light of the reason are much like those wonderful, gelatinous dwellers of the sea when brought into the dry atmospheric light,—shapeless, pulpy masses of inanition which were erst such marvels of delicate, waving beauty.

Whether, then, the individual, the single principle, or the whole play be the object of thought, the pupil has, aided by her previous training, prepared herself for the rich repast before her, and need not

> 'Watch the wine flow, by herself but half-tasted;
> Hear the music, and yet miss the tune.'

Nor need she believe in her heart that she is to conclude with Prospero (*Tempest*, IV. i. 156) that —

> "We are such stuff
> As dreams are made on, and our little life
> Is rounded with a sleep,"

—whatever may become her conviction after she has reached Prospero's age and experience. Rather is she convinced by the noble creations of the poet's magic, and in spite of the evil ones,—which make indeed, like Caliban, the noble more noble by contrast,—that she should cry out with the fresh young heart of Miranda, worthy daughter of her sire, beautiful in her faith, —

> "O, wonder!
> How many goodly creatures are there here!
> How beauteous mankind is! O brave new world,
> That hath such people in't!"

Would that all young hearts could be brought so to feel and believe, or could be enabled to retain their young hope in life! Especially is it needful in this age when, on the one hand, the scientific men (so the theologians say) tell us that we are only wonderfully developed animals, — fine, strong, but ape-descended, probably simian in soul; and the theologians themselves, on the other hand, tell us that we are wicked, are devil's spawn before we are born, and suck in sin with our mother's milk. So that too many of us, young and old, are prone to look upon the fair face of creation, upon the star-lit heavens themselves, and see in them, as Carlyle did, only "a sad sight."[1]

Applying now these principles, if such they can be called, my method of work is this: One of the plays in the *Clarendon Press Series* is selected and, after some brief introductory matter, the class begins to study. Each pupil reads in turn a number of lines, and then is expected to give such explanations of the text as are to be found in the notes, supplemented by her own knowledge. She has pointed out to her such other matters also as may be of interest and are relevant to the text. These matters may be passing æsthetic criticisms upon characters; suggestions as to Shakespeare's style and art; citations of other authors, in the way of illus-

---

[1] *Cf.* Mr. Hudson's Preface to the *Harvard Shakespeare*, pp. xiii-xv, which I had not seen before writing these lines.

tration, or for comparison of their way of treating the same or similar themes; paraphrases of Shakespeare's language into modern English when needful; grammatical notes; in a word, whatever may be found helpful in stimulating the pupil's interest without distracting her attention. In order to keep the thread of the story plainly before the eye, it is frequently necessary to refer the pupil back, from time to time, to the language or actions of the characters as given in previous scenes; especially so when there is any change, real or apparent, in the development of the character,—*e.g.*, Gertrude in *Hamlet;* Macbeth and Lady Macbeth after the banquet scene.

When the play has been finished or when any character disappears from the play,— as Polonius in *Hamlet*, Duncan in *Macbeth*, the Fool in *King Lear*, — the class have all those passages in the play pointed out to them wherein this character appears or mention is made of him; and then, with this, Shakespeare's biography of him before their eyes, they are required to write a *composition* — bane of pupils, most useful of teachers' auxiliaries — on this character, without other æsthetic assistance or hints than they may have gathered from the teacher in the course of their study. This is to be *their* work, and to express *their* opinions of the man or the woman under discussion, and is to show how far they have succeeded in retaining their thoughts and impressions concerning the character, and how far they wish to modify them under this review. They are thus compelled to realize what they do and do not think; what they do and do not know; in how far the character does or does not meet their approval, and why. That is, the pupils are compelled to pass judgment upon themselves along with the Shakespeare character.

Here again, there is really but little danger of too conscious a knowing that they know. For, in fact, the consciousness that a criticism of self is a real part of the composition does not occur to the pupils, and yet is none the less felt and none the less effective; and false opinions and wrong principles will be self-condemned. When these compositions are examined, any errors of judgment can be noted by the teacher; questionable views can be questioned and misapprehensions corrected. Further, the teacher can express his own opinion more freely, and can read aloud the better class of critics or give the substance of their views. This should be done only *after* the pupil has formed and expressed an opinion. Thus used, the critics become a valuable standard of suggestive comparison and do not serve merely as the crude stuff of a dead cram. It is sometimes surprising to find how much and how rapidly dull, heavy pupils improve in clearness of expression and, of course, clearness of vision, in the composing of a few of these criticisms; and how much greater their interest in Shakespeare becomes when they once find that an opinion or opinions of their own have been entertained by some distinguished critic. Nothing so fixes impressions as putting them down in black and white; and therefore nothing is more useful to the Shakespeare teacher than this writing, followed by revision and comparison. For the pupil, each character successfully outlined is henceforth a distinct acquaintance and no longer one of a group.

Every important character in the play is thus dealt with. Not only each character, but particular scenes between characters will naturally afterwards become objects of composition and discussion, *e.g.*, the interview between Hamlet and Ophelia, or Duncan before Macbeth's castle,—

where the character and the occasion are examined in their mutual relations; so, too, for particular scenes in themselves and in their relation to the whole play, as the "devil-porter" scene in *Macbeth*. (See *Mac. Ex.* 50; *Ham. Ex.* 64 and 67.) And finally, the play itself is examined in the same way, as to its pictures of life and civilization and as to its ethical aim and value.

Before finishing this series of writings, but after reading through the play once, the pupils have parts assigned them and go through it again. This time they read scenes or pages as may be convenient, and then the attention is directed to the *grammatical* points. This is really a difficult subject to discuss or to teach. It is so easy to do too much, and so easy not to do enough. I am not altogether satisfied that my method is best. It is this: to assign, as stated, a certain part of the text upon which the grammatical references given in the index to the play in Abbott's *Shakespearian Grammar* are to be looked for and studied. From these references all are excluded which treat of prosody, accent, lengthening and shortening of words and syllables, — versification, in a word. Abbott's explanations often need explaining for young students; and yet when made plain, they do very much towards making the text clearer and more forcible. When it is read subsequently in the light of these explanations by pupils who take the parts of the various characters, the interest is much increased. And profit is nearly always in proportion to interest.[1] Furthermore, additional opportunity is thus given to the pupil for reflection upon the development of the characters and upon the progress of the

---

[1] The "Notes and Questions" on *Macbeth* given by Abbott at the end of his grammar are suggestive as a guide to the use of the book.

play and its meaning; and to the teacher to call attention to particular matters, and to general ones too, which were not so intelligibly suggested in the more confined first reading; for then the aim was to get upon the eminence, as it were, in order to look around.

I am disposed to think this separate dealing with the grammatical structure of Shakespeare's text is better than having it studied along with the word-forms and the philological content of the words. For it almost necessitates a review of the whole play and the pupil's work on the play; and the value of review is very great and too well known to be insisted upon.

The essay-criticism of characters and scenes is kept up all the while. And, of course, as each essay is returned and criticised, and its subject made more plain to the understanding, the whole play grows in luminousness and in coherence, and the magic of the poet wins its way more and more into the minds and hearts of the students.

It is well at this stage to suggest comparisons with other characters in other plays; for the pupil can now understand that the comparison may mean a definite something, knowing one of its terms. If time afford, Hudson or Dowden or Gervinus or Taine may be introduced and their criticisms read in class; for then they profit, whereas before one play is studied and learned, they simply confuse, and teach the average pupil to be superficial.

After the play is finished, Dowden's *Shakspere Primer* is taken up, and Shakespeare, the man, is read about, and something more of the play just studied is learned, and its interest enhanced. If possible, another play is then read more rapidly. Thus it will be seen that perhaps the whole half-session may be spent on one play; and it is time well spent if one play be really learned. My Shakespeare Class meets three times a week; when more time can be given it, more work can be done.

All this may seem to smack too much of the pedagogue with one idea. Perhaps it does. But my experience has been that those in a class who have worked on Shakespeare most enjoy him most, and are therefore most apt to profit by his teachings. As I have already said elsewhere, work, loving and persistent work, is the meaning of such study. It is ennobling and self-sustaining, such communion with Shakespeare, and through him with other great minds, just as similar work in music or painting is ennobling and productive of good taste and good morals.

And it is not true that this takes too much time for Shakespeare and from other things; and if it does, do let the children take time enough to learn something. They spend time, because it is "the thing" to do, in acquiring a gibble-gabble which they fondly hope will prove to be French on the proper occasion, and in toiling over a "Kauderwälsch," so-called German. Now, to learn to read both French and German is a desirable thing, and to know either or both is valuable. But many people believe that the value of such real knowledge is often counterbalanced by the tendency towards vagueness and unreality, ending in discontent, which a foreign medium of thought is apt to generate in young minds. A very young lady, able to express her opinions in glib French or doubt-suggesting German, is quite prone to imagine herself for a time greatly superior to the people around her on that account alone, while the fact may be that she is able merely to show herself foolish at bottom in two languages instead of in one. But it will probably take nearly twice the time for her to find it out; for, being word-crammed, she is word-deceived as to herself. Real possession of a foreign language tends to make anybody in part a foreigner. Our school-girls usually set before them as their aim the acquisition of just enough French or German to do them the harm of the abuse of those languages, without the real benefits of their use. Unless offset by solid training in their mother-tongue, these foreigners do much to unfit American girls for their daily life with its plain duties. Of all the educational shams and affectations, the "modern languages" have done probably the most harm to the women of this country. To "modern languages" time immeasurable has been given by the generation of American women now under fifty. How much of it was time wasted? But nobody was ever yet hurt by learning and taking to heart the utterances of Shakespeare's great, sound soul. So it would be wise to give the rising generation time enough to try, at least, to learn something from him.[1]

As a subject for study for young women, Shakespeare is peculiarly the best thing that they can study in English literature, because he calls forth the best in them by the manly soundness of his thought, and because the value of contact with true manliness of thought in the development of a true womanliness is not to be estimated. And because, further, Shakespeare is in an extraordinary degree healthfully objective in his effect upon the mind, whereas many, perhaps most women have a tendency towards over-refine-

---

[1] I remember a reply, much to the present point, made by my wise professor of Latin. When it was objected that the English University young men spent so much time on Latin, — reading Latin, studying Latin verse, and writing Latin odes, — he replied: "Yes; but when they have finished, *they know Latin.*" And it is strikingly characteristic of English statesmen that they have shown in their work the good effects of having learned in youth to *know something.*

ment of subjectivity — towards putting other people in their places instead of putting themselves in the places of other people. Contact with such sane, large-souled impartiality of mind as Shakespeare's is therefore peculiarly beneficial in a woman's education.

The teacher of Shakespeare is probably exposed to more temptations and liable to more errors than any other instructor. It is worth while to consider briefly some very common errors which have peculiarly harmful influence on the pupil studying Shakespeare. The teacher should guard against the temptation on his own part of befogging the pupil's mind with comparative readings and emendations which he may happen to know. It is better to know and to think about one thing than to try to think about half-a-dozen things. It is therefore better for the pupil to get a definite notion about one reading than to know that Shakespeare may have written several things instead of that one thing. This view is the result of that same experience which has brought me to the conviction that expurgated texts should alone be used in class work, — a conviction based upon observation of the bad effects of the diversion of thought otherwise produced; a conviction, therefore, independent of, though coincident with the moral aspects of the teacher's position. And the teacher should guard his pupil as well as himself from the habit of trying to improve on the text, since it produces neglect of an actual thing for the sake of an imaginary thing, — and few habits of mind hurt more than that. It either discourages the student or makes her superficial and conceited in an incredibly short time. And for the proper study of Shakespeare, reverence of mind is a great advantage, be it natural or acquired. That does not imply lack of boldness of thought.

As has been suggested elsewhere, the foisting upon Shakespeare of any more "Old English" work than may be necessary is silly. In this school the effort has been so to arrange the English course as to lead from modern English back to Shakespeare, and as far as possible from Anglo-Saxon down to Shakespeare. But when on Shakespeare, the pupils are neither persuaded nor allowed to think that they are merely dealing with a branch of middle English study, the exercise being for the nonce in Shakespeare. Undoubtedly, the pupil familiar with Anglo-Saxon and with dialectic forms of middle English will understand the confusion of constructions (see *Mac. Ex.* 13) better than one who merely has Abbott's explanation to rely upon. So the girl who has read Chaucer will see all the more clearly the gerundial infinitive construction when it occurs. But it is enough to understand those usages in Shakespeare's language clearly, without knowing all that can be learned about them.

The crowding of the young mind with a multiplicity of ideas, all vague, as is frequently done when one character is elaborately compared with another character which is known only to the teacher, is a pernicious practice, and one into which a teacher is easily betrayed. But it blunts the pupil's interest in the character under discussion by giving her the hopeless feeling that there is something about it which she cannot know until she has read, in the indefinite future, some other play. Now Shakespeare does not make any character in any play depend upon any comparative notion somewhere else. I think this is true even of such continuous characters as King Henry in the two parts of *Henry IV.*, or of Prince Hal or Falstaff in the same plays. Unless the outlines of characters have time to arrange themselves, to crystallize in the pupil's mind, no definite and exact portrait can be retained and no adequate benefit can result from the time and labor given to the work. The element of time, indeed, must be allowed and provided for, even in our hothouse style of educating, if we wish to accomplish any real result beyond barrenness and exhaustion. Time is necessary to us all, and to all other things where reproduction is hoped for after absorption. And, as I think somebody remarks, one of the striking characteristics of the Elizabethan mind is this need, of which it was conscious, for rest — for time for reflection — for escape from doing and seeming to the privacy and liberty of merely being. Spenser was wholly given up to it. Bacon sought opportunity for it again and again, and was perhaps half-reconciled to a disgrace which brought quiet with it. Raleigh found it in his prison and made noble use of it. And most striking of all and least comprehensible to our eager-eyed age, Shakespeare, with his splendid powers, with his prolific creativeness, seems to have sought during years, possibly from the very time of first leaving Stratford, the opportunity of going back there and being able to give himself up to a quiet life, to contemplation; if, at least, we can trust to what he did, what he did not do, and to the tone of his last "romance" plays, particularly of *The Tempest*. And the last of the Shakespearians, John Milton, deliberately decided from his boyhood that his life was to be one of reflection, from which only the call of duty diverted him for a time. All of which teaches us over again that

"The gods approve
The depth and not the tumult of the soul—"

an admonition which of all people teachers should take most to heart. They should see to it lest they keep continually distorting and destroying, by throwing in the pebbles of their opinions, the image cast by the genius of Shakespeare upon the young soul as upon a placid lake.

And here I would repeat more emphatically what has been said in part already. Do not allow the pupils' minds to be hurried unduly into forming opinions about the characters by reading what Gervinus or somebody else has said. They should neither read it nor hear it read too soon. They should not read *about* Shakespeare until they have read Shakespeare himself and written down their own opinions. Of course, they should be guided in forming opinions by remarks of the teacher during the reading; for no method of instruction is more fruitful than the incidental and unexpected association of ideas by a skilful teacher. But this incidental character of the criticism is its value. Harm is done when somebody's opinion is thrust upon the pupil while she is elaborating only half-consciously her own. This is the meaning of Mr. W. Aldis Wright's protest against "sign-post criticisms," as he calls æsthetic notes, in the Preface to his Clarendon Press edition of *King Lear* (p. xiii.) — which title, by the way, seems to have called forth unnecessary gall. When the time comes, the æsthetic criticism of others is most beneficial to any mind, young or old. But in this much taught, much reading, much talking age of newspapers and magazines and sham writers and small-eyed learning, the poor school-children have a hard struggle at best to keep free of superficiality; and their teachers should help them, not do them the cruel wrong of showing them how to deceive themselves. Too many will do that in the magazine, from the pulpit, in the text-book; too many of whom Hamlet might still say that they have, "and many more of the same breed that I know the drossy age dotes on — only got the tune of the time and outward habit of encounter; a kind of yesty collection, which carries them through and through the most fond and winnowed opinions; and do but blow them to their trial, the bubbles are out" (Act V., Sc. ii., 176-181).

And we teachers ought to bear in mind that commonplace is sometimes so much better than genius; for thereby we can console ourselves for the violence we do the glowing heart within us which makes us yearn to "electrify" our pupils by brilliant displays of our powerful "personal magnetism," whatever that may mean. When pupils say they have studied this or that and yet show that they know nothing about it, oftener it is the fault of the teacher's wrong way of working than of the pupils themselves.

Teachers should be willing for their pupils to begin, as they did or ought to have done, at the beginning; and then be willing to wait long enough for results to come in their "kindly season." We should work soberly and not demand presently of the child-mind what we feel that we ourselves are only acquiring gradually after years of slow work. Most of us may read with profit, in more senses than one, what Hans Andersen says the moon heard the little child read in her corner:—

> "Into the dust with Talent's glory,
>   But commonplace is fortune made;
>   In truth, 'tis an old, old story,
>   Yet daily the piece is played."

It is certainly wrong to encourage pupils to think they can be manufactured into Shakespearians, "in an eminent sense," and all teachers should "read, mark, learn, and inwardly digest" Mr. Hudson's remarks on this subject, in his essay on *How to Use Shakespeare in Schools*. A high standard of attainment in Shakespeare should be kept before pupils, of course, as possible and desirable; but they should be taught so as to help the girls, not so as to make conceit-bags of them; and they can be helped very greatly.

The most valuable thing any woman can bring from school life to the real daily life is the *habit of good healthy reading* in the literature of her own land. If she has acquired that, she has indeed passed from mere instruction to that education of which so much stuff is talked, and which is an individual, voluntary thing; it being no more possible to *educate* boy or girl against his or her will than it is to make a horse drink after you have led him to the water.

If the aim of Shakespeare study be to employ him as a text-book in classes of elocution, then certainly the pupils ought to be helped as far as possible to understand adequately the passages to be read, since understanding must precede good reading. Otherwise, they will be almost sure to succeed in reading Shakespeare in that peculiarly awful way so much affected by those declamatory people who give "marvellous renditions," as the newspapers tell us, but who would have made Shakespeare confess that he "had *liefer* the town crier spoke his lines," had he ever heard them "mouth it" once. Few things attainable by any course of instruction, however, are so desirable as the accomplishment of expressive, tasteful reading of Shakespeare. For whoever can read Shakespeare well, can read any other English author well.

One other point of great practical importance may be made. Teachers should be very chary of allowing their pupils to be diverted to side-issues, to Shakespearianisms in the place of Shakespeare himself. Among these may be reckoned the chronological order of his plays — the sources whence he drew his materials — the settling of disputed readings — the evidences of his private opinions and experiences as found in his works — his versification, and of this last more particularly. All of these things, be it said, are of value, of utmost value, for the scholar and the editor of Shakespeare; but from the school-girl in the class-room they should not demand either time or attention beyond a very limited extent. Among these I include Versification even with the fear of Dr. Abbott before me. (See Abbott's *Shakespearian Grammar* and the Preface thereto.) Mr. Hudson's experience in teaching Shakespeare's verse [1] would be the experience of many teachers if their classes were consulted. I do not believe that it makes any difference to the ordinary pupil's apprehension of a line whether it be metrically right or wrong; and such lore does not belong in the class-room and should be kept out of it. I have never yet been able to see any good come of making school-girls learn more of Shakespeare's versification than that his blank verse is supposed to contain ten syllables, an unaccented and an accented syllable being joined, and in that order; and that Shakespeare uses more than ten or less than ten syllables as he sees fit, and changes the order of their accents as his taste directs. Even if Shakespeare's verse be a proper object of school work, there are other things too valuable for the time to be so misapplied, if not wasted outright. A class had better read half a dozen plays instead of spending time trying to make believe that they are learning Shakespeare's versification in any one play.

This paper would hardly accomplish its aim fully without some mention of *Text-books;* although each teacher must decide that matter for himself. I have spoken of Mr. Hud-

---

[1] *How to Use Shakespeare in Schools*, p. xv.

son's little volume of essays and of their value; yet Mr. Hudson's method of instruction is not a practicable one, I think, for schools, as schools are in this country. He says: "I never have had, never will have, any recitations whatever; but only what I call, simply, *exercises*, the pupils reading the author under my direction, correction, and explanation; the teacher and the taught thus communing in the author's pages for the time being." (*How to Use Shakespeare in Schools*, p. x.) Mr. Hudson may be theoretically right as to the intrinsic value of most recitation and examination; yet the determination of results, in a real way or in a sham way, is a necessity for our schools. Only thus can they attain and maintain their standards. And without some standard of scholarship, I do not see how an unendowed school can honestly support itself. We school-teachers must work as we can, not as we would. So, too, while agreeing with Mr. Hudson in the main, in his "protest against Shakespeare's being used . . . for carrying on general exercises in grammar and philology," I make bold to suggest that only sufficient study of this kind can enable the student to realize that Shakespeare's "language is the medium, not the object, of thought"; and that without such study, therefore, the pupil will be quite sure to learn, not Shakespeare, but the *teacher's* Shakespeare alone; and that, too, almost in proportion as the teacher is half-learned and without self-restraint. Nothing but such study, it seems to me, can save the pupil from that "thrusting himself between the author and the reader" on the part of the teacher, which Mr. Hudson strongly deprecates on the part of the editor. (Preface, *Harvard Shakespeare*, p. x.) This brings us to consider the question of the place for notes in class-room editions of

Shakespeare's plays. Mr. Hudson, acting on his experience, prints the notes at the foot of the page. Mr. Aldis Wright, in the *Clarendon Press Series* of plays, puts the notes at the end of the play; so does Mr. W. J. Rolfe in his editions. These are all three admirable editions, and the ones generally used in our schools.

For a class beginning the study of Shakespeare, my experience has decided me in favor of Mr. Wright's *Clarendon Press Series*. I prefer them, as compared with Rolfe's series, because his are really little *variorum* editions, and such notes are apt to bewilder beginners by their frequent over-suggestiveness; and because I believe it is injurious to put so much tempting æsthetic matter before pupils who should make up their minds for themselves. Mr. Rolfe's books seem to me most excellent for Shakespeare reading-clubs, and, perhaps, for advanced classes. Mr. Hudson's editions have the objectionable foot-notes. I speak of a Class of beginners. Mr. Hudson's reasons for his decision certainly have much force, and they may convince me should I ever teach as much as he has done. His reasons apply particularly to authors whose *individual words* are to be explained, *e.g.*, a learned writer like Milton. But, in Shakespeare, not the word alone, usually the word and the whole expression of the thought are involved, so that the thought itself is the difficulty. To understand thought, we must think; and to think, time is necessary. Now, as I have already suggested elsewhere, foot-notes on the same page certainly do much to hinder the formation of the proper mental habit, and to generate dependence and superficiality. They help a sluggish mind to become confirmed in its lazy habits, and they prevent the active mind from exercising its powers.

Our book-makers and teachers strangely overlook, it seems to me, the immense value of this element of time, — time for reflection. The young student *must have it.* The older students, — men like the three Editors named, saving their presence, — can only do without it then, when their associations of ideas, resulting from long habit, enable them to make quantity of ideas, or mental space, supply the lack of time. The disregard of this plain dictate of common sense in other departments of instruction is simply scandalous. All sorts of bad books and questionable methods are used to deceive parents and children into believing that much has been attained because a wicked system of cramming has been made to submerge, so to speak, the child's mind.

But, to continue, there is this advantage in foot-notes, that they carry us faster over the ground, thus giving more repetition, and thereby both more familiarity and better opportunity for comparison. But, on the other hand, the trouble is that, quickly learned being quickly forgotten, we carry with us, through all the repetition, just those errors to which we are most liable, and which time for reflection, and nothing else, will rid us of. Thus, we merely read ourselves and our errors into Shakespeare a dozen or so times instead of once. These considerations seem to me fatal to attaining the greatest benefit by foot-notes for pupils *beginning* to study Shakespeare. But I use gladly Mr. Hudson's editions in my Shakespeare reading club, or in an advanced class, after an introductory study of one or more plays.

It would, however, be a glad day for any teacher of Shakespeare to expect to do half as much good work *on* Shakespeare, and half as much good *with* Shakespeare, as Mr. Hudson has already accomplished.

I would advise any teacher to get the same play in all three editions, and then decide for himself. He will surely learn something from each edition.

Dowden's *Shakspere Primer* I find useful; and Abbott's *Shakespearian Grammar* is almost indispensable for a teacher, whether he use it as a class-book or not. The chapter on Shakespeare in Taine's *English Literature* is valuable. I do not see that a teacher needs anything more in the ordinary class-work, whatever he may study for himself and his own growth. Whoever has a volume of the Furness *Variorum* edition needs little else for the play edited. The introductory essay on the "Teaching of English," by Mr. Hales, in *Longer English Poems*, is an excellent discussion of the subject.

My fervent wish in giving to my countrywomen these pages containing the work of their young sisters, is that more of them may be induced to commune habitually with the master-spirit of our race; that those who are already spreading his influence may be helped to do so more effectually; and that all our study may issue in that true life for the individual which brings about the true life for the whole people. God keep the homes of America, — the true strongholds of her freedom!

I would like to extend this paper into a plea for the healthful education, the English education, the Shakespeare education of American girls, especially the girls of the South, upon whom is laid a burden grievous to be borne. I would like to raise my voice, not for that education which is sham and debilitating, intellectually and morally, but for the schooling which is sound and bracing and full of the free spirit of our race, the race of Shakespeare and of

Milton. For our great need throughout our whole country is not for women more intellectual, more scientific than they are now; let them be all that too, but not unless they can add to it true womanhood, sweet motherhood. It is the mothers who make men patriots, and we need more men who love their country.

FEBRUARY, 1883.

The experience of four years of teaching since the foregoing *Remarks* were written, confirms, in general terms, the trustworthiness of the conclusions therein set forth as to the practical effect of such a method of dealing with Shakespeare in the class-room, — that it makes his works the most valuable of all text-books for undergraduate students of English Literature.

Upon the value and the effect of requiring compositions (see pp. 254–256) to be written on the various characters in any given play in hand, it is not easy to insist too much. It stirs sluggish thought, awakens sympathy, and trains the mind to loyal discrimination of character, not to mere coldhearted criticism, as nothing else, in my experience as a teacher, does or has done.

As to the amount of study and time to be given to the purely grammatical examination of Shakespeare's English by the average pupil, I can only repeat with emphasis what I have already said (p. 256) : "It is so easy to do too much, and so easy not to do enough." My present inclination is to think it may be best to rely upon the notes for the explanation of obscure passages until the class — in schools where they are carried so far — have read something in Chaucer, and then to return to the grammatical discussion (p. 261).

But it seems altogether probable that for the average pupil the time spent on Abbott's *Grammar* would be better spent in reading another play of Shakespeare.

To regularly organized clubs containing persons who have at all devoted themselves to the study of Shakespeare, I do not presume to give any advice; but to those who are unfamiliar with such work, I would respectfully suggest that some such plan as follows will be found profitable and agreeable: Take, say, the *Merchant of Venice*, and let it be read through without much comment of any kind; then at successive meetings, let the various characters and incidents of the play be taken up for discussion by one or more persons during a part of each meeting, and the rest of the meeting be devoted to reading other plays or parts of plays bearing upon the characters or subjects under discussion. For instance, Portia naturally calls up for comparison her sisters Rosalind, Beatrice, Miranda, Desdemona and others; as Bassanio suggests Orlando, Romeo, and Hamlet, and as Shylock's lust of will and thirst for power make us think of Macbeth and Iago, of Claudius and Edmund. Shakespeare will thus be constantly compared with himself and will afford a commentary upon himself of surpassing interest. Such work can be made as strenuous, or as little so as time, inclination, and other circumstances may dictate.

For reading aloud in Clubs of this kind, the annotated and expurgated edition of the separate plays by Rev. H. N. Hudson seems to me decidedly the best. The notes are hardly so full as in the *Clarendon Press* or in Mr. Rolfe's edition; but they are at the bottom of the page, and the expurgation is much more thoroughly done than in those editions, and prevents a great deal of needless embarrassment to the readers. To Mr. Hudson, Mr. W. J. Rolfe, and Mr. W. Aldis Wright the thanks of English-speaking people are due for the loving care and scholarly research with which they have edited the plays of Shakespeare and made them accessible to the vast majority of their countrymen. They have done a splendid work, one whose effects are showing themselves already. And the New Shakspere Society of London has earned and is earning the gratitude of the present and of the future for the aid its work is giving to a right understanding of the age of Shakespeare, as well as for its publications directly affecting his works, and for its generosity in giving schools prizes for encouraging Shakespeare teaching and study.

MAY, 1887.

The observation and experience of the past summer months induces me to add — at the risk of repeating an oft-told story — a brief outline of a *book-club*, practicable, and most profitable, for persons not having access to good libraries, and yet desirous of reading in connection with Shakespeare, or in any other direction. These book-clubs are well known in the larger cities.

Five, ten, fifteen, twenty people, let us say, subscribe from two to five dollars apiece, and buy through some agency, or directly from the publishers, their books at about wholesale prices. Each book is sent by the secretary of the club to each member in succession, a record of books and persons being kept to establish responsibility and priority of claim. Any one wishing to buy any one of the books sends in his or her name and the name of the book, and, after the book has gone the rounds, it is sold for half-price and the money turned into the treasury for new purchases. Books not thus sold to club members are sold to book-dealers for what they will bring, and this money, too, is put into the common fund. By-laws and regulations to suit different communities can be easily made. And instead of reselling the books to its members, any club might donate them to the circulating library of its town or neighborhood, and thus not let their charity end at home.

For Shakespeare book-clubs, some such course as the "Course of Shakespeare Historical Reading" in the numbers of *Shakespeariana*[1] for the current year would be found interesting.

SEPTEMBER, 1887.

---

[1] *Shakespeariana*, 1104 Walnut St., Philadelphia.

CHAUCER EXAMINATION:

THE PROLOGUE; THE KNIGHT'S TALE;
THE NUN'S PRIEST'S TALE.

MISS VIRGINIA STRICKLER,
OF LURAY, VIRGINIA.

HOLLINS INSTITUTE, VA.

1886.

NOTE.

THE Chaucer questions were given to Miss Strickler, a few at a time, and were answered by her without referring to the text at all. The questions did not then have the references either to the lines or to the pieces marked as now. That has been done since for the convenience of those who may wish to use the examination; the numbers standing first are the line-numbers of the *Clarendon Press* edition;[1] the numbers in parenthesis are taken from Gilman's *Chaucer*. Miss Strickler did her work without assistance, and it is given, a few unimportant matters of form, not of substance, excepted, as it came from her hands.

I desire to express my grateful sense of obligation to Professor Child for his kindness in preparing the examination.

WM. TAYLOR THOM.

HOLLINS INSTITUTE, VA.,
April, 1887.

---

[1] *Chaucer's Prologue, Knightes Tale,* etc., ed. R. Morris, *Clarendon Press Series,* Macmillan & Co. *The Poetical Works of Geoffrey Chaucer,* ed. Arthur Gilman, 3 vols. Houghton, Mifflin & Co.

PRIZE EXAMINATION ON CHAUCER.

THE PROLOGUE; THE KNIGHTES TALE; THE NONNE PRESTES TALE.

JUNE, 1886.

Questions by Prof. F. J. Child, of Harvard University, with additions (marked by asterisks) by Wm. Taylor Thom, of Hollins Institute.

I.

1. Give the important facts in the life of Chaucer from the year 1370.
2. Under what kings did he live?
3. What reason had they to befriend him?
4. Describe Chaucer's personal habits.

II.

5. Why is the plan of the Canterbury Pilgrimage a particularly good one?
6. How many pilgrims are there, and how many tales are told?
7. Name some of the other works of Chaucer.
8. Compare *The Knight's Tale* with the poem on which it is founded.

III.

9. Describe, as far as you can in Chaucer's words, the Clerk and the Parson.

IV.

10. Give the history of Palamon and Arcite down to the tournament.

11. Write as much as you can of the theory and practice of medicine in Chaucer's time, using all three of the poems as sources.

12.* State briefly the versification of *The Canterbury Tales;* as compared with Anglo-Saxon poetry; importance of final *e* in Chaucer's verse, and what it represents in his language.

Explain all that seems to you to need explanation as to the matter and the verbal form of the passages which follow, whether particular questions are asked or not.

V.

Prologue.

13. "The yonge sonne hath in the Ram his halfe cours i-ronne," 7, 8. Notice *yonge, i-ronne.*

14. "The martyr that hem hath holpen when that they were seeke," 18. Notice *hem, holpen, seeke.*

15. "The condicioun of eche of hem and whiche they weren and of what degree," 38-40.

16. "He hadde the bord bygonne aboven alle naciouns in Pruce," 52-53. Why Pruce and afterwards Lettowe and Ruce?

17. What is the Prioress's especial ambition? 132, 139-141.

18. "The reule of St. Beneyt," 173. Can you distinguish between the regular and the secular clergy?

19. "As Austin byt." Notice *byt,* 187.

20. "I not how men him calle," 284. What other negative verbs are used by Chaucer?

21. "St. Julian he was in his countre," 340.

22. (The doctor) "Kepte that he wan in pestilence," 442. What is the humorous explanation?

23. What were the chief pilgrimages in those days out of England?

24. "Him were levere," "ful loth were him," 486.

25. "No wonder is a lewed man to ruste," 502. Grammar. What was "a lewed man"? Compare with the Maunciple.

26. "The Reeve was a colerik man," 587.

27. "Ful. lowde he sang, Com hider, love, to me," 672. The *e* in *loude, love*, and the absence of *e* in Com.

28. "Him thoughte he rood al of the newe get," 682. Give as many impersonal verbs from Chaucer as you can. *Impersonal verbs show what about a language?

29. "A chaunterie for soules," 510.

30. "From Gootland to the cape of Fynystere," 408.

31. "Telle he moste his tale," 847. Compare with the English *must*.

32. "Good mester," 613; "lymytour," 209; "forward," 33; "solas," 798; "vileinye," 70; "vernicle," 685. Meanings.

33. "Cometh ner," 839; "God you speede," 769; "to schorte with our weie," 791; "at oure alther cost," 799; "herkneth if you leste," 828. Grammar.

VI.

The Knightes Tale.

34. "King Capaneus that starf at Thebes," 74, 75 (932).

35. "Him thoughte that his herte woulde breke," 96 (954); the *es*.

36. "At the sonne upriste," 193 (1051).

37. "I nam but deed; these nys no more to seye," 264 (1122). Rule as to negatives in Chaucer.

38. "Palamon gan knytte his browes," 270 (1128). Use of *gan?*

39. Arcite's justification of himself for loving Emily, 295-313 (1153).

40.* "Let him be war his nekke lith to wedde," 360 (1218).

41. What is the "selle fantastyk"? 518 (1376).

42. "Three yeer in this wise his lyf he ladde," 588 (1446); other uses of *yeer?*

43. "*Needes cost* he moste himselven hyde," 619 (1477).

44. How came Theseus to be hunting the very day of the duel?

45.* "And it am I that loveth so hoote Emily," 878, 879 (1736). Grammar?

46. What does Theseus say of the folly of lovers after he has come upon Palamon and Arcite? 927-956, (1785).

47. "Frely withouten raunsoun or daunger," 991 (1849).

48. Describe the theatre (not the temples), 1023-1055 (1881).
49. "Wisdom ne richesse, beauté ne sleighte, strengthe, ne hardynesse, ne may with Venus holde champartye," 1089-1091 (1947). The examples which prove this proposition?
50. Describe King Lygurge and his array, 1271 (2129).
51. King Emetreus, 1298 (2156).
52. "Namely oon that with a spere was thirled his brest boon," 1851, 1852 (2709).
53. How much time does the story cover?

VII.

The Nonne Prestes Tale.

54. The poor widow's way of life, 1-26 (8433).
55. "My lief is faren on londe," 59 (8491). Meaning.
56. What must a good husband be, according to Partelot? 94-97 (8526).
57. "Catoun *which that* was so wise a man," 120 (8552).
58. "The humour of malencolie," 113 (8545).
59. "Me mette I was in such meschief," 74 (8506).
60. "This night I *shall* be mordred," 185 (8617).
61. "The hostiler so sore engyned," 240 (8672).
62. "He lith gapynge upright," 222 (8654).
63. "To that oon man fel," 256 (8688).
64. "Forslouthe wilfully thy tyde," 276 (8708).
65. "Bad him for to kepe him wel for traisoun," 296 (8728).
66. "The brighte sonne in the signe of Taurus hadde i-ronne twenty degrees and oon," 372 (8805): what day?
67. "Undern," 401, (8834).
68. "Goddes worthy forwetynge," 422 (8855).
69. "I were worse than a feend," 465 (8898): why wor*se?*
70. "Daun Russel," 512 (8946).
71. "As saith us *Eneydos,*" 538 (8971): why *Eneydos?*
72. "Certes he Jakke Straw and his menyé," 573 (9006).
73. The concluding moral of the Cock and the Fox.

VIII.

74. Inflect the Anglo-Saxon and the Chaucerian pronoun *he*.
75.* The same pronoun in Modern English, and explain the intruding and surviving forms.

IX.*

76.* What seems to be Chaucer's attitude towards religion and the clergy, as compared, for instance, with the author of *Piers the Plowman?*
77.* What seems to be his opinion of women?
78.* Chaucer's general attitude towards mankind, especially with reference to the opinions of his age?
79.* Chaucer's rank and importance to English Literature as an artist, and the artistic elements of his poetry.

I.

1. The first event of impórtance in the life of Chaucer after 1370 was the Italian journey of 1372-73, undertaken for the purpose of negotiating a commercial treaty with the Genoese. In the course of it, Chaucer visited Florence and Padua. At Arqua, near Padua, he is supposed to have met Petrarch, and from him to have learned the story of the Patient Griselda.

The Italian mission seems to have been successful, for, in the April after his return, Chaucer was rewarded with the grant of a daily pitcher of wine, afterwards commuted to a money payment of twenty marks. Later in the same year, he was appointed to the important and lucrative post of Comptroller of Customs and Subsidy of Wools, Skins, and Hides at the port of London. The duties of the office must have been engrossing, and for years he was not allowed to appoint a deputy; but no doubt the daily contact with diverse classes of practical men was not without its compensations, or even charms, to the writer of *The Canterbury Tales*.

In this same year, 1374, the Corporation of the City of London granted to Chaucer the house over the gate at Aldgate on condition that he keep it in repair.

This was probably also the year of his marriage, for at this time and afterward the pension of Philippa Chaucer was paid to her through him, and in this year the Duke of Lancaster granted an annual pension to Geoffrey Chaucer and his wife Philippa in consideration of services to himself, his consort, and his mother the queen. Mention is indeed made in 1366 of a Philippa Chaucer, maid of honor to the queen, who may have been Geoffrey's wife, but she may also have been his cousin and namesake; and we should prefer to think that the personal revelations in the *Boke of Blanche the Duchess* come from the lips of a disappointed youth — not from those of a married man. The supposition that Chaucer's wife was a daughter of Sir Paon de Roet and sister of the third wife of John of Gaunt seems to be without foundation.

In the next few years Chaucer was sent abroad on several diplomatic missions, some of them of great delicacy and importance. In 1386 he was elected Knight of the Shire for Kent. In the same year, when the Duke of Gloucester and his party came into power, Chaucer was dismissed from office. The following year his wife died, but in 1388 he took his merry Canterbury pilgrimage. In 1389 he was appointed Clerk of the King's Works at Westminster, and the next year Clerk of the Works at St. George's Chapel, Westminster. In 1392 he lost both offices, and in the years that followed he seems to have been considerably straitened in money matters, for we find him raising money on his two pensions. Upon the accession of Henry IV. in 1399 Chaucer's former pension was doubled, and he soon after covenanted for a fifty-three years' lease of a house in the garden of St. Mary's chapel at Westminster. There, in October, 1400, he died. His grave is in Westminster Abbey, the first of the poets buried there.

2. Edward III., until 1377; Richard II., 1377-99; Henry IV., 1399-1400.

3. Chaucer must have been a valuable public servant. His knowledge of men, his reticence, his knowledge of foreign tongues — he was certainly conversant with French and Italian — fitted him peculiarly for diplomatic service abroad, and we accordingly find him frequently thus employed. That he was a man of sound common sense and practical ability, knowing how to make himself useful under any circumstances, we may well believe. Furthermore, the office of the poet was then, even more distinctively than now, to afford pleasure, and such an inimitable story-teller as Chaucer was sure of an honorable position in a court that craved amusement. Twice, at least, Chaucer played the part of Poet Laureate, gracefully celebrating, in the *Book of the Duchess*, a royal bereavement, and, in the *Parliament of Fowls*, a royal matrimonial negotiation. The manner of these two performances was such as could scarcely fail to win gratified recognition. No doubt, too, there was much that was personally attractive in the poet, and perhaps personal friendship cemented his long official connection with the court.

4. In appearance, he was small of stature and inclined to corpulence. His face was small, fair, and intelligent, and he had a habit of looking down "as he would find a hare." He was a close observer, and not a great talker, though he loved good company. He tells us himself that "his abstinence was little." He was devoted to study, coming home from his

office work to pore over a book until his eyes were dazed and his head ached. When he was "making songs and ditties," nothing could divert him from his work, save the song of birds and the fresh beauties of a May morning. He was fond of solitary communings with nature, and when he was alone he walked quickly.

II.

5. Because the occasion — a journey with a religious object in view — was one that encouraged the disregard of conventionalities and arbitrary distinctions of rank, and permitted free play to individual traits. The incidents of the journey and the free comments of the travellers upon the tales, give excellent opportunity for the natural and spirited development of the various characters that have been broadly sketched in the Prologue.

6. Thirty-two, the Canon and his Yeoman having joined him on the way. Twenty-four tales are told.

7. The Boke of the Duchess, Compleynte to Pite, Anelida and Arcite, Boece, Compleynte of Mars, Compleynte of Venus, Legende of Good Women, Troilus and Creseide, House of Fame, Parlament of Foules, and other shorter poems.

8. *The Knightes Tale* is borrowed from the *Teseide* of Boccaccio, with numerous omissions, additions, and changes of plan. The additions are mainly in the imaginative and descriptive parts, and are admirable. Chaucer omits the account of the conquest of the Amazons and of the marriage of Theseus, and abridges the description of the battle. He deviates from Boccaccio in making Palamon, not Arcite, first see Emily, in representing the two princes

as furiously jealous of each other, and in supposing that Emily sees neither of them. The changes of detail are very numerous.

III.

9. The Clerk is described as looking "holwe and thereto soberly," riding a horse that was "thin as is a rake," and wearing a "thredbare courtepey." He had as yet gotten him no benefice, nor was he so worldly as to have office, but it pleased him to have at his bed's head twenty books of Aristotle, bound in black and red; in fact, he had quite "gone to logic." He spent all he could get from his friends at school, busily praying for the souls of his benefactors, "and gladly wolde he lerne and gladly teche."

The outward appearance of the Parson is but meagrely described: the description of him is an expansion of the statement that "Cristes lore and his apostles twelve, he taughte, but first he folwede it himselve." He did not leave his village charge to the care of a hired substitute, while he himself ran to London to seek a chantry at St. Paul's. He guarded well his flock, going on foot, his staff in hand, to visit the poorest and remotest in his parish if they were sick or in trouble. He was not exacting in the matter of tithes, and was always ready to share his scanty income with the needy.

IV.

10. They were the sons of two sisters, and of the royal family. From childhood they have been sworn friends, and in the defence of Thebes they fall side by side. Theseus carries them to Athens as prisoners, not to be ransomed or

released. One day, from his prison tower, Palamon sees Emily, Theseus' sister-in-law, walking in the garden, and he becomes deeply enamored. He calls Arcite, whose heart is likewise smitten, and from this time a violent jealousy divides the two cousins. Arcite is released at the request of Perithous, on condition that he shall not show himself again in the dominions of Theseus on pain of death. After spending a few years in Thebes, he returns to Athens in disguise, attaches himself to the court, and works his way into high favor. On a certain morning in May, he goes to the green wood, and as he rambles he falls into a soliloquy. The night before Palamon had escaped from prison, and was now hiding in the same grove. He overhears Arcite, reveals himself, and a conflict is arranged for the following day, in the midst of which Theseus and his train, out for a day's hunt, suddenly come up. The duel is stopped, explanations given, and an agreement made for a combat, with a hundred famous knights on each side, to be held a year later.

11. Astrology still played an important part in medicine in Chaucer's day. His "doctor of physicke" "coude keep his patient wonder well in houres by his magic naturelle," and he also knew how to "fortunen the ascendant." He made use of "dragges" and "letuaries" intended to help one another. Litharge, ceruce, oil of tartar, "ointments that would clense and bite," are among the remedies which failed to relieve the Summoner's "sawceflem." Melancholy was believed to be actually caused by black fumes rising into the head, and Madame Pertelot alludes to the four humors, attributing Chanticleer's troubled visions to "the greete superfluite of youre reede colera." The remedies she prescribes are mostly herbs, among them "salve," or sage, which was highly esteemed in the Middle Ages. The resources of the

healing art seem, on the whole, to have been limited, and Chaucer no doubt expresses an opinion fairly justified by the practice of his time, when he declares, commenting on the treatment of Arcite's wound, that if the vigor of nature be seriously impaired, there is small help in physic.

12.* With the exception of the *Tale of Melibœus* and the *Parson's Tale* they are written in heroic couplets — five accents in a line. Sometimes, however, an unaccented syllable is added at the end of the line, making eleven syllables, and sometimes the first foot consists of a single accented syllable, giving but nine. The Anglo-Saxon poetry was alliterative, two important words in the first section of the line and one in the second beginning with the same letter. Chaucer adopted the Romance system of versification, rhymed and accentual.

The pronunciation of the final *e* is often necessary to the harmony of the verse, while, on the other hand, the *e* is often to be slurred for the same reason. Grammatically it represents the dative case of nouns, the definite declension, the plural number, and the vocative case of adjectives. In the preterite of strong verbs it distinguishes the plural from the singular number.

V.

13. "The *yonge* sonne hath in the Ram his halfe cours *i-ronne*."

The sun entered the sign of the Ram the 22d March; his "halfe cours in the Ram" for April would, accordingly, carry us somewhat beyond the middle of the month.

Yonge alludes to the fact that it was early in the year. The final *e* here shows the definite form of the adjective.

I-ronne is the past participle, the prefix representing the A.-S. *ge*.

14. "'The martyr . . . that *hem* hath *holpen* when they were seek."

The "martyr" is of course Thomas à Becket. *Hem* is the accusative case from the A.-S. dative, *him*, afterwards supplanted by *them*. *Holpen* is the past participle of *helpe*, A.-S. *helpan*. *Seeke* is the plural form of the adjective.

15. "The condicioun of eche of hem, and whiche they weren and eek in what array."

Hem may be further noticed as the form which gives the modern colloquial *'em, each of 'em*. *Whiche* retains here the force of its derivation, *wha + lic*, and means "of what sort or character."

16. "He hadde the bord bygonne aboven alle naciouns in Pruce."

The bord bygonne may mean "opened the tournament," in Low German, *boort;* or it may mean, "sat at the head of the table."

Pruce is mentioned because it was customary at this time for knights in England and elsewhere to go to Prussia to assist the Teutonic Knights in their warfare with the heathen inhabitants of Lithuania and Russia.

17. "To counterfeite cheere of court and been estatlich of manere and holden digne of reverence" — this is the good lady's pet ambition.

18. "The reule of St. Beneyt," or Benedict, was the oldest form of monastic discipline in the Western Church, and, as the Monk thought, "somewhat strict."

The regular ecclesiastics were those who had assumed monastic vows, and embraced a life of seclusion and religious contemplation, such as the Monk; while the secular clergy, to which the Parson belonged, preached, wrought, and taught in the world.

19. "As Austin byt." *Byt* is from *bidden*. A.-S. *biddan*, to pray, enjoin, bid. The final *t* is a contraction of *d* of the root and the ending of the third person, — *th*, — in A.-S. *dth = t*.

20. Chaucer contracts *ne* with the forms of *have, will*, and *be*, as *nath, nolde, nis*.

21. "St. Julian in his countré." St. Julian was the patron of hospitality.

22. "Kepte that he wan in pestilence." The humorous explanation is that because "gold in physike is a cordial *therefore*"—excluding the suspicion of avarice—"he lovede gold in special."

23. To the Holy Land, especially to Jerusalem, to Rome, to the shrine of St. James at Compostella in Galicia, and to Cologne, where the bones of the Three Wise Men were preserved.

24. "Him were levere," "ful loth were him." The construction is, in each case, impersonal, and, expressed in full, would be, "it were levere, or pleasanter, to him," "ful disagreeable to him." There has been a confusion of the implication of choice of possession contained in this expression, with the idea of simple possession, resulting in the change to *have* in modern usage.

25. "No wonder is a lewed man to ruste." "A lewed man to ruste" is to be taken as the subject, and the full sense is, "that a lewed man should ruste is no wonderful thing." "A lewed man" is an unlearned, ignorant man, or a layman. In the description of the Maunciple the former meaning is intended; here, the latter.

26. "The Reeve was a colerick man." *Colerick* means having an abundance of "reede colera," or blood, hence disposed to anger.

27. "Ful *lowde* he sang, Com hider, love, to me." The *e* of *lowde* changes an adjective into an adverb, that of *love* shows the vocative case of a noun, originally an adjective, while the absence of *e* from *com* indicates the singular of the imperative.

28. "Him thoughte he rood al of the newe get." *Thoughte* is the preterite of the impersonal verb *thinke*, to seem, "it seemed to him." *Like* is also used impersonally, while the expressions, "him were levere," "were loth," are common. *Wo* is used similarly, though there is frequently confusion, and such expressions as "I am wo" occur. *Lust, mette, game, smerte,* are more or less frequent. * A large number of impersonal verbs in a language indicates an early stage of development, showing that the people who use it had not yet developed the ability or formed the habit of referring effects back to themselves as personal causes.

29. "A *chaunterie* for soules." An endowment for the payment of priests to sing mass for the soul of the founder. The connection shows the author's opinion of the establishment of St. Paul's.

30. "From Gootland to the cape of Fynystere"— "from Jutland to Cape Finistere," on the coast of Spain.

31. "Telle he moste his tale." *Moste* was in Chaucer's time the preterite of *mote*, whose present was — first and third *mot*, second *most*, plural *moten* or *mote*. It meant sometimes, as in this case, *must*, but the more frequent meaning was *may*. Gradually, the idea of obligation or necessity came to be the usual one, giving our English *must*. This comes from the preterite, which early acquired a present sense, the Chaucerian present, itself at first a preterite, dropping out of use except in a few set forms.

32. "Good mester." *Mester* means trade, profession, comes from the Lat. *ministerium*, through the Fr. *métier*. *Lymitour* was a begging friar assigned to a certain limit or region of country. *Forward* = compact, A.-S. *forwcard*. *Solas* = comfort, pleasure, a Romance word. *Vileinye* means ungentlemanly speech or conduct, such as might be expected of a *vilein*, or serf of the manor, villa. Already an evil moral sense was beginning to be imposed upon the word, though it did not have then the idea of simple wickedness belonging to it in modern usage. *Vernicle*, a miniature copy of the head of Christ, which was said to have been miraculously imprinted on a handkerchief of St. Veronica, preserved at St. Peter's. Pilgrims usually brought back such tokens.

33. "Cometh ner." *Cometh* is the imperative plural, often used through respect in addressing a single person. *Ner* is comparative of *neigh*, not yet used as a positive, as it came to be in later stages of the language. "God you speede." The verb has a causative force and is in the subjunctive; *you* is accusative plural — in full, "May God cause you to prosper." "To schorte with our weie." The position of *with* suggests its usual prepositional force, but it is properly an instrumental adverb, qualifying the expression "to schorte oure weie," and the true sense is more clearly expressed by our modern idiom which would have it "*to shorten our way with.*" "At oure alther cost." *Oure* is here, not a pronominal adjective agreeing with *cost*, but the genitive plural of the first personal pronoun, with *alther* agreeing — "cost *of us* all." "Herkneth if you leste." *Herkneth* is again the imperative plural, and *leste* is the present of the impersonal verb *leste* or *luste*, to be pleasing; *you* is dative plural.

VI.

34. "King Capaneus that starf at Thebes." *Starf* is the preterite of *sterve*, which meant to perish by other means as well as hunger. Participle *i-storven* or *i-storve*.

35. "Him thoughte that his herte wolde brek*e*."

The *es* of *thoughte* and *wolde* are the ordinary endings of the first and third persons of the past of weak verbs; the *e* of *herte* descends from Anglo-Saxon, where the *e* of *herte* serves to distinguish it from *heort*, our modern *hart*, and the *e* of *breke* represents the *a* of the Anglo-Saxon infinite termination *an*.

36. "At the sonne upriste."

Upriste, dative case of a verbal noun from *rise*, A.-S. *riesan*. *Sonne* retains the declension of the weák feminine noun, which had the genitive originally in *an*, subsequently *en*, and later, as here, in *e*.

37. "I nam but deed." "There nis no more to say." Two negatives in Chaucer do not make an affirmative; two, three, or even four, may be found in the same sentence, only emphasizing the negation. *Ne* coalesces with the following word whenever possible. *Ne . . . but* has very nearly the sense of the Fr. *ne . . . que;* only, no more, or no better, than.

38. "Palamon gan knitte his browes."

Chaucer uses *gan* in much the same way that *did* would now be used, and he employs the past tense oftener than the present. He regularly uses *gan* for the singular, and *gonne*, *-en*, or *gunne*, *-en*, for the plural preterite.

39. Arcite first attempts to clear himself of the trespasser's guilt by proving a difference of kind between the affection of Palamon and his own. "Yours," he says, "is

affection of holiness, you do not know whether she is woman or goddess; whereas mine is love to a creature." The broken promises of fidelity and friendly assistance he excuses by quoting the "the olde clerkes sawe" to the effect that, no matter who the law-giver is, a lover can be expected to obey no behests but those of his affection. This defence he strongly urges, declaring that for himself he wills no other than to love Emily.

40.* "Let him be war; his nekke lith to wedde."

War is here an adjective, A.-S. *waer*, cautious, prudent. *Lith to wedde* = stands for surety. *Wedde* means a pledge, and is the dative of purpose, destined position, office, etc., as in "to lady" and "to wife"; *cf*. A.-S. "settan to abbode." In the Modern English *wed, wedding*, the idea is limited to a particular kind of pledge, the assumption of particular vows.

41. A certain division of the brain, lying in the front part of the head, where fantastic visions and imaginings were supposed to originate.

42. "Three *yeer* in this wise his lyf he hadde."

Yeer, like *folk, good, hors, thing*, and a few other nouns of the neuter gender in Anglo-Saxon retained the unchanged plural which had originally belonged to them, as some of them do still in Modern English.

43. "Needes coste he moste himselven hyde."

Needes cost = *needes coste* = by the force of necessity. Adverbial expressions similar in form and meaning are found in other Teutonic languages.

44. I do not recall any special reason. I believe it is stated that Theseus loved the sport and hunted nearly every day, and this particular day was fine and clear.

45.* "And *it* am *I* that loveth so hoote Emilye."

The Anglo-Saxon construction was "*ic eom hit*"; the Modern English, "*it is I.*" Chaucer's form represents the transition, the pronouns having exchanged places, but the verb still agreeing with the pronoun of the first person, as in Anglo-Saxon.

46. Theseus recognizes that such exaggerated passion is not unprecedented, but he is inclined to have little patience with it, and his first impulse is to deal harshly with the combatants, from which course he is dissuaded by the entreaties of the ladies.

47. "Frely withoute raunsoun or daunger." Without the ransom for which prisoners of war were ordinarily released, and without the conditions which made Arcite's return dangerous. *Danger* means by derivation not only "peril," but "penalty" and "jurisdiction," coming from the Low Latin *damnum*, which means both.

48. It was a circular space, a mile in circumference, enclosed with a wall of stone and a ditch. Within, seats were arranged as in an amphitheatre, so that no one prevented another from seeing. Toward the east was a gate, with the temple of Venus above; to the north, another, under the temple of Diana; and still another in the west, under the temple of Mars.

49. "Wisdom ne richesse, beaute ne sleighte, strengthe ne hardynesse, ne may with Venus holde champartye." King Solomon, Crœsus, Medea, Hercules.

50. Lygurge, the greete king of Thrace," is described as "like a griffon" in countenance, with his black eyes and shaggy brows. On his smooth black locks he wears a crown of gold, ton-great, and he sits high on a golden chariot, drawn by white bulls. With him comes a train of hunting-dogs with jewelled collars.

51. "Emetreus" wears a suit of cloth of gold, inlaid with pearls and rubies, his eyes are "bright citrine," his nose "high," his hair yellow, and his looking like a fierce lion. He rides "a steede bay."

52. "Namely oon that with a spere was thirled his brest boon." *That ... his = whose*, so *that ... he = who*, and *that ... him = whom*. *Thirled*, from *thirle*, means pierce, thrill, occurs in the compound *nose-thirles*.

53. Seven years intervene between the capture of the princes and the escape of Palamon, thence to the tournament is one year, and from that to the end of the tale, I think, three years; so the whole period is about ten years.

VII.

54. The poor widow lives in a cottage whose compartments consist of a "hall" in which Chanticleer and his wives, the swine, and other humbler members of the household have their abode, and a "sooty bower" occupied by the widow herself and her two daughters. Her board is spread in brown and white; brown bread, singed bacon, and sometimes an egg or two constitute her simple fare. She has no need of costly wines and condiments, for she knows nothing of repletion and luxurious maladies. All her life is ordered in simplicity and is peaceful with "hertes suffisaunce."

55. "My lief is faren on londe." This was no doubt the refrain of a popular song, and the meaning is, "My love is gone away."

56. "Hardy, wise, discreet, not a coward, not a boaster."

57. "Catoun *which that* was so wis a man." *Which* was originally an interrogative, and it had not in Chaucer's time

quite lost the interrogative force. Accordingly, *that* was affixed to show that it was used as a relative. But Chaucer also used *which* alone as a relative.

58. "Humor of melancolie." *Humor* is state of body, disease. *Melancolie* was so named from the supposed material cause, black fumes, the result of excess in eating and drinking, rising to the head and troubling the brain.

59. "Me mette I was in such meschief." *Mette* is an impersonal verb, to seem in a dream, and is properly accompanied by the dative case, *me*. *Meschief = trouble, misfortune*, is from the Fr. *meschef*, — *mes* from *minus*, and *chef* from *caput*.

60. "This night I *shall* be mordred." *Shall* in Chaucer retained more or less of the idea of obligation or necessity which belonged to it distinctly in the older forms of the language. The sense is here, "I am destined to be."

61. "The hostiler so sore engyned." The hostler was then the master of the *hostelrie*, or inn, not, as now, the servant who attends to the horses. *Sore* is an adverb, though the final *e*, as it belongs to the adjective as well, cannot be taken as determining. *Engyned* is "put to torture," French, *engin*.

62. "He lith gaping upright" means "he lies on his back with his mouth gaping open."

63. "To that oon man fel." *That oon* is a survival of the somewhat extensive use in Old English of *that* as the definite article. *Fel* is the preterite of the impersonal verb *falle*, to happen.

64. "Forslowthe wilfully thy tyde." *Forslowthe* is to lose through sloth, *for* having as sometimes in Anglo-Saxon, when used as a prefix, the idea of loss or destruction. There seems to be no valid reason for not regarding the prefix as iden-

tical with the preposition. The primary sense of the latter is *before*, and may mean in a hostile as well as in a favorable attitude.

65. "*Bad* him *for to kepe him* wel *for* treason." *Bad* is the preterite of *bidden*, A.-S. *biddan*, to pray, to bid, or enjoin. *For to kepe* is gerundial infinitive in form, but the idea of purpose usually belonging to it is not very distinctively conveyed, *for* being at this time often added to strengthen the infinitive sign *to* when the use of the infinitive was only complementary. *Him* is reflexive without *self*, as is frequently found. *For* = *for fear of*, and is a development of the second signification of *for*, before.

66. "The brighte sonne in the signe of Taurus hadde i-ronne twenty degrees and oon and somewhat more."

We are told in this connection that thirty and two days had passed "since March began," but Mr. Skeat observes that the words "since March began" are parenthetical, and concludes that they may be disregarded, and that we are really to understand that thirty-two days had passed since March, which would bring us to the second of May. Referring to the "Astrolabe," he finds that the sun would at that time be, at the point indicated, about twenty-one degrees in Taurus. The third of May seems, then, to be the day indicated.

67. "Undern." This word seems to have been used with several meanings. It probably meant first the second quarter of the day, from 9 A.M. till noon. It was then applied sometimes to the beginning, sometimes to the end of that period. Dr. Morris says it means here the time of the mid-day meal.

68. "Goddes worthy forwetyng." *Forwetyng* = *foreknowledge*. *For* used in its simple primary sense of "before," *wetyng*, from *witan*, to know.

69. "I were worse than a feend." The *e* of *worse* represents the *a* of the A.-S. *wyrsa*, and was, I suppose, retained because *worse* did not, as did most comparatives in Old English, resume the connective vowel before the comparative suffix. *Worse*, like *less*, did not follow the rule of changing the *s* of this suffix to *e*.

70. "Daun Russel." *Daun* is from the Lat. *dominus*, and was a title widely applied in the Middle Ages, though belonging particularly to monks. *Russel* is the name given on account of the reddish brown or russet color of the fox.

71. "As saith us *Eneydos*." Chaucer uses *Eneydos* like the name of an author, but it can hardly be inferred from this that he was not acquainted with *The Æneid*. It is probably a mere carelessness of expression.

72. "Certes he Jakke Straw and his meyné." This is an allusion to the Peasant Rebellion, 1381. *Meyné* means train, retinue, household, domestics, from O. Fr. *mesne*, or *maisgneé*, Low Lat. *maisnada*, Lat. *minores natu*.

73. Towards the close of the piece a parallel is drawn between the wily fox and the flatterers and liars that impose upon the vanity of lords and princes, and a warning is held up in Chanticleer's misfortune, but I suppose what may be called the concluding moral is the sage reflection of Chanticleer, that he who winks when he should see, deserves never to prosper, extended by Daun Russel, under the smart of his loss, to those that "jangle when they should hold their peace."

VIII.

74.   A.-S.   SINGULAR.   Chaucer.
        Nom. he   *Nom.* he
        Gen. his   .   *Gen.* his

Dat. him   *Dat.* him
Acc. hine   *Acc.* him

PLURAL.

Nom. hie   *Nom.* they
Gen. hiera   *Gen.* here
Dat. him   *Dat.* hem
Acc. hie   *Acc.* hem

75.* Modern English.

SINGULAR.   PLURAL.

Nom. he   *Nom.* they
Poss. his   *Poss.* their, theirs
Obj. him   *Obj.* them

The two main differences between the Anglo-Saxon and Chaucerian pronoun are, first, the disuse of the accusative *hine*, and the substitution for it of the dative *him;* and second, the use of *they* instead of *hie* in the nominative plural. In O. E. *hie* had become *he*, the same as the nominative singular, and as the feminine pronoun. To establish a distinction in form, a nominative plural derived from the demonstrative pronoun came into use, and this Chaucer adopted. He does not, however, make use of the oblique forms *their* and *them*, which afterwards became the established ones. *Their* gave rise to *theirs*, after the analogy of *oures* and *youres*, forms of the Northern dialect, and these forms in *s* were limited to use in predicate relations.

IX.*

76.* In matters of religion, Chaucer seems to have been a person of easy faith, accepting his creed with very little questioning, pretty much as he found it formulated for him. With the vexed questions of "Fate, Foreknowledge, and Freewill," — questions much and eagerly discussed in those days — he troubles himself but little. When he touches upon them, as he frequently does, he has an air of being interested, slightly curious, as to the probable answer, without feeling an absorbing interest, much less a personal stake in the matter; he lays the problem before us, as it were, with a quizzical, "Well, what do you make of it?" When it comes to the direct statement of his own views, he turns away, "he cannot bulte it to the bren," "he wol not han to do with such matere." He is ready to accord admiration and reverence to whatever is beautiful or healthful in the established faith; he yields it a poet's appreciation and a right-minded man's support. Just as he does not perplex himself with unnecessary doubts and questionings, so he does not strain his faith to believe in what is exaggerated and unreasonable. His piety is as far from superstition as from fevered dubiety.

It was not possible for so clear-sighted an observer to fail to observe the corruption of the Church, patent to all eyes, or for a man so candid and upright to refrain from expressing his disapprobation. The weapon he employs is satire, keen, delicate, unsparing. Doubtless his ridicule lacks the stinging force of Langlande's bitter invective, for it was not like Langlande's, the out-glow of a white-heat of moral indignation; it meant only to prick, not to pierce. But in the rank of society to which Chaucer belonged, and which he most strongly influenced, Langlande's unveiled denunciations would have been utterly ineffective; the most destructive attack that could be made on any institution was just the gay mockery which Chaucer lavished on the worldly and sinful ecclesiastics. Langlande's convictions made him a thorough-going reformer; Chaucer's have not the same apparent energy, but the difference of temperament and of social environment must be taken into account. In his own way Chaucer was just as earnest, and in his own sphere of influence achieved as much.

77.* Full as much of the satire of the Middle Ages was levelled at the foibles of women as at the corruptions of the Church, and Chaucer fell in with the current literary fashion with a readiness increased no doubt by the infelicity of his own personal experience of marriage. He has an intimate knowledge of the ways of women, and his portrait of the Prioress is marked by sympathy as delicate as its humor. He does not spare her affectations, but he casts no reflection upon her "conscience and tender herte." Nor should it be overlooked that two of the most considerable of the Canterbury Tales, the "Clerkes," and the "Man of Lawes," celebrate instances of heroic womanly fidelity, and at the same time contain high tributes to the sex, and an exalted ideal of marriage. Still the mass of evidence looks the other way. *The Wife of Bath's Tale* is sufficient to offset the two mentioned, and throughout the series accusations of inconstancy, changing with fortune, querulousness, and the like, are brought against the sex, pilgrim after pilgrim making his jest or gibe. On the whole, though Chaucer's estimate of women was far more exalted than was ordinary in the Middle Ages, he did not rid himself of convention and prejudice, and accordingly failed to be entirely consistent or perfectly just.

78.* Chaucer's attitude was that of an observer and student of mankind. He shared in active life, we know, and was one of the real workers in the world. But he was not a partisan. His ability to see both sides of a question was too great, and his sympathies too wide and generous; it was mankind and human life that he loved, not a party or section of either. This is what we should gather from his writings, and there is nothing in the known facts of his life to contradict it. His adherence to the interests of John of Gaunt was not such as to cost him more than a temporary loss of office in a violent political reaction; otherwise the course of his life was but slightly ruffled by political changes, and this could hardly have been the case had he been an active politician. There is still less reason for believing that he took sides in the religious controversies of his time. We have seen what was his attitude towards the Church, and he was no more a Wyclifite or Lollard than he was a Churchman. Likewise, in the social agitations of the time, though his personal and official connections were with the aristocratic party, he had a generous appreciation, frankly and courageously expressed, of the nobleness of soul so often to be found among the lowly. The description of the Plowman is a conclusive proof of Chaucer's broad-minded liberality, fitly confirmed by that other description of the real gentleman, as the man gentle in heart and pure and brave in life, whether his lineage be high or no. In short, Chaucer, in relation to public affairs, may be not inaccurately described as a thoroughly independent conservative. In temper and in sympathies he belonged not to an age, but to all time.

79.* In all stages of English literature, Chaucer's rank has been undisputed as "the father of English poetry," "the Homer of his country," and "the well of English undefiled." Before him there were no great literary models in the native speech. He represented the national spirit of England rising into independence of foreign influences and foreign models, and into a just consciousness of its own superb capabilities. Perhaps his first importance is due to what he did for the language in raising it from a confusion of rude dialects to be the noble vehicle of expression which, to use the words of Dunbar, "surpasses every terrestrial tongue as midnight is surpassed by a May morning." This he was enabled to do by reason of his just and true sense of the values of words, their affinities and power of combination. In the manipulation of words, Chaucer is a consummate artist.

In the plot and conduct of his narrative his art is not, perhaps, so fine — is a little too palpable and conscious. It was not that he did not possess the artistic perception, for it was that which guided him to the choice of Romance forms; that which impelled him to modify in some way all that he borrowed; that which, in the frequent happy arrangement of incident and fitting of speech to speaker, gives such charm and vigor to his narrative. That it did not reach its utmost perfection was not a defect of natural ability, but of training, consequent upon his having worked without the assistance of a literary past and its traditions.

In the works of Chaucer we are able to discern the beginning of much that we account most valuable in the later literature. He was to some extent conventional, especially in his satire against the Church, women, and marriage, and perhaps in the bent of his description. But the first was far more than a fashion, animated as it was by a serious purpose or sharpened by personal experience, while conventionality never renders artificial his genuine love of nature. He alludes again and again, as a matter of course, to the beauties of May, but his allusions have always an air of sincerity and freshness, his descriptions of nature are marked by the minuteness of a careful and loving student, and he gave a new and deeper meaning to the fashionable adoration of the daisy. In fact, it is not too much to say that the power of fascinating and vivid natural description which constitutes so valuable an element in English literature has its real beginning in him.

Mr. Ward also points out — and this is to be noticed in connection with his opinion of women — that Chaucer is the first English love poet, though it must be allowed that here he was largely — perhaps more largely than in any other respect — influenced by the French.

He is, moreover, our first great humorist. It is Chaucer's quaint, rich humor quite as much as anything else that makes *The Canterbury Tales* such delightful reading at the present day — a fact that speaks well for the quality of the humor itself. It is rare fun that will keep five hundred years.

But Chaucer's greatest power is that of portraying character. He is the first English writer to set before us characters that have a distinct individuality, characters "whose past we can calculate and whose future we can foretell." It is the first appearance in a new field, and a field well suited to it, of "the English positive common sense and ability for seeing the inside of things." It is the beginning of the English drama and the English novel of character, the twin glories of our literature.

It has been questioned whether Chaucer has really any dramatic ability, whether he is not, after all, only an inimitable story-teller. This is the view maintained by the Rev. Stopford Brooke. It is to be questioned, on the other hand, whether the power to tell a story extremely well — which no one denies to Chaucer — does not of itself imply dramatic power in some degree. It includes, certainly, the power to individualize characters, to conceive strong situations, and to present both in fitting words. The dramatist goes further and exercises his art in arranging the plot so as to develop the characters. This Chaucer does distinctly in *The Canterbury Tales*, and it is hard to believe that, had the drama been ready as a literary form, he would not have left incontestable evidence of his possession of a gift which is, in some aspects, the highest form of genius.

I have not been assisted in this examination.

VIRGINIA STRICKLER.

"*Taketh the fruyt, and let the chaf be stille.*"

EXAMINATION ON SOME ASPECTS

OF

WOMANHOOD

IN

CHAUCER, SHAKESPEARE, AND TENNYSON.

MISS BESSIE PORTER MILLER,
OF MARYLAND.

HOLLINS INSTITUTE, VA.

JUNE, 1887.

NOTE.

THIS examination or discussion was written under the same general conditions as the other examinations in this volume. While revising the first draught of the examination Miss Miller was allowed access to the texts of Chaucer, Shakespeare, and Tennyson for purposes of quotation and verification, and, also, I reminded her of Chaucer's *Moder of God*, which she had overlooked in the discussion of Motherhood, and recalled to her the quotation from Lessing, familiar to her for two sessions, with which the paper ends; other corrections were unimportant matters of detail affecting materially neither the form nor the substance of her work.

The aim and scope of this paper seems perhaps too ambitious; but it should not be criticised otherwise than as what it purports to be and is — school work, since it represents, in part, some of the work of the senior composition class during the two last sessions, in part, the results of a session of post-graduate reading and study.

I have availed myself of the delay of this edition in passing through the press to insert this examination in order that my fellow-teachers — and my fellow-students, their pupils — may get from it the suggestion, if it has not already come to them otherwise, of the great pleasure and profit to both teacher and pupil there is to be found in this kind of comparative reading and study, in this following reverently the development of the spirit of our race in and through the utterances of her greatest children.

WM. TAYLOR THOM.

HOLLINS INSTITUTE, VA.,
July, 1887.

SOME ASPECTS OF WOMANHOOD IN CHAUCER, SHAKESPEARE, AND TENNYSON.[1]

JUNE, 1887.

I. MOTHERHOOD. —
   Its beautiful, ennobling, or opposite aspects.

II. WIFEHOOD. —
   1. The relative rank of husband and wife in the three poets, as to fact of civilization and as to ideal of married life.
   2. As cause and means of development of types of women, and the resulting effects on lives of husband and wife: —
      a. Mistaken Wifehood.
      b. Disloyal Wifehood.
      c. True Wifehood.

III. DAUGHTERS. —
   In relation to mothers; to fathers. Childhood in Tennyson as compared with Chaucer and Shakespeare.

IV. As to development of character with regard to general and personal truth in and through the relations as women.

I.

In the discussion of Motherhood as given by our three great poets, Chaucer, Shakespeare, and Tennyson, perhaps the easier method will be to proceed from particular illustrations to general conclusions rather than from general

[1] Gilman's *Chaucer;* *Globe Shakespeare;* Tennyson's *Works.*

conclusions to individual illustrations. And first among the mothers of Chaucer's poems comes, of course, the world-renowned figure of the "patient Griselda." Though she appears chiefly as an instance of surpassing wifely obedience and loyalty, there are in the *Clerkes Tale* a few verses setting forth most touchingly the tender affection she felt for her children. Few as the words are, with their absence the sanctity which now hangs about her would be lost; for without the deep, firmly controlled distress which for a moment gains the mastery over her, though it is still subservient to her loyalty to the Marquis, even that loyalty must have lost its charm and strength of example. In each instance when she is commanded to render up her child, — to execution, as she thinks, — her beseeching words to the executioner and her pathetic words of farewell to her child reveal a mother-love so deep and strong that only an equally strong love and an additional and powerful sense of duty could have prompted her to any action in even seeming contradiction to the dictates of the maternal affection. After that display of emotion, it is impossible to think that her subsequent silence covers indifference — the suffering is there, though so heroically concealed. Convincing proof of this is given in the reunion scene, when, her unmerited trials at last over, she is restored to her place of honor as wife of the Marquis Walter, and her children are again placed at her side. Twice she swoons from excess of joy; and her words, few and broken, betray as much happiness over the recovery of her son and daughter as of her husband. Nor does it seem to me that her affection as a mother was without a very considerable influence in the prevention of the exhibition of any feeling of resentment as a wife when she found that all the trials and sufferings of years had been purposely brought upon her by Walter as a cruelly useless test of her fidelity. Again, in Constance, of the *Man of Lawes Tale*, Chaucer has given us a very beautiful picture of motherly devotion, though, as in the case of Griselda, it appears only as a hasty and subordinate sketch rather than as a fully developed theme. When, owing to the wicked schemings of her mother-in-law, Donegilde, preparations are being made to launch her and her little child upon the ocean alone, her sorrowful words come straight from her heart, as she beseeches that the child at least be not sent forth to perish upon the waters. But her prayers are of no avail; and after calling down blessings upon the infant head, she yields herself and it up to the Unseen Power which had already guided her through one solitary voyage, and which again brings her to a haven of rest. Through the years that she remains at Rome, believing herself an abandoned wife, her love for her son keeps her affections fresh and pliable; and it is through the child that recognition, explanation, and reconciliation at least ensue. Another very beautiful and more distinctive picture of motherhood is given in the *Prioresses Tale*, in the mother of little Hugh. Again it is the attitude of deep distress that is depicted. Her grief and alarm at the disappearance of her son, her distracted search for him, her acute anguish after the discovery of his body, her pitiful lamenting over the child when prepared for burial, — all are feelingly portrayed by the gentle old poet who could mourn with those that mourned as well as smile with the smiling and laugh at all mankind.

These three, I think, comprise Chaucer's pictures of worthy and attractive phases of motherhood, while those of the opposite nature are even fewer and more in outline. Of the old "sowdanesse," mother of the sultan whom

Constance was expected to marry, we do not know whether ambition had destroyed motherly love, or whether she was guided by perverted religious zeal, in murdering her son and banishing Constance. In the case of Donegilde, mother of King Alla, who appears in the same tale, the same remarks will hold good; but in either instance the imperfect outlines furnished us give little room for excuse-making.

Rather aside from the ordinary delineations of motherhood is Chaucer's representation of the Virgin Mary, — the "Moder of God." The deep significance attached to the ideal presented in the Virgin is characteristic not only of Chaucer's time, but of the whole of the Middle Ages. A few lines from the "Invocation" at the beginning of the *Seconde Nonnes Tale* present the picture as it was universally conceived (ll. 16,436–16,456 [1]) : —

> "Thow mayde and mooder, doghter of thy sone,
>   Thow welle of mercy, synful soules cure,
>   In whom that God for bountee chees to wone,
>   Thow humble, and heigh over every creature,
>   Thow nobledest so ferforth oure nature,
>   That no desdeyn the Makere hadde of kynde,
>   His sone in blood and flessh to clothe and wynde.
>
>   * * * * *
>
>   Assembled is in thee magnificence,
>   With mercy, goodnesse, and with swich pitee,
>   That thow that art the sonne of excellence
>   Not oonly helpest hem that preyen thee,
>   But often tyme, of thy benygnytee,
>   Ful frely, er that men thyn help beseche
>   Thow goost biforn and art hir lyves leche."

It was to the Mother of Christ, and not to Christ, nor to God, that prayers were addressed, and always with firm

---
[1] Gilman's *Chaucer*.

faith in the intercessory power of her meek and long-suffering womanhood; and the powerful influence which the popular conception of her had upon the existing modes of thought is distinctly traceable in the gentle resignation with which Griselda, for instance, yields up her children even to death upon the demand of what seems to her a higher authority than her own. This influence is even more plainly seen in the case of Constance, who says in her prayer to the Virgin just before she and her child leave the shore of England (ll. 5270–5276 [1]) : —

> "Thow sawe thy child yslayn bifore thyne eyen,
> And yet now lyveth my litel child, *parfay!*
> Now, lady bright, to whom alle woful cryen, —
> Thow glorie of wommanhede, thow faire May,
> Thow haven of refut, brighte sterre of day, —
> Rewe on my child, that of thy gentillesse
> Ruest on every reweful in distresse."

As we glance over the list of mothers that appear in Shakespeare's plays, the first one that attracts our attention is another Constance, — the Constance of *King John*. Indeed, I do not know of any other more immediately striking figure among all of Shakespeare's women, unless it be Margaret of Anjou as she is depicted in *Richard III.;* and in both instances the terrible effect seems to be largely due to the peculiar horror of curses from a woman's lips. Many others are equally intense in their emotions, and a few are even more so; but none have more facility or vividness of expression than Constance. She is the impersonation of feminine rage and vehemence, roused by injustice done to her offspring. I do not look upon her as influenced by ambition for herself, but only for her son; for had

---
[1] Gilman's *Chaucer*.

it been so, her impulse-governed nature could not have refrained, either in her conversation with Elinor or in her lamentations after the loss of her son, from giving some clearer evidence of the existence of distinctly selfish motives. Whether she raves, storms, curses, or entreats, she is the same woman, finding in her son the centre of all her hopes and the abiding-place of all her love.

In striking contrast to Constance, and yet equally impressive in her own majestic way, is Hermione as a mother. She is as self-contained as Constance is fluent; but though the effect she produces is not as instantaneous, I am inclined to think that it is in the end as powerful. The mother-love is the sustaining force within her, and it is that which moves her to defend herself against the unjust charges of Leontes. After the loss of his confidence and esteem, she has for herself little desire to live; but she defends her honor for the sake of those whom her dishonor would plunge into life-long shame.

> "For life, I prize it
> As I weigh grief, which I would spare: for honor,
> 'Tis a derivative from me to mine,
> And only this I stand for."

It is the news of the death of Mamillius which, coming in the midst of her trial, administers the final stroke; and she is carried off, to remain for sixteen years a voluntary exile from her "life and use and name and fame." And when, in the final scene, she descends from her pedestal into the midst of the awe-struck group before her, her first words are for Perdita, and not for Leontes: —

> —— "You gods, look down
> And from your sacred vials pour your graces
> Upon my daughter's head";

and for a woman of Hermione's disposition, it would seem probable that, though her forgiveness of Leontes might be thorough and sincere, the chief part of her happiness for the future will be found in living in and for her child.

The chief attraction of Queen Gertrude is her deep affection for Hamlet. It would seem that she had, during his lifetime, been sincerely attached to the elder Hamlet; but her lack of depth and her confirmed habit of self-indulgence make it easy for her, only a few weeks after her husband's death, to marry his brother, a man bad at heart, whose chief attraction for her was probably the power she had over him. But through all her errors, her love for Hamlet remains unchanged; and it is through his words that she is brought to realize how far she has strayed from the right path. Her love as a mother was her salvation, though even its strength could not atone wholly for her weaknesses and misdoings; and her death came finally in the guise of defeat, as far as the true aim and scope of her life was concerned.

The affection which the queen in *Cymbeline* bears for Cloten is not only her chief, but her sole attraction. In connection with every one else in the play, she is ruled by scarcely concealed malignity; but that her love for her son has prevented the complete deadening of her moral nature is proved by the confession she makes upon her death-bed, — an honest endeavor on her part to correct, even so late in life, the ill effects of her many errors and her attempted crimes.

So in Margaret of Anjou the one redeeming trait is her love for the young prince. Her life as a wife is a crime; as a queen, it is a failure; as a mother, it is at best a pitiful attempt. Except for this one ennobling element, her emotions and passions are all of the baser sort, — ambition, arrogant pride of the rankest kind, dishonorable love, wanton cruelty, and ungoverned rage. With the loss of her son, all restraining influence is gone; and she sinks into the terrible plight in which we see her in *Richard III.*, all the force and vehemence of her nature being expended in curses, the blackest and deepest that she can conjure up, upon the enemies who had murdered her son; and the development is all the more awful from its very appropriateness.

Volumnia is strong in many ways, and yet it is her devotion as a mother which constitutes the real strength of the character. Her life is wholly bound up in Coriolanus; and his brave deeds and high renown are her glory. But though she has courage to propose and push forward the most daring schemes for the advancement of her son, the nobility that there is in her love cannot submit to any violence on his part toward his country; and after she has forced him into a false position and has unintentionally been instrumental in causing his exile, her final act in the play is one of self-abasement, where she pleads with Coriolanus to spare his native city. Nor is her intercession in vain. He, recognizing the depth and sincerity of her love, even though it had not always been happy in its modes of action, also recognizes the correctness of the motive in this instance, and yields; though he himself declares —

> —— "all the swords
> In Italy, and her confederate arms,
> Could not have made this peace."

All the beautiful elements of the mother-love — its strength, tenderness, unselfishness, and devotion — are revealed in the love of Cordelia for her father, poor old King Lear, that most sublimely pitiful of all Shakespeare's creations. Her tender, watchful care and her real self-sacrifice, her deep sympathy and devotion in things both great and small, are well-known aspects of her whose words are so few and whose influence is so deep and far-reaching.

The only ones of Shakespeare's women that I can think of who were unfaithful to their instincts as mothers are Lady Macbeth and Tamora; and of these Lady Macbeth was not unfaithful in deed, though her open declaration that she could be so is scarcely less terrible than the reality. With all earnestness she vows to her husband that, though she knows all the tenderness of a mother for her child, yet could she dash its brains out had she so sworn as he had; and that one sentence contains enough of evil to brand her forever. The character of Tamora is throughout so black and revolting as almost to forbid discussion; and the destruction of all feeling as a mother is by no means the least repulsive of her characteristics.

Turning to Tennyson, we find in the *Idyls of the King* but little concerning the direct influence of motherhood. It appears to some extent in *Enid*, where the wife of Yniol rejoices over the betrothal of her daughter, is delighted over the recovery of the dress "all branch'd and flower'd with gold," is wholly mystified and a little provoked at Geraint's request that Enid shall wear instead the dress of faded silk in which he had first seen her, and yet is willing to let her daughter, now about to leave her authority, act as her own judgment dictates. The only other woman in the *Idyls* who appears in the relation of mother is good Queen Bellicent in *Gareth and Lynette*. Two of her sons, Gawain and Modred, have already sought the court of "the blameless King"; and her unwillingness to part with Gareth, the youngest, tallest, and best of the three, is a very beautiful touch of nature. So also is the imposing of the condition upon his going, and her subsequent removal of it long before the appointed time, for the sake of the good it will do him.

Among Tennyson's poems, the mother-influence appears strongly in *The Princess*. The love of her child keeps Psyche unharmed by Lady Blanche's evil power, while Ida, who had no such safeguard, is with much more difficulty reclaimed. One of the things which most turns us against Lady Blanche is her apparent indifference to, and her after scorn of, the lovely little Melissa, whose winning ways and pure soul prove that the mother does not wholly form the character of the child. A striking instance of the maternal capabilities of self-sacrifice is given in *The Victim*, where, upon the demand of the priest that the king's dearest shall be offered to the gods as a means of averting the trials under which they were suffering, at the last moment the queen-mother throws herself upon the knife in order to save the life of her child.

So in *Rizpah*, an infinitely pitiful picture is drawn of the poor old mother, who still believes, after years of raving and suffering, in the innocence of the boy who had been hanged, and who has removed, by painful efforts through many nights of darkness, the bones of her darling from their first resting-place into consecrated soil.

Of a different order from anything else which Tennyson has written is *Despair*, — a poem rightly named; for it is the wail of a soul utterly lost and hopeless with the relinquishment of all the beautiful sustaining belief of humanity in the existence of an unseen, all-wise and all-powerful Ruler who guides all things aright. The story is told by the husband, who was saved from drowning by the minister with whom he talks; but mention is made of the wife and mother, who succeeded in her attempt to perish by the waves, and whose faith in God and man was first shaken by the discovery that her own son had been guilty of crime.

Lady Blanche and Lady Aylmer are the two most conspicuous examples given by Tennyson of the ugly phases of motherhood. Lady Blanche is not only unattractive, but even repellent in every way; while Lady Aylmer is merely a mild, weak imitation of her weak, vain old husband, who rests so securely in his pride of birth that he never dreams of an attachment between Edith and Leolin, and whose inordinate worship of rank makes him ruin his own greatest hope through what is really the murder of his child. The lesson of *Aylmer's Field*, — that of iniquity on the part of parents who marry off their children through worldly consideration without regard to their real happiness, — is the same which receives such emphasis in *Maud*, and again in *Locksley Hall* and *Locksley Hall Sixty Years After*. In *Maud*, however, the dead mother of the girl seems to have wished to provide for her daughter's true welfare; and it is the father and brother who endeavor to dispose of her according to their own selfish interests. The young man in *Locksley Hall* is bitter in his protest against the parental affection which bars the child behind gates only to be opened by golden keys; and even sixty years after his indignation has not ceased.

In many instances, with all three of the poets, the mother-influence is conspicuous through its absence. Griselda has no mother; neither have Ophelia, Desdemona, Portia, Helena, Isabella, Rosalind, Celia, Beatrice, Hero, Cordelia, — in fact, the vast majority of Shakespeare's young women; neither have Guinevere, Elaine, Lynette, Ettarre, the Princess Ida. In most cases, the resultant defects in character are plainly discernible; but in very few are they serious enough to destroy the real beauty and dignity of the creation. Thus, a mother might have infused more of self-control and self-reliance into Ophelia and Desdemona, more of gentleness into Beatrice, more of truth into Guinevere, more of humility into Ida and Lynette; but despite these deficiencies and many more, there is yet an abundance of good to establish beyond a doubt the intrinsic worth of young womanhood, even when that most beneficent of all influences, the mother-love, is absent. In some few instances, as Miranda, Marina, Hero, and Portia also, as far as we can tell from the few words she utters concerning him, the father seems to have supplied in large measure the place of a mother, and generally with fair success,— one of the many transformations that true and unselfish love may undergo.

Chaucer's pictures of worthy motherhood are all gentle, tender, and submissive,— a common trait of all his pictures of attractive womanhood, with the possible exception of Meliboeus' wife, Prudence, who has the right on her side and finally persuades her husband of the fact. There is both strength and beauty in his delineations, but the coloring is always soft and subdued. We find nowhere the intensity and vividness of Shakespeare's Constance, nor the unyielding power of a Volumnia, nor yet the calm, mild force of a Hermione; but though neither Chaucer nor Tennyson may equal Shakespeare in this as in many other particulars, it is yet no reflection upon the power of either. In the action of Griselda as a mother, the influence of feudalism is easily apparent; while Tennyson shows forth many of the same gentle and pitiful phases of motherhood in the light of the now existing social system. But the great Shakespeare has given us the mother-love in all its most impressive phases; and in no instance, I think, has he given it untruthfully.

II.

1. In the progress of civilization in the last five centuries, changes have of course been made both in the real and ideal system of relations existing between husband and wife. In the time of Chaucer, the influence of feudalism was still supreme, as appears in many of his poems. We find, in almost every case, that the authority of the husband and the dutiful submission of the wife is due almost if not quite as much to the fact that he is a feudal lord as that she is his lawful wife. Especially is this felt to be the case in Griselda, who, even if it had not been that she loved the Marquis as she did, would yet have been forced by the social habit of the day to render up obedience in all things. But Chaucer takes away the hard glare of fact and infuses much of his own high ideal of the proper state of things by representing Griselda's action as due, not to any compelling external custom, but to a loyalty and sense of duty which have their origin in love and gratitude alone. But though he has given us in Griselda nearly his ideal of a wife, he has no praise to bestow upon Walter as a husband. The mutual duties of husband and wife are fulfilled probably more nearly according to his ideal in the story of Dorigen and Arveragus, where the loyalty of both is tested without the contrivance of either, and where each proves true. Without the *L'envoy de Chaucer* we might not suspect Chaucer of insincerity in his delineation of Griselda's character, but with it, we may fairly judge that he deemed it much more an ideal thing than a thing attainable, however desirable; while in the story of Dorigen there is nothing to rouse such a suspicion. The character of Dame Prudence is drawn with all gravity; but the conversation which he puts in the mouths of the pilgrims afterwards

makes us doubt whether the old poet regarded a convincing flow of reason and a faculty for managing a whole family connection as a very desirable thing in a wife, even if attainable. Certainly he leaves no room for doubt concerning his disapproval of a further development of the same thing into the noisy loquaciousness and rough bullying of the Wife of Bath. Neither does he leave a doubt in our minds that, in his opinion, loyalty of the one to the other is the first duty between man and wife; that the husband is the proper head and controller of the household; and that there is due to him wifely as well as filial obedience.

In the age of Elizabeth, civilization had progressed so far that there was no existing contemporary ground for the portrayal of a Griselda, even had Shakespeare chosen to try his hand upon one. The feudal spirit, in many of its real and superficial aspects, was still strong in the land; but there is also plainly discernible a strong underlying tendency towards a freer and more independent manner of life. Thus Imogen and Hermione are placed in positions as trying as that of Griselda, and very similar to it; but in neither case is there exibited the unresisting submissiveness which Griselda shows. For the sake of her children, Hermione makes a brave attempt to defend herself; and Imogen, when she finds she is suspected and repudiated by Posthumus, gives vent to eloquent and indignant protest; though each of them loves her husband so devotedly that after the loss of his affection she does not greatly care to live. Griselda aids her lord in the maintenance of his high position; but nowhere in Chaucer is given on the part of the wife that active and independent helpfulness in external affairs which Shakespeare has portrayed in the two Portias and many others of his women. And so, by way of contrast, he shows us in Desdemona and Ophelia the effect of the lack of that independent helpfulness. Shakespeare, in common with Chaucer, places loyalty as the foundation bond between husband and wife; but there is according to his conception much more of mutual dependence than existed in the ideal of the earlier poet, though in his view also the husband is the proper head and ruler of the family.

Our nineteenth century poet, Tennyson, has chosen, in the *Idyls of the King*, to go back to a time previous even to that of Chaucer; but though the relations therein depicted are outwardly those of long ago, the underlying thought and feeling is modern. The general tendency of the *Idyls*, of *The Princess*, and of many of his minor poems, serves to establish clearly Tennyson's ideal of the relations which should exist between husband and wife. In it he too makes of loyalty the foundation; but there is more of correspondence and of equality in difference between the relative ranks of husband and wife than appears even in the great Shakespeare. The effect of civilization is constantly to broaden views, to divide responsibilities, to increase mutual dependence, and at the same time to develop independence; and while the three poets, in drawing the characters and relative ranks of husband and wife, each build upon the same foundation, and in large measure with the same material, there are in detail, and partly in substance, changes due to growth, modification, and development, which speak well not only for the poets but for our race and age.

---

2. *a.* There is no case, I think, in which the development of character as a wife is more distressing than in that of Lady Macbeth. There was no element of disloyalty in the affec-

tion she had for Macbeth; indeed, she regarded him with a love whose intensity is seldom equalled, and it was from this very intensity that its harmfulness arose. Her passion for her husband absorbed every other healthful emotion, — her instincts as a mother, as a friend, and we might almost say, as a human being; until, from being a lovable and commendable emotion, its result is actual spiritual deformity. Ruled by ambition for her husband, she leads him on with an inexorable hand from one crime to another, until there is no longer any escape for him nor any need for her assistance or instigation. Instead of helping, she has ruined him. Her punishment — the loss of her husband's love, for which she had dared all — is as severe as it is unexpected; and it is only after her realization of her failure, her conscious perception of the fact that she has alienated him from her instead of binding him to her, that repentance gains a hold upon her fiercely loving and deeply criminal heart. But even then, through her own instrumentality, her husband has sunk beyond recall. I know of no instance in either Chaucer or Tennyson that can compare with this infinitely pitiful picture of mistaken wifehood. There is a bare interlinear suggestion of what might have been in the case of the Princess Ida; but it is little more than that.

b. In Chaucer's poems, the type of disloyal wifehood, of which the Wife of Bath may be taken as a fair specimen, is uncomfortably well represented, especially in the *Canterbury Tales;* and it is a relief to find little or nothing of the same gross character in either Shakespeare or Tennyson. Of the degrading influence and effect of such a type upon both husband and wife, it is needless to speak. I can think of no instance given by Chaucer of disloyalty on the part of a wife of higher rank.

It seems harsh to put Gertrude down as a disloyal wife, yet I suppose that is where she belongs. During the lifetime of her husband she was faithful to him in deed, if not entirely so in thought; but as soon as his sustaining strength was withdrawn, her weak nature yielded to unworthy suggestions, and her lack of fidelity was none the less a reality and none the less degrading because it was only unfaith to a memory. And so the disloyalty to her first husband, revealed to her by the words of her son, made loyalty to Claudius an impossibility; and thus was added to the lives of each another foothold for Defeat to seize upon.

In addition to all their other faults, Goneril and Regan are disloyal as wives. Each loves Edmund, and the dishonorable affection is the cause of the death of each. Goneril, discovering her sister's passion, poisons her; and then, when the loss of Edmund is assured, stabs herself to the heart. But in this case, at least, the effect upon the husband is salutary rather than otherwise. Albany is, of course, deeply wounded and shocked at the intense wickedness of the beautiful princess he had married; but he is much more of a man at the end than at the beginning of the play.

In the *Idyls of the King*, the disloyalty of Isolt brings death upon herself and Tristram and the sin of murder upon the soul of her husband, King Mark; but in Guinevere, Tennyson shows us the disastrous effects of a wife's disloyalty upon herself, and all connected with her, in a way seldom equalled, and, so far as my limited knowledge goes, never surpassed. In the first place, the origin of her disloyalty is so plausible and so often repeated in every age and clime. There are few things more natural than that she, with her fresh, impulsive young nature, should be delighted with the gallant Lancelot, the best and bravest of all the Table Round, whom Arthur had sent to convey his bride to Camelot. And when, upon her arrival at the court, she finds her husband less responsive, more grave and earnest than she had expected or than she cared to understand and appreciate, to whom should she turn but to Lancelot for the personal warmth and sympathy without which she imagined she could not exist? And so, by almost imperceptible degrees, her passion grew, weakening and deforming her own character, spoiling the lives of the two men who most loved her, causing indirectly the death of Elaine, "the lily maid of Astolat," polluting the morals of the court, and dragging with her a whole kingdom in her fall. At first she is unconscious of all this, then the feeling of it grows upon her, then the partial knowledge; but the words of King Arthur bring upon her the full realization in all its overpowering force. As far as she herself is concerned, by a life of self-consecration and devotion she atones for the wrong she has done; but the effects upon others lived after her. Not only the whole purpose of the king's life had been spoiled, but its achievements had been utterly destroyed, never to be regained. Her influence had permeated through every stratum of society, and had injured thousands in a way for which she never could atone. Such is one great lesson of the *Idyls of the King*.

The thought of Guinevere and Lancelot naturally brings to mind the story of Francesca da Rimini and Paolo, so beautifully told in Dante's *Inferno*, where Francesca, being married to a man of much mental ability, but of deformed body, bestows her love upon his brother Paolo, who had been sent to conduct her to her husband; and in reading one day of the love of Lancelot and Guinevere, their mutual passion is disclosed, and they act over again the old story, as a punishment for which they are doomed to everlasting union in hell, the victims of perpetual desire and of the utter absence of hope.

Guinevere has also many traits in common with the Northern Brunhild, though without the elements of great physical strength and really masculine courage. By a trial of strength instituted in accordance with her own interpretation of the decree of the oracle, Brunhild is forced to marry Gunther, thinking that it was he who conquered her, when it was in reality Siegfried whom she loved. Kriemhild, Gunther's sister, who becomes Siegfried's dearly loved wife, arouses at once the hatred and jealousy of Brunhild; and her scorn of Gunther, her contemptuous treatment of Kriemhild, her tempting of Siegfried, her despair at the ill success of her attempts, her terrible revenge, and her subsequent remorse, are all powerfully portrayed in Geibel's tragedy; and while she and Guinevere are widely different in many respects, there is that in the general effect of each which reminds us of the other.

c. The beautiful and ennobling effects of true wifehood are shown by all three of the poets in a variety of most attractive phases. The submission and perfect truth and loyalty of Griselda, so long continued without a sign of giving way, renders her almost saintlike, and the inspiring and uplifting force of her love enables her to step from her place in the humble home of her father Janicle into the great palace of the Marquis Walter, where she performs the duties of lady and mistress with a grace and dignity which win the applause of all. And the effect upon her husband of her behavior through the whole trying affair must certainly have been to remove all lingering traces of unworthy suspiciousness, though most of us would have been loth to trust him as Griselda did.

Perhaps the closest analogy between any two characters as given by the three poets is that existing between Griselda and Enid. The same tender love and submission, the same complete surrender of self to the husband who is dearer to her than life itself, is apparent in each; and the effect produced upon Geraint is the same as that upon the Marquis. Though neither Griselda nor Enid had in the beginning that perfect love which casteth out all fear, they gained it in the end, and received in return the affection of their husbands purged from all distrust; for they will "henceforward rather die than doubt."

In the story of Dorigen, the ennobling effects of true wifehood are shown immediately in the life of Aurelius as well as of herself and her husband Arveragus. By a thoughtless condition, prompted only by her deep love and anxiety for her husband, and seemingly impossible of fulfilment, she places herself in the power of Aurelius, and when he, having fulfilled the condition, comes to her to claim the performance of her promise, she goes at once to her husband in her difficulty. With noble self-forgetfulness, he encourages her to keep her promise, and she goes, expecting to meet with what is worse than death; but Aurelius, overcome by her truth and her husband's magnanimity, renounces his evil claim and leads afterwards a better life.

Shakespeare places before us the inspiring and uplifting power of true wifehood in many beautiful lights. The helpfulness of Portia, who saves her husband from dishonor and her husband's friend from a horrible death, is as invigorating and as well sustained as it is attractive. So the sympathy and congeniality of Brutus' Portia is a picture not soon to be forgotten. To the honest and long-continued efforts of Helena are due her own happiness and usefulness as a wife and the salvation of Bertram as her husband and as a man. Her influence appears in the play amidst much that is dark and disagreeable, but it is in itself so pure and sweet and holy as to support almost entirely the rest of the play.

Imogen reminds us in many ways of Constance of the *Man of Lawes Tale*. In either case the wife is exposed to danger through her husband, but Posthumus is deceived, and the commands of King Alla are changed by his mother Donegilde; and the change from the groundless suspicions and voluntary ill-treatment by Geraint and Walter of Enid and Griselda is a grateful relief. But while Imogen and Constance are alike constant and devoted, they are considerably unlike in actions and even more so in words. Imogen both feels and expresses some indignation and resentment at the treatment she receives from Posthumus; but Constance expresses none, and probably does not feel it. Imogen, having lost her chief interest in life with the loss of her husband's respect and esteem, finally attempts to poison herself; Constance, having still her child upon whom to lavish her affection and for whom she may live, has no thought of seeking death. In either case, the wife comes out elevated and strengthened, Posthumus is purified from all taint of suspicion, and Alla is refined by suffering.

Hermione presents a picture of wronged, noble wifehood, so reserved and majestic as almost to forbid pity even while it demands our homage. She falls a victim to the cruelly unjust suspicions of Leontes when she is only trying to comply with his wishes, and is so far the one of Shakespeare's women most nearly akin to Griselda and Enid; but in general character she is far removed from them. I do not know that after the trial scene there would have been any way for her to approach the king; certainly she does not attempt it, nor am I sure that she would have done so had the way been ever so clear. The blow to her self-respect had been too cruel; and it was only after sixteen years of silence and seclusion that she could feel willing to attempt a reconciliation. In the meantime the nature of Leontes has been softened and subdued, and his eyes opened to the gross injustice of which he has been guilty; and his intense self-reproach and repentance as expressed before the supposed statue of Hermione are sufficient to convince her that happiness is still in store for them both. Queen Katharine has much of the same dignity in her sorrow that Hermione has, and equally good cause for her sorrow. Indeed, it is impossible to read of the trial of either queen without thinking at once of the other; and one scarcely knows which is more deserving of sympathy.

Next to Enid, Tennyson's most striking instance of true wifehood is the suggestion he makes at the close of *The Princess* of the wife that Ida is to become. In the ideal which the Prince and the Princess set for themselves, he gives us a glorious picture of the strength of union of two complementary lives,

> "—— side by side, full-summ'd in all their powers,
> Dispensing harvest, sowing the To-be,
> Self-reverent each and reverencing each,
> Distinct in individualities,
> But like each other ev'n as those who love.
> . . . . . . Each fulfils
> Defect in each, and always thought in thought,
> Purpose in purpose, will in will, they grow,
> The single pure and perfect animal,

The two-cell'd heart beating, with one full stroke,
Life."

In mentioning the instances of true wifehood given by Chaucer, it would be a grave oversight to omit the Duchess Blaunch, whose death her husband so sincerely mourns. She is not only represented as being the model of feminine beauty and grace, but she was ruled by reason and a love of truth, and served as an inspiration and spiritual guide to her husband.

III.

Chaucer represents Griselda as being as dutiful and lovable as a daughter as she is as a wife; and her life with her old father Janicle, where she seeks the herbs they live on and makes her bed of boughs, is touching and beautiful in all its rude simplicity. Equally beautiful is the life of her other self, Enid, in its filial relations. "Sweet and serviceable" she was, and fully deserving of the affection she enjoyed from both father and mother. There is something about these two daughters which reminds us of Cordelia, though she, in her whole-souled devotion and entire self-sacrifice to her father, goes far beyond them. Not that she neglects her wifely duty to France; but her first aim, naturally and rightly, is to defend and care for the poor, rash old man whose tremendous soul has probed to its very depths the bitterness of filial ingratitude, and who knows by fearful experience, "how sharper than a serpent's tooth it is to have a thankless child." And of those thankless children, Goneril and Regan, what is there to say? It is hard to say anything severe enough,—impossible to say anything too severe. They are all that is detestable, without a single touch of palliating emotion. Portia's respect for the memory and wishes of her dead father are most beautiful. Not only does she vow that unless she is won by the lottery of the caskets, as provided for in her father's will, she will remain unmarried all her lifetime, but even when Bassanio, the true object of her affections, arrives, she gives him no hint in his choice of a casket, for —

> "I am then forsworn;
> So will I never be."

Portia's obedience reminds us of Ophelia's, but with what a difference ! Portia's is the means of securing to her the happiness most necessary to her development; Ophelia's is a death-blow to her already tottering chance of happiness. By her heed to Polonius' words instead of to the dictates of her own heart, she is led into a course utterly hateful to Hamlet, and is finally betrayed into a palpable falsehood; and he renounces her at once and completely.

In Celia and Jessica we are forced to make excuse for their disregard of the duties of a daughter, but we excuse them upon rather different grounds. There may be cases in which even the worst of fathers should be clung to and cared for; but neither the Duke nor Shylock needed any real service which Celia or Jessica could perform for them, and they naturally drift off to where their purer impulses would lead them.

The gentle, motherly affection which Elaine's father shows for her is as delicate and moving as all else connected with the "lily maid"; nor is there any lack of fondness on her part. Only even the father-love, strong and pure as it may be, is not enough for her sensitive nature; so she dies, her slight hold upon existence broken down by the strength of her own unrequited affection. It must be confessed that Ida does not show any very profound emotion for old Gama, nor is it to be expected that she should, though certainly she reveals no lack of affection for him. There is in his small nature nothing that she needs; for he cannot supply, even in part, the place of a mother to her, as Prospero does to Miranda and Elaine's father does to her; but bearing her noble nature in mind, one feels no fear of any serious filial shortcomings on the part of Ida. Except for Enid, Constance of the *Man of Lawes Tale*, and Marina and Perdita, I can think of no principal female characters of the three poets whose mothers are represented as being alive; and even here, in the last two cases, there is all the effect of orphanage. It seems at first thought a little strange that all three poets should, in such a majority of cases, represent their young girls as having fathers but being motherless; but there is thus gained for them a tender consideration and compassion and a conviction of worth in and for themselves which it would otherwise have been difficult to attain.

An exquisite picture of the same beautiful relation between daughter and father is given by the great Lessing in his *Nathan the Wise*. It is hard to conceive of anything more perfect in its way than the mutual help and comfort rendered by Nathan and his adopted daughter, Recha; and one scarcely knows whether to admire most his sage paternal benevolence or her docile filial responsiveness.

Nor can we dwell upon this relation without having occur to our minds the corresponding relation, as set forth by Hamlet and his mother. The devotion is equally great on both sides, and Hamlet accomplishes in one way for Gertrude what Cordelia accomplished for Lear. Certainly, without their affection for each other, there would be little to attract us to the Queen of Denmark; and without his consideration for her, there would be much less excuse for Hamlet.

In Tennyson's *Dora*, the relationship of daughter and father exists in effect if not in fact. Indeed, Dora displays towards her hard-headed old uncle an unusual amount of daughterly affection and forbearance; and the simple, unostentatious dignity with which she bears her disappointment in love, and afterwards endeavors to reconcile the father with his son, and later still with his grandchild, raises her from insignificance to true heroism.

The softening and irresistible effect of the child upon the hitherto obdurate heart of his grandfather leads us naturally into a consideration of childhood as it appears in the three poets.

As to the distinctive phases of childhood, there is a marked difference between the delineations of Tennyson on the one hand and those of Chaucer and Shakespeare on the other;—not a difference in the nature of childhood itself, but in the view taken of its meaning and importance by society at large. For instance, as far as the child-nature is concerned, little Hugh of the *Prioresses Tale* might live to-day as well as in the fourteenth century; and nothing could be truer to nature than Master William Page's frequent and candidly confessed lapses of memory and desire for a holiday. Though in the majority of the children in Shakespeare's plays there is a good deal of shrewdness and precocity, it is not beyond the range of possibility, and in every case the surrounding circumstances are such as to warrant the development of such traits. But while the consideration of childhood and its influences occupies a secondary place with Chaucer and Shakespeare (of necessity if not by preference with Shakespeare), Tennyson considers it as an element of the first importance in civilized human society. Especially is this the case in *The Princess,* where Psyche's baby is "the conquering heroine of the epic." It is she who keeps alive in Ida's haughty breast the really tender emotions by means of which she is recalled from her ways of error. As has been pointed out by more than one critic, wherever the action is most rapid, there the infant Aglaia appears, and never without her influence being apparent. So the songs which are placed between the cantos, consist for the most part of variations upon the idea of the necessity of unity of feeling and aim in the home, and of the enlivening and sustaining influence of children as a bond of union. Thus, in the first song, where a misunderstanding has arisen between husband and wife, it is over the grave of the child they have lost that they "kiss again with tears." In the second, the mother is sustained and comforted in the absence of the father and feels that they are not in reality apart because she has his child to care for. In the fourth, the warrior hears, even through rolling drums, the voice of wife and child, feels new strength in his arm, and strikes his foe to the ground. In the fifth, the wife is inconsolable for the death of her husband until the old nurse sets *his* child upon her knee; then the refreshing tears burst forth, and new life comes to her with the thought, "Sweet my child, I live for thee." And so we might go through Tennyson's poems, finding everywhere the same interpretation of the significance of childhood, — another result of a civilization which endeavors to work from cause to effect, and which foresees in the training of the children the future destiny of the world.

IV.

Upon first thought it might seem that Griselda was untrue to her duties both as a wife and a mother,—that she overdid the first and neglected the second; but, as I have before stated in part, I do not think such a view can with justice be maintained. There is too much of real suffering in the few farewell words to her children to support the idea of any lack of maternal affection, and upon a little reflection there is revealed, to my mind at least, a sufficient compelling cause for her course of action. This cause is found in the fact that her obligations as a wife are peculiarly extensive and binding, and assume under all circumstances the position of primary importance. Her husband was the Marquis of the land, while she was only the daughter of an humble tiller of the soil; he had raised her to his lofty station and placed her at his side on terms of equality. He had chosen her in preference to all the great and good ladies of the country, and had gained her solemn promise of obedience and loyalty. All this constitutes to her firmly dutiful and conscientious nature a bond which nothing else can supersede or even equal, even leaving out of consideration the deep and abiding love which forms so strong a tie between her and her husband; and she adheres with noble self-forgetfulness to what is for her the highest truth and duty.

And so in the case of Enid, we are apt to feel a little impatience with what at first seems to be her over-submission to the will of her husband; but in thinking over the matter in all honesty and sincerity, we are forced to confess that her actions were in full accordance with the highest light of the truth of life as it was revealed to her. There were not in her case, as in Griselda's, any apparently conflicting claims of duty and affection. She had only to decide what course was best for the welfare and happiness of herself and Geraint, and few will deny that her choice, viewed in connection with its results, was the proper one. She, too, owed to her husband a heavy debt of gratitude in behalf of her parents as well as of herself; and her love for him and her admiration of his generosity and prowess were the strongest forces in her life. That her obedience to her husband is slavish cannot for a moment be maintained, for she disobeys him where it seems to her to be to his advantage that she should do so; it is born of no servile emotions, but of deep distrust of self and of implicit faith in Geraint as one higher and better than she is. She says distinctly: —

> "I needs must disobey him for his good;
> How should I dare obey him to his harm?
> Needs must I speak, and though he kill me for it,
> I save a life dearer to me than mine."

With the loss of Geraint's faith and love, her desire for life would be gone; and the true thing for her was to keep herself worthy of them and to convince him of her worthiness by her deeds, since words were forbidden her. She and Griselda stand together, utterly unresisting in their intense meekness and lowliness of spirit, yet rendered unconquerable by the subduing strength of virtue.

Dorigen and Arveragus are both wholly and consistently loyal to their conception of truth, though we, looking upon their conception by the light of nineteenth century views, are bound to consider it a strange mixture of exaggerated truth and untruth. To understand the position they take, it is necessary to go back to the notions of chivalry, which combined the loftiest and purest ideals with so much that was base and ignoble. In this instance, it is the strained sense of honor, the leading idea of chivalry, which is brought into prominence, and to which they give the exalted name of "trouthe." But though the ideal is a perverted one, the husband and wife who could at the bidding of conscience adhere to it at the expense of all earthly happiness, prove themselves of noble stuff. After Dorigen's confession, Arveragus says to her: —

> "Ye shul youre trouthe holden, by my fay!
> For God so wisly have mercy upon me,
> I hadde wel levere ystiked for to be,
> For verray love which that I to yow have,
> But if ye sholde youre trouthe keep and save!
> Trouthe is the hyeste thyng that man may kepe," —

which, in the modern interpretation of the term "trouthe," is a noble sentiment for all mankind.

Lady Macbeth loves her husband as devotedly as Griselda and Enid love theirs, but she fails utterly in the fulfilment of her true duty as a wife and as a woman. The words she utters upon her first appearance in the play reveal her deliberate and voluntary unfaith to her woman's nature, —

> "Come, you spirits
> That tend on mortal thoughts, unsex me here,
> And fill me from the crown to the toe top-full
> Of direst cruelty! make thick my blood;
> Stop up the access and passage to remorse,
> That no compunctious visitings of nature
> Shake my fell purpose, nor keep peace between
> The effect and it! Come to my woman's breasts,
> And take my milk for gall, you murdering ministers
> Wherever in your sightless substances
> You wait on nature's mischief!"

She yields to the selfish and unworthy dictates of her heart and brain until the wrongful concentration of power becomes the one aim of her life. Everything gives way before her overmastering ambition for herself and her husband; and her excessive regard for the external goods of life as compared with the internal brings its certain punishment. Her life is almost wholly devoid of that beautiful heart and soul life, without which true womanhood cannot exist and humanity becomes hideous.

In striking contrast with Lady Macbeth stands Portia, whose beautiful and healthful instincts of soul and intellect make her the power that she is in all the womanly relations of life. Her adherence to the wishes of her dead father is an admirable exponent of the strict integrity and loyalty of her nature; and her action in the play is a beautiful earnest of the life she will lead and the beneficent power she will exert as the wife of the man she loves. In some respects she has been criticised as unwomanly, but, I think, without the faintest tinge of justice. Her half-conscious revelation of affection to Bassanio in the beginning of the casket scene has, in my opinion, nothing in the least unmaidenly about it, but is only an additional indication of the beautiful transparency, innocence, and truth of her fresh young heart. No one thinks of accusing Miranda of a lack of maidenly delicacy in her conversation with Ferdinand, and it seems to me that Portia is quite as little in need of defence. As for her action in connection with the trial of Antonio, what else could she have done? Would it have been the part of a true woman to allow her husband to be dishonored in the eyes of the world, and his friend to perish when it lay in her power to prevent it? On the contrary, it was the intense truthfulness and sincerity of her womanhood which caused her to step to the front as she did, not in defiance, but in noble forgetfulness of the accusation of over-boldness which might be brought against her. She is at all times and under all circumstances loyally true to her own healthful and vigorous nature, whether indulging in good-natured ridicule of her discarded lovers, whether acting with gracious tact towards the Princes of Morocco and Aragon, whether talking with those she truly loves, or acting out what presents itself to her mind as a duty, and the result is a woman, made

> " By thought and deed, thro' guidance of the soul,
> Tho' not a perfect, yet a noble whole."

Gertrude was as tactful in her way as Portia, and we feel that she must have possessed and exercised many true womanly traits in order to exert the charm that she did over all with whom she came in contact. She seems to have been regarded with a very genuine devotion by the elder Hamlet, for even after her unworthy action in hastening into a second marriage, the Ghost solemnly commands Hamlet to contrive nothing against his mother; and the affection and consideration with which she meets from Claudius, otherwise so cold, wary, and unfeeling, are very evident. But beyond the outward graces there was little of truth or depth within her. Her affection for Hamlet was as powerful and genuine an emotion as she was capable of; but even that was far from consistent in its promptings to action. She was shallow and weak rather than actively false, her true womanliness being confined to the little things of life.

Though many characters are drawn with more distinctness of outline and fulness of detail, none can excel Cordelia in exquisite and absolute truth. Even in her first appearance, when her just indignation makes her almost brusque in her replies, her spotless integrity of soul is revealed; and at no subsequent time is its purity dimmed. As a wife, she is irreproachable; as a sister, she utters fearlessly her convictions and entreaties to the false, malignant creatures she sees opposed to her; as a daughter, she is exquisite beyond words to describe. She scarcely seems like a woman,— rather like a creature from another sphere; and yet each one of us bears within the joyous conviction that even such a character is not beyond the range of our human nature.

We are apt to look upon Ophelia as a tender, beautiful creation whose weakness lay in her lack of mental stamina and in her emotional excess; nor is this view an incorrect one. And yet it is the undue action of her head rather than of her heart to which the failure of her life is due. One of the few lessons Polonius had taught her was obedience; and she had fastened upon the idea with all the tenacity of a weak nature for the one or two sustaining notions which preserve it from collapse. And so, when the crisis of her life comes, she allows the lesser duty to prevail over the greater, only to discover afterwards that she has made an irretrievable mistake.

Desdemona, too, ruined her last chance of happiness by as downright a lie as Ophelia's. In leaving her father, I do not think there was any real violation of her duty as a daughter; as was the case with Griselda, she only followed what was to her a higher call. But when she feels, rather than perceives, the snare which the fiendish Iago has thrown around her and Othello, there are no simple alternatives for her to choose between; she becomes confused and perplexed, and knows not which way to turn for escape. Othello asks her for the handkerchief; she perceives dimly the importance which he attaches to her reply, and yet lacks the moral courage to tell him the truth, which is her only chance of salvation. But if one untruth can ever atone for another, surely it does so in her case; for her last words — the declaration that it was herself and not Othello who had been the cause of her death — go far to restore our faith in her high conception of what was truth for her and in her ability to live up to that truth.

Goneril's spiritual nature seems to have been one dark mass of falsehood and treachery. Her one approach to human affection is her disgraceful attachment to Edmund, whose wickedness is only equalled by her own. Towards her father she is the concentration of all that is undutiful and cruel. She treats the honest frankness of Cordelia with insolent defiance; and the real nature of her seeming loyalty to Regan in the early part of the play is shown when, seeing that her sister may interfere with her plans, she murders her without an instant's hesitation. Her behavior towards her husband is the very perfection of infidelity; and the final touch is added to her desperate career when she dies at her own hands, as she sees the failure of the last of her unholy plans; — and dies with no word or sign of remorse.

Imogen and Juliet resemble each other no little in their passionate natures and ardent poetical temperaments, and especially in their conviction that love is the only thing that makes life worth the living. Their absolute loyalty to their husbands is indisputable. The only question that could arise would be whether, in seeking to take their own lives, after they have been deprived of the love which could alone make life really tolerable to them, they were acting truthfully towards themselves; and when considered in this connection, they must invariably meet with condemnation. In either case our sympathies are so powerfully aroused that a position of impartiality is hard to attain; but after that has once been gained, our feeling for them must of necessity contain an element of disapproval. Of the two, Juliet's ill-regulated and wildly beautiful nature is the more intense in its effect upon us, but the greater stability of Imogen's character enables her to command more real respect; and while we feel less of a compelling impulse to excuse Imogen for the attempted deed, she was yet really and sorely tried. Both of them were but human, and after the loss of the love and hope which was their support, they gave way under trial; but while neither of them is justifiable, sympathetic human nature finds them easily excusable.

The influence of Isabella's true womanhood is as widespread as it is powerful. Not even to save her brother will she yield herself up to dishonor, yet she struggles bravely for, and finally accomplishes his release, and, in addition, rights a wronged woman, convicts Angelo of error and brings about his repentance, and helps to show the Duke the errors in his government as no one else had done. Hers was a difficult road to follow, but she maintained her truth to herself, and reached the goal at last — a saintly victor.

As for Guinevere, while our judgment condemns her, we feel in our hearts a sympathy for her that is almost painful. Without the slightest intention on her part of being untrue to herself or to Arthur, her very natural desire for the expression of personal sympathy and affection leads her by almost imperceptible degrees from the straight and narrow path into ways of crookedness and error, because, in her search for present enjoyment, she lost sight of the standard of perfect truth. Then, when the movement in the wrong direction has once been started, she persistently blinds herself to the fact that she is going astray, and will not realize what it is that she is doing. Not only is she false to the king, but her unjust suspicions of Lancelot's fidelity, owing to the sleeve he wore in his helmet, and her final discovery that Arthur, and not Lancelot nor another, was for her the highest, whom she must have loved had she known, awake within us the suspicion that she might in time have been disloyal even to Lancelot. That her love for him is not of the pure, true nature which would have him avoid even all appearance of evil, is proved by the deception she makes him practice upon the king, when Lancelot, misunderstanding her glances, and thinking only to please her, refuses to fight in the tournament for the ninth diamond. What was at first a natural and easily excusable mistake on her part was allowed through weak self-indulgence to broaden and deepen into sin, foul and dark, which in turn, from its necessary action upon a kingdom's welfare, became absolute crime. What an emphasis is here given to the divine command, "Keep thy heart with all diligence, for out of it are the issues of life."

The Princess Ida came near making a fatal error by mistaking "true for false, and false for true"; but her eyes were opened before it was too late, and the final impression she leaves upon us is that of a grand woman whose true mission in life will be grandly fulfilled. Except perhaps excessive ambition, and the half-unconscious assertion of self which is ever attendant upon the conscious possession of power, she has no great fault which may not be directly or indirectly traced to the influence of her preceptress, the Lady Blanche. She has had placed before her ideals that are as false and impossible as they are alluring to one of her natural enthusiasm; and she pursues them with an ardor and devotion which in a better cause would have been well-nigh sublime. But through all her errors, the instincts of a true and noble womanhood are readily discernible; and even when her false ideas make her appear almost repellently inhuman and cruel, we cannot for a moment doubt her sincerity and integrity of purpose. And when at last she comes to view the affairs and relations of life through the flawless transparency of reason and healthful human affection, her genuine repentance for sins committed, her anguished confession of weakness and her deep humility of spirit are luminous heralds of the glorious future which yet awaits her, where warm realities shall be substituted for hollow shows, inspiring love for vain ambition, the true life for an empty dream.

In every case, we find success or failure in life following as an inevitable consequence upon the observance or non-observance of the crowning maxim of our master-artist, Shakespeare: —

> "This above all: to thine own self be true;
> And it must follow, as the night the day,
> Thou canst not then be false to any man."

Not that the fulfilment or non-fulfilment of this supreme duty of utter truth to self will always bring its visible reward or punishment in this present stage of existence, — in what we are commonly pleased to call life; but that it will undoubtedly do so in that infinitely beautiful or infinitely despairing stage of existence where the soul shall first perfectly realize itself, is the belief which makes human nature divine. And along with this belief comes the further hope-inspiring conviction that "not the truth of which any one is, or supposes himself to be, possessed, but the upright endeavor he has made to arrive at truth, makes the worth of the man. For not by the possession, but by the investigation, of truth are his powers expanded, and therein alone consists his ever-growing perfection. If God held all truth shut in his right hand, and in his left nothing but the ever-restless instinct for truth, though with the condition of for ever and ever erring, and should say to me, 'Choose!' I would bow reverently to his left hand, and say, 'Father, give! Pure truth is for Thee alone!'"

BESSIE PORTER MILLER.

Hudson's Expurgated Shakespeare.

For Schools, Clubs, and Families. Revised and enlarged Editions of twenty-three Plays. Carefully expurgated, with Explanatory Notes at the bottom of the page, and Critical Notes at the end of each volume. By H. N. HUDSON, LL.D., Editor of *The Harvard Shakespeare*. One play in each volume. Square 16mo. Varying in size from 128–253 pages. Mailing Price of each: Cloth, 50 cents; Paper, 35 cents. Introduction Price: Cloth, 45 cents; Paper, 30 cents. **Per set (in box), $12.00. (To Teachers, $10.00.)**

SOME of the special features of this edition are the convenient size and shape of the volumes; the clear type, superior presswork, and attractive binding; the ample introductions; the explanatory notes, easily found at the foot of the page; the critical notes for special study; the judicious expurgation, never mangling either style or story; the acute and sympathetic criticism that has come to be associated with Dr. HUDSON's name; and, finally, the reasonableness of the price.

Oliver Wendell Holmes: An edition of any play of Shakespeare's to which Mr. Hudson's name is affixed does not need a line from anybody to commend it.

Cyrus Northrop, *Prof. of English Literature, Yale College:* They are convenient in form and edited by Hudson, — two good things which I can see at a glance.

Hiram Corson, *Prof. of Rhet. and Eng. Lit., Cornell University:* I consider them altogether excellent. The notes give all the aid needed for an understanding of the text, without waste and distraction of the student's mind. The introductory matter to the several plays is especially worthy of approbation. (*Jan.* 28, 1887.)

C. F. P. Bancroft, *Prin. of Phillips Academy, Andover, Mass.:* Mr. Hudson's appreciation of Shakespeare amounted to genius. His editing accordingly exhibits more than learning and industry, — it reveals insight, sympathy, and conviction. He leads the pupil into the very mind and heart of "the thousand-souled Shakespeare."

Byron Groce, *Master in Public Latin School, Boston:* The amended text is satisfactory; the typography is excellent; the notes are brief, always helpful, not too numerous, and put where they will do the most good; the introductions are vigorous, inspiriting, keenly and soundly critical, and very attractive to boys, especially on account of their directness and warmth, for all boys like enthusiasm. (*Jan.* 22, 1887.)

C. T. Winchester, *Prof. of English, Wesleyan University:* The notes and comments in the school edition are admirably fitted to the need of the student, removing his difficulties by stimulating his interest and quickening his perception. (*Feb.* 10, 1887.)

A. C. Perkins, *Prin. of Adelphi Academy, Brooklyn:* In the preparation of the School Shakespeare, Mr. Hudson met fully the capacities and needs of students in our schools and colleges. (*Feb.* 4, 1887.)

HIGHER ENGLISH. 27

The series consists of the twenty-three plays enumerated below
We furnish of the Old Edition, in paper covers, the plays starred in the
following list (Mailing Price, 25 cents; Introduction, 20 cents):—

*A Midsummer-Night's Dream.³ *Henry the Fifth.²
*The Merchant of Venice.¹ *Henry the Eighth.³
*Much Ado About Nothing.⁸ *Romeo and Juliet.⁸
*As You Like It.¹ *Julius Cæsar.¹
Twelfth Night.¹ *Hamlet.¹
*The Tempest.² *King Lear.²
The Winter's Tale.² *Macbeth.²
King John. Antony and Cleopatra.¹
Richard Second. *Othello.⁸
Richard Third.² Cymbeline.³
*Henry Fourth, Part First.¹ *Coriolanus.³
Henry Fourth, Part Second.¹

Hudson's Three-Volume Shakespeare.

For Schools, Families, and Clubs. With Introductions and Notes on each Play. 12mo. Cloth. 636–678 pages per volume. Mailing Price, per volume, $1.40; Introduction, $1.25.

The plays included in the three volumes respectively are indicated by figures in the above list.

The Harvard Edition of Shakespeare's Complete

Works.

By HENRY N HUDSON, LL.D., Author of the *Life, Art, and Characters of Shakespeare*, Editor of *School Shakespeare*, etc. In *Twenty Volumes;* 12mo; two plays in each volume; also in *Ten Volumes*, of four plays each.

RETAIL PRICES.

Twenty-vol. edition, cloth . $25.00 | Ten-vol. edition, cloth . . $20.00
Half-calf. . . . . 55.00 | Half-calf. . . . 40.00

☞ *Buyers should be careful in ordering not to confound the* **Harvard Shakespeare** *with an* **Old Edition** *made in 1851, and sold under another name.*

THIS is pre-eminently the edition for libraries, students, and general readers. The type, paper, and binding are attractive and superior, and the notes represent the editor's ripest thought.

www.ingramcontent.com/pod-product-compliance
Lightning Source LLC
Chambersburg PA
CBHW030314240426
43673CB00040B/1165